Ian Martin is a   *EP*)
and co-author of *The Thick o*
edits the satirical website www.martian.fm and writes a
column for the *Architects' Journal*. He was born in London but has
lived since 1988 in Lancaster, where he is a comedy grandfather.

IAN MARTIN

FUCTUM EST DE REPUBLICA

The Coalition Chronicles

faber and faber

First published in 2011
by Faber and Faber Limited
Bloomsbury House
74–77 Great Russell Street,
London WCIB 3DA

Typeset by Ian Bahrami
Printed by CPI Mackays, Chatham

A CIP record for this book
is available from the British Library

ISBN 978–0–571–27691–2

2 4 6 8 10 9 7 5 3 1

Contents

Mr. Brown Takes His Leave

[The Prime Minister entered the Chamber dressed in his Going-Away Clothes, a costume in style 'New Romantic': to wit, a blouse most billowy and trousers piratical, as once deemed fashionable by Lord Byron and Mr. Ant. The Government Benches then cheering the Prime Minister, the Opposition Benches jeering him with great clamorousness. Mr. Speaker then exercising his Authority over the House.]

Mr. Speaker: Order, order! We have a great deal of business to get through today, and I would appreciate it if . . .

Hon. Members: Wanker!

Mr. Speaker: Order! This is intolerable. Hon. Members will settle down now or I'll get really cross. Order, the hon. Member for Northampton & Peeping will refrain from making those appalling gestures at the Prime Minister. Oh, and at me too now. How dare you? I am not stupid. Oh, I am VERY familiar with the 'cocksucking' gesture, thank you very much. The hon. Member will . . . no, no, put it away now, nobody's impressed. I'm warning you . . .

Hon. Members: *[chanting]* Cock visible! Cock visible!

[A flurry of unsheathed penises in the Chamber then did most sorely aggravate Mr. Speaker.]

Mr. Speaker: Bailiff, the Gelding Secateurs!

The Bailiff of the House: Yo ho, Mr. Speaker! *[addressing the House]* I will sunder any man from his dependent signifier whose dependent signifier remains visible, in accordance with the Protocol of the House, yo ho!

[Hon. Members then re-trousering and occluding their penises, in aspect fearful of the Gelding Secateurs.]

Mr. Speaker: Thank you for your co-operation. Questions to the Prime Minister. And could we please keep the blooming noise down, my neurasthenia is very bad today.

Mr. John Lewis-List (Luton Selfserve): Will the Prime Minister itemise his engagements for today? And can I just say he can count on my support, certainly until the General Election. After that, I'll probably be spending more time with my public-relations colleagues and my extensive contacts book.

Hon. Members: Wanker! Bastards like you are the reason so many ordinary people hate our fucking guts! Have you got a number for Max Clifford, I've committed adultery again!

Mr. Speaker: Order! Please. All this hubbub is giving me a blooming headache. Prime Minister, pray continue.

The Outgoing Prime Minister (Mr. Gordon Brown): Thank you, Mr. Speaker. Ugh. This morning I rose at 0230 hours. After returning to bed with a bowl of fortified porridge and coughing loudly for a few minutes ugh, I was pleased to welcome Mrs. Brown, my wife Sarah, to the day's proceedings ugh. In fact, Mr. Speaker, she gave me this note *[opened envelope]* to read to the House, with your indulgence ugh:

Dear House of Commons,
Hi. Just wanted to give a little sigh and shake my head and say the Prime Minister may be a 'gwouchy bear' sometimes but he is a man of great substance, both laterally and vertically. I just wanted also to say that I . . . I love him . . .

Hon. Members: *[nausea, retching, genito-urinary discomfort]*

. . . and to remind people at home that if they're not entirely happy with Downing Street, they can follow me on Twitter instead. I am very much the sole remaining acceptable face of clapped-out Labour rhetoric. When I reach a million followers, I will do something silly for charity. Best regards, Mrs. Sarah Brown.

Mr. David Cameron (Whitney Whoseturn): Mr. Speaker, would the Prime Minister not agree that he is a useless bloody great wobbling titpump? Does he not accept . . .

Hon. Members: Wanker! Wanker! Wank! Er!

Mr. Speaker: Order!

Mr. David Cameron: Does he not accept, Mr. Speaker, that he is an international laughing stock, especially when his face freezes

3

into that grotesque sex doll face after every sentence?

The Prime Minister: *[inaudible, possibly 'It's a fucking miracle, the wooden boy can speak!']* Mr. Speaker, at 0400 hours I held meetings with ministerial colleagues and others ugh, planning legislative proposals for after the General Election, with a straight face, in my pyjamas. At 0600 ugh I had a private meeting with my counsellor in the study – I mean, personal trainer in the gym. At 0630 I had a working shower and video conference with Mr. and Mrs. Sarkozy, during which I made a joke ugh about Napoleon. *[regarded the hon. Member for Whitney Whoseturn]* And from roughly 0800 until the present moment ugh I have been preparing myself to face you across the Dispatch Box, you piddling sanctimonious public-school JOBBIEFUCK!

Hon. Members: Yeah! No! Boo! Fat cunt!

Mr. David Cameron: Mr. Speaker, does the Prime Minister seriously expect the people of Britain . . .

Hon. Members: Wanker!

Mr. Speaker: Order, order!

Mr. David Cameron: . . . seriously expect the people of Britain to believe him? Or what? Mr. Speaker, the Prime Minister is an arse-faced juddering casket of phlegm who couldn't run a fucking bath, let alone the country. 'New Labour'? *[mime: unreadable, possibly 'spitting' or 'whistling']* The people of Britain are sick sick sick of this useless thicket of blunt, winky-fiddling bumsacks. On our television all the time, ruining the news and dodging important questions about gardening costs. And they are sick sick sick of a Prime Minister who, if anonymous Tory bloggers are to be believed, literally has NO VISION. Because in addition to being clinically DEPRESSED, the Prime Minister is physically COMPRESSED. And addicted to BARBITURATES, and fucking BLIND!

Mr. David Blunkett (Sheffield Masturbeighton): You sightist bastard! Mr. Speaker, on behalf of all registered blind folk I'd like to say the only plus is we don't have to see the Leader of the Opposition's face. Which, I am reliably informed, looks like the puckered end of a FUCKING SAVELOY!

[The House fell to uproar, hon. Members exchanging opprobrium most noxious. The Bailiff of the House then summoned the Royal Cudgellers Response Unit, which did subdue the Chamber, also cudgelling into quietude the hon. Members for Belfast Wholly Cross and Belfast Stormout, whose violent disagreement over matters theological had escalated into a sword fight. Decorum then returning to the Chamber, hon. Members to their places.]

The Prime Minister: Mr. Speaker, I am sure the whole House will want to join me in paying tribute to the brave men and women . . .

Hon. Members: *[groaning]*

The Prime Minister: . . . brave men and women who have laid down their political lives in the service of this Government. They made the ultimate sacrifice in the defence of democracy and freedom against the forces of Nihilism and Eton who would ugh destroy our way of life . . .

Mr. Nick Clegg (Sheffield Shagnotch): Mr. Speaker, is it not the case that, as the *Guardian* has said, 'The liberal moment has come'? Yes, yes, the hon. Gentleman opposite may mince around impersonating me at the moment of ejaculation for as long as he thinks his lower spine can stand it. He is a fat testicular doughnut. Hm. Let us see, Mr. Speaker, what else the *Guardian* has to say:

The Liberal Democrats were green before the other parties, and remain so. Their commitment to education is bred in the bone . . . Great credit goes to Nick Clegg . . .

Call it credit. Call it making love to the British public while they stroke my cables and say my name. Mr. Speaker, let us consider what ELSE the *Guardian* has to say . . .

Hon. Members: Oh, fuck the *Guardian*! Oh, I like the Review section on Saturday! Who's that muppet with the shit-eating grin who's always writing about wacky family life? All of them! Ha ha! I'm going down the pub! Yeah, bollocks to this!

Mr. Speaker: Order, order! We are not here to discuss the journalistic merits or otherwise of the *Guardian*, although I will concede . . . Order!

Hon. Members: Wanker!

Mr. Speaker: Order! I will concede that they were very fair in their assessment of my plans to reinvigorate this House. Now, where is it?

[Mr. Speaker produced a copy of the Guardian *and put on his reading glasses, signalling gravitas. Began to read.]*

Mr. Bercow *[indicated self]* said the public believe that 'most MPs attend the chamber to make zoo noises during Prime Minister's Questions . . .' adding that . . .

Hon. Members: *[noises of monkeys, tigers and comical tourists]*

Mr. Speaker: Order! Order! Hon. Members are proving my exact point here, so the joke's on you, I'm afraid.

> **Mr. Bercow** *[indicated self]* **said, 'We have too many general debates which are indeed extremely general and rather lengthy, but too few short, snappy exchanges on subjects which are immediately relevant . . .'**

Ms. Theresa May (Fuckmeshoeburyness): Point of Order, Mr. Speaker. The hon. Member for LL Cool Wokingham is being an elephant, and he's just turned out his pockets for the ears! It's disgraceful!

Mr. John Redwood (LL Cool Wokingham): Mr. Speaker, our so-called political commentators have made merry sport with my physical features for years. Yes. Yes. They always draw me with big Vulcan ears. Well, Mr. Speaker, let the cartoonists enhance THIS! Yes! If they can!

[The hon. Member for LL Cool Wokingham directed his 'trunk' at the hon. Member for Camberwell Betspread and sang the first verse of 'Nelly the Elephant'.]

Hon. Members: Ha ha! I bet that cartoonist from the *Guardian* does him cock out from now on! He's gone off a bit, don't you think? Shut up, I like the penguins!

Mr. John Redwood: And might I urge you, Mr. Speaker, to make the most of your time as the Self-Styled Elf King up there in your oversized clothes? Because when the Tories get in, we're turfing you out, you irredeemable control freak. You jumped-up office clerk! You, you . . . bumhole!

Hon. Members: *[braying, handbags, croaking]*

[The hon. Member for LL Cool Wokingham then quit the Chamber, followed by Heralds and Pursuivants unto the corridor, then being decisively intercepted by Cudgellers.]

Mrs. Patricia Hewitt (Leicester Grimcow): Mr. Speaker, may I make a personal statement, pretending it's a question by putting a question mark at the end of the sentence? Mr. Speaker, hon. Members may know me as a tireless worker in my role as highly paid special adviser to various private healthcare operators. Older members will perhaps remember me in my previous role as Secretary of State for Health. Alas, it is with a heavy heart, Mr. Speaker, that I now turn my back on the Commons, having been suspended from the Parliamentary Labour Party after my entrapment by undercover journalists. And it is with the same heavy heart – as heavy, Mr. Speaker, as compacted ice – that I now say, 'Good riddance, you gnarled lump, you clenched buttock, you indented tumour,' to my right hon. Friend the Prime Minister . . .

Hon. Members: Wanker! Traitor! You look like Deirdre off *Coronation Street* but 'on the blanket'!

Mr. Speaker: Order. The hon. Lady, if she will forgive me for saying so, should never have married Ken Barlow. Question to the Prime Minister!

Mr. Spencer Count (Perkton Haverbung): Mr. Speaker, I speak for many hon. Members when I say I am shocked at the continuing persecution of hon. Members of this House for gardening costs, etc. Will the Prime Minister assure us that this madness will stop? Does he know how much it costs, this shit, keeping three buggering gardens looking trim? And will he please not get me started on anything else that may emerge *[indicated 'downstairs'].* I have absolutely nothing to say on this matter.

Hon. Members: Hear, hear! Wanker!

The Prime Minister: Mr. Speaker ugh, I refer my honourable Friend to an answer I gave previously on the Andrew Marr programme. There were plenty of answers in that. He's welcome to ugh iPlayer it and choose one of those.

Mr. Nick Clegg: Will the Prime Minister explain how in the last twelve years the poverty gap has widened during a period when he as Chancellor presided over . . .

[The Prime Minister cleared a space before the Front Bench and signalled his readiness to the Band of the Coldstream Guards, who struck up their funky martial arrangement of the Dead or Alive musical number 'You Spin Me Round (Like a Record)'. The Prime Minister began to dance as if tormented by Neurological Demons, making 'wanker' gestures towards the Leader of the Opposition.]

Mr. David Cameron: Mr. Speaker, the hon. Gentleman may carry on like this until he is blue in the face. I'm sure the country would be enormously grateful, as that condition would indicate a fatal fucking heart attack!

Mr. Nick Clegg: I like to think I speak for everyone in the country who cares passionately about Dance, Mr. Speaker. I know and care passionately about everything, and I KNOW about Dance. This is not Dance, Mr. Speaker. It's *[facial expression: imperceptible, possibly 'smile']* as if the Prime Minister is falling down a fire escape while somehow, in defiance of the laws of physics, remaining on his feet! He is a joke, Mr. Speaker. If I were a judge on *Strictly Come Dancing* I wouldn't give him a mark at all. I'd simply hold up a card with 'FAT SPAZZO' written on it.

Hon. Members: Ha ha! Wanker! Yeah, he looks like a fucking roasted ox!

[The Dance concluded, the Prime Minister returned, self-towelling, to the Dispatch Box, then drawing his cutlass and presenting it to the hon. Member for Whitney Whoseturn, unto the Line of Division.]

The Prime Minister: Mr. Speaker, the hon. Gentleman opposite tries, like the pathetic little ugh spindle of shit he is, to discredit the very real achievements of this Government. Economic success. Ugh. A plan in place to deal with the period after economic success. A promise of change. Ugh but change, Mr. Speaker, at a sustainable rate. Change people can trust. Fair change. Oh, the hon. Gentleman may mime 'execution by hanging'. Very clever, I'm sure. The fact remains, Mr. Speaker, that the Leader of the Opposition appears not to have so much a face ugh as a prolapsed fucking NECK STUMP.

Hon. Members: *[howling, shrieking, gargling]*

Mr. George Osborne (Tatton Cosplay): On a Point of Order, Mr. Speaker. My hon. Friend is using his tie to strangle HIMSELF. Surely, cruelly, this is a mime not of execution but of auto-erotic asphyxiation. If one . . . *[in reverie]* if one were being fellated, in the nanny's bedroom cupboard, say, one would definitely do that . . . thing with the tie and the citrus fruit. And the bitch could be dressed as Britannia, and one could be saying cruel things like, 'Oh yeah, bitch. The party's over. Your pussy's the economy now, bitch. How do you like THIS harsh measure?' Oh.

[The hon. Member for Tatton Cosplay then aware of a silence in the House, himself falling silent, then indicating his Order Papers.]

Mr. George Osborne: That is why, Mr. Speaker, the country needs strong, cruel leadership from people who understand pain. Real pain. What? What are you laughing at, 'Priscilla'?

[The hon. Member for Tatton Cosplay administered a Chinese burn to the hon. Member for Midsomer Boxset.]

Mr. Oliver Letwin (Midsomer Boxset): Ouch, you rotter! Mr. Speaker, the hon. Gentleman has an erection!

Mr. Speaker: Order, order. Oh God, again? Really? The hon. Member for Tatton Cosplay must understand here and now that I will not allow this wilful and persistent engorgement on his part to stand. The hon. Gentleman will recalibrate his ambition at once, thank you. Prime Minister . . .

Mr. George Osborne: I can't fucking help it, Mr. Speaker. It's the inflation.

Mr. Speaker: Order! Prime Minister, pray continue.

The Prime Minister: Mr. Speaker, I think the hon. Gentleman will look a lot less cocky after the General Election, ugh, when the nation firmly rejects all his Tory bullshit. Unless the nation ugh is some kind of giant, aggregated mongbrain and actually wants to be governed by this bunch of ugh toffs and bummers. They clearly want to dismantle the Welfare State. The people don't want this, Mr. Speaker. They don't want to be told what they think or how they feel. They don't want to be patronised, abstracted or triangulated into some sort of fucking pie chart, because there's always ugh too much jelly between the pastry and the policy, Mr. Speaker. The people want steady governance, familiar faces and a controlled IMPLOSION of the Welfare State ugh. You know, I was in conversation just yesterday with the *Daily Mirror* chicken . . .

Hon. Members: Yah, yah, yah, yah, yah, rhubarb.

Mr. David Cameron: Mr. Speaker, let me put the hon. Clanking Bollock opposite right on a few things. When we form the next Government, and I am being very clear about this, there will be no reductions in front-line services. No increase in VAT. No more pointless reorganisation of the NHS. No means-testing of child benefit. No scrapping of the Education Maintenance Allowance. No free ride for bankers. No two-tier schools system . . .

Hon. Members: Wanker! Don't fuck about with our two-tier schools system!

Mr. David Cameron: From the hysterical squawking opposite, Mr. Speaker, and from certain shrill commentators in the *[gestured in the direction of the Members' Dining Room]* 'real world out there' anyone would think my colleagues and I aspired to be a Cabinet of millionaires shitting on the poor!

Mr. Nick Clegg: Oh, do me up the Bilbo with a truncheon, Mr. Speaker. Listen to them. You *[indicated the Prime Minister]* and you *[indicated the hon. Member for Whitney Whoseturn]* are hypocrites. Hypocrites and gobblers. I know it. The nation knows it. I despise you both, and your clapped-out parties, and everything you stand for. I cannot wait for one of you to come creeping round with your 'Oh, Nick, I've got a hung Parliament, can you show me how to dress on the left?' They are yesterday's men, Mr. Speaker. It is time for them to retire. Time to return to their constituencies – and prepare for *Countdown*.

Hon. Members: *[confused and poorly executed version of the* Countdown *thinking-time theme]*

Mr. Speaker: Order, order now. Hon. Members must calm down. I will not allow 'uncoordinated singing' to join the list of irritating blooming interruptions the House must endure. This is most unseemly behaviour and . . .

[Hon. Members continuing to 'sing' the Countdown *theme, more loudly and with less co-ordination.]*

Miss Ann Widdecombe (Maidenhead Singular): Silence! Stop this bally noise, I say, at once!

[The House then falling silent, Mr. Speaker indicating his displeasure with the hon. Member for Maidenhead Singular by pulling faces at her.]

Miss Ann Widdecombe: Mr. Clerk, perhaps Mr. Speaker should be escorted to the Infirmary. I fear he is having a stroke.

Mr. Speaker: *[inaudible, possibly 'That's one more than you've ever had, you fucking Spacehopper']* Order. Just because this is the hon. Lady's last appearance in This Place, she needn't think she can undermine my Authority.

Miss Ann Widdecombe: Say 'Aye aye yo ho ho' all those who wish to see Mr. Speaker removed to the Infirmary.

Hon. Members: Aye aye yo ho ho!

[Mr. Speaker accompanied by the Clerk of the House then leaving the Chamber in disposition flounceful. The Prime Minister texting his publisher. Miss Ann Widdecombe then taking to the Floor of the House, where she skipped a light fandango to a swing version of 'A Whiter Shade of Pale' issuing from a portable CD player. The Prime

Minister joining her for a heavy fandango, both exiting the Chamber to applause and jeering.]

The Prime Minister: This is not goodbye, my friends, but au revoir. I'll see you back here with *[attempting to lift the hon. Member for Maidenhead Singular into the air, failing]* a hefty majority . . .

Moment of Scepticism.

The Mind of Gordon Brown

A Re-Imagining of Events Occurring upon the 28th of April 2010

PRAYERS AND MENTAL PROJECTIONS

[Mr. Brown in the Darkened Room]

BIGOTGATE –
The Director's Cut

INT. MINISTERIAL CAR. THE M1 MOTORWAY – DAY

The PRIME MINISTER (Colin Firth) stares solemnly out of the window. His face – ordinary yet powerful – reveals an inner turmoil and mild moral indigestion. Beside him, fielding calls, taking notes, his beautiful aide 'FRENCHIE' (Helena Bonham Carter). She finishes a call and turns to him, concerned.

Frenchie: Prime Minister, you really must stop working – and thinking – all the TIME. I know it is all so very worthwhile, but the Electorate . . . Honestly.

CUT TO: EXT. BURGER KING, TODDINGTON SERVICES – DAY

Glimpsed from the car, a blurry pass.

CUT TO:

INT. BURGER KING, TODDINGTON SERVICES — DAY
A ragged scrum of working-class extended-family members shuffling about, squinting at the menu pictures. They are all dressed as footballers, with the same name on the back of their shirts.

BACK TO:

INT. MINISTERIAL CAR — DAY, DARKENING

Frenchie: They're just SO fickle. And SO ungrateful, Prime Minister. They don't appreciate you, really they don't.

He turns to look at her. She lays a hand gently upon his massive load-bearing shoulder. The DRIVER (Clive Owen) speaks via an intercom.

Driver: If it's OK with you, skip, I'm staying on the M1 all the way up to Dewsbury, then back down the M62 to Rochdale. On paper, the M6–M6 Toll Road–M62 North looks quicker. But trust me, chief, it ain't. It really ain't.

Frenchie: *(answering phone)* Hold please. *(covering the mouthpiece)* Up to you, Prime Minister. M1? Or M6? It's your call . . .

The PRIME MINISTER smacks his fist into his palm and shows his teeth.

Prime Minister: Fuck it, Frenchie. No more 'this way, that way' bubble and squeak. *(to DRIVER)* M1! Tell security we're going M1! The right way. The steady way. The way of experience, and justice. To Rochdale! And Victory!

They all laugh, confidently.

EXT. ROCHDALE TOWN CENTRE — DAY, OMINOUSLY GREY

A jubilant crowd surrounds the PRIME MINISTER and his ENTOURAGE, chanting 'Five more years!' As he shakes hands, we hear shouted words of encouragement: 'By 'eck lad, you make that Tony Blair look a right jessie!' 'Marvellous job, difficult circumstances. Top marks, son!' 'Ee, Ah tell thee what, tha can come back to our 'ouse and Ah'll show thee mah Yorkshire puddings, eh!'

CUT TO:

INT. PRIME MINISTER'S HEAD — PERPETUAL DAWN
He's scanning the crowd. Everyone supportive and positive. Who's that, though, away there by herself, lost in her own thoughts and muttering grimly?

CUT TO:

CLOSE-UP: BIGOTED WOMAN'S FACE — MAD HAIR AND CRUMBS
A slightly dishevelled BIGOTED WOMAN in her fifties (Susan Boyle) is listlessly tossing bits of bread to the birds. She sings softly to herself: 'I dreamed a dream . . .'

BACK TO:

EXT. ROCHDALE TOWN CENTRE — DAY
FRENCHIE is steering the PRIME MINISTER towards the ministerial car, which is now draped in flowers. But he's keen to talk to BIGOTED WOMAN.

Frenchie: Prime Minister, we must leave now. You have to open a new steelworks in Sheffield at one.

Prime Minister: Frenchie, do you know the Parable of the Lost Sheep?

Frenchie: I . . . think so. Does it, I don't know, turn out to be the Lamb of God?

The PRIME MINISTER is already heading towards BIGOTED WOMAN. He stops, turns back to FRENCHIE and laughs.

Prime Minister: Look it up, Frenchie. It's probably on the Internet. You have to go after the lost sheep. That woman *(indicates BIGOTED WOMAN)* is the one that got away. And I'm bringing her in, Frenchie. I'm bringing her in . . .

EXT. ROCHDALE TOWN CENTRE, IN FRONT OF 'HALF PRICE OR LESS' — DAY, DRIZZLING
The PRIME MINISTER approaches BIGOTED WOMAN, camera crews and well-wishers clamouring after him. He stands before her, hands clasped. He looks away, into the far distance, as if recalibrating the scale of development aid required in Africa. He looks back at BIGOTED WOMAN. A beat. He offers his hand. Still mumbling, she shakes his hand, avoiding eye contact.

Prime Minister: Hi. I'm Gordon Brown, the Prime Minister.

Bigoted Woman: I know who you are. Are you going to do these cutbacks then, or what?

Prime Minister: Of course, fiscal prudence is . . .

Bigoted Woman: Fiscal prudence? You come up here with your fancy words. When are you going to cut the public sector, eh? Because that community centre won't shut itself, lad. You've got to cut spending. There's buggers just sitting about in that library, being *(jabbing him in the chest)* kept. Warm. At. Other. Folks'. Expense.

Prime Minister: Publicly owned civic space is a privilege that people were prepared to die for, Ms. . . .

Bigoted Woman: Mrs. Mrs., if you don't mind. Widower. Do I LOOK like a bloody gaylady?

Prime Minister: And what does a gaylady look like, exactly?

Bigoted Woman: So, I look like a gaylady, do I? Well, that just about takes the bloody dog's biscuit, that does. And another thing: where's Eastern Europe? And why are people coming from there to live in Rotherham? There aren't enough potatoes to go round.

Prime Minister: There are always enough potatoes. Let's look at these potatoes for a moment.

Reporter 1: Are you asking to see her potatoes, Prime Minister?

Bigoted Woman: They steal our dogs and make them race round the park at night in little dog cars.

Prime Minister: You mention Eastern Europe. Many of those who've come here in the last few years are from Poland. Their grandparents stood with ours and fought and died in the struggle against fascism . . .

Reporter 2: Prime Minister, are we to understand that you're going into this General Election as a pro-immigration socialist, backing the unions against the bosses in some crazy rerun of post-war Britain?

A beat. The crowd falls silent.

Prime Minister: Yes.

An eruption of joy and revolutionary fervour.

Prime Minister: *(cont'd, to BIGOTED WOMAN)* I promise you this. No longer will I tolerate the marginalisation of white working-class people. We cannot simply ignore those we disagree with, dismiss them as chavs and racists. It's time to sort this country out. Yeah?

All: So say we all!

Frenchie: Prime Minister, we really have to go. Now.

Bigoted Woman: Oh, Gordon. I believe you. I've been so mean-spirited, but now I'm going to be part of your New Society . . .

Prime Minister: Not just new. We must build an inclusive society. A sort of Wide Society . . . I have to go. All the best. Love you. Love you.

The BIGOTED WOMAN stands amid the cheering crowd, watching him disappear into the ministerial car. She's singing 'Happy Talk' and moving in a vaguely South Pacific *way.*

INT. MINISTERIAL CAR, MOVING OFF — DAY, BRIGHTENING

The PRIME MINISTER and FRENCHIE collapse, happy, into the back seat. DRIVER oddly quiet as he negotiates the dense crowd of well-wishers, laughing policemen, etc.

Frenchie: So how did it go with your lost sheep?

Prime Minister: Oh, she was just some very unhappy woman. Lost all trust in Government. And people, I think. It's my job – our job – to put that right. (*A beat. To DRIVER*) You OK, mate?

Driver: (*dabbing at eyes*) Heard you on the radio, Sir. Had me right choked up, it did. Wide Society. Yeah. I like the sound of that. I'm with the overwhelming majority of people in this country. I'm backing you all the way. God bless you.

The PRIME MINISTER unbuckles his seatbelt and, to FRENCHIE's horror, slides back the partition, steadies himself and manages to exchange a fistbump with the DRIVER.

Driver: I'll let you have your privacy now, Sir. You have lots to think about.

The security screen slides into place. The PRIME MINISTER rebuckling, and chuckling. FRENCHIE still cross.

Frenchie: You MUST wear a seatbelt at ALL times, Prime Minister. Suppose something had happened to you.

A sheepish grin. A twinkle in his eye.

Frenchie: *(cont'd)* You're very naughty. Oh, what's that on your lapel? It's not . . . that's not the Sky News mic, is it? Is it still picking up your voice, do you think?

The PRIME MINISTER looks at the mic with disdain, removes it and speaks deliberately into it.

Prime Minister: Testing, one–two. Now I'm assuming that in line with your impeccable fucking standards this microphone was disabled at the conclusion of the visit. Because, if it IS still on, you're technically in breach of the Official Secrets Act. Bugging the Prime Minister's car? Are you SURE? My memory's not what it was, but isn't there some sort of inquiry into phone-hacking and illegal eavesdropping scheduled soon? I THINK the newspaper concerned is owned by Rupert Murdoch. Your boss. Who wants a bigger stake in the British media. He wouldn't condone anything like this. Oh, Frenchie, could you just check . . .

An almost imperceptible sound signals that the mic is no longer live. Not taking his eyes from FRENCHIE's, he lowers the window and tosses the mic out of the car. She moves closer, becomes more intimate.

Frenchie: You are a very, very naughty Prime Minister indeed.

They kiss, more passionately. The Prime Minister notices a figure out-side the car, knocking on the window. It is a CLEANER. She's bored. She's done this before.

Cleaner: . . . this sofa. Wake up, please. You have fallen asleep in your office again. I'm sorry, but I need to hoover this sofa you are lying on. I found half a pork pie down the back of this sofa yesterday. Half a pork pie! In this sofa! AND dry-roasted pea-nuts! AND a hard-boiled egg! In this sofa!

> Moment of Interruption.

Number 10 Downing Street

Upon the Feast of St. Dude, the 12th of May 2010
SOUNDCHECKS
[Mr. Cameron and Mr. Clegg in the Garden]

Broken Britain Back Again

[Mr. David Cameron and Mr. Nick Clegg approaching the double lectern at a saunter, exchanging pleasantries behind their hands.]

The New Prime Minister (Mr. David Cameron): Shit. *[indicated the Deputy Prime Minister's Downstairs Area]* Look. Your flies are undone, you utter bloody chav.

The New Deputy Prime Minister (Mr. Nick Clegg): Fuck! *[inspected crotch]*

The Prime Minister: Ha. Made you look, made you stare, green grow the rushes-o!

The Deputy Prime Minister: Oh, you buggering tossball. I'll get you back, you see if I don't, you sodding turd, you. Ha ha, do you think all this bullshit looks convincing from over there?

The Prime Minister: Are you kidding? *[punched the Deputy Prime Minister playfully on the shoulder]* They're fucking journos. No scruples, no values. They don't care what we're saying. They assume it'll all just be piss steam. This is us, dude, joshing for the cameras. Remember what Andy told us: keep talking, and if you can't think of anything to say, just say 'shitake stroganoff' or 'lesbian' because that keeps the face animated and human. Shitake stroganoff.

[The Prime Minister punched the Deputy Prime Minister playfully on the shoulder again. The Deputy Prime Minister playfully jabbed the Prime Minister in the kidneys.]

The Prime Minister: Fuck! That hurt! Lesbian. Lesbian. Lesbian. Stroganoff, you cunt.

The Deputy Prime Minister: Oh, check it out, dude. Nick Robinson's such a bummer. He looks like an albino lizard. Ha ha. Shitake stroganoff.

The Prime Minister: Yeah, ha ha. Awful lesbian lesbian stroganoff little mingeflap. Hey, wasn't he 'above you' at Westminster, shitake?

The Deputy Prime Minister: Oh, up your ARSE lesbian. Blue Robbo? He went to some squitty little school in Cheshire, I think . . .

The Prime Minister: CHAVshire. Ha ha. Up YOUR stroganoff.

The Deputy Prime Minister: Yeah. OIKhampton in CHAVshire. Ah ha ha stroganoff stroganoff lesbian shitake.

[The Prime Minister and the Deputy Prime Minister removed their hands from their faces.]

The Prime Minister: No, up YOUR arse, you total spaz. Good afternoon, everyone, and welcome. On the steps of Downing

Street yesterday evening, as the sun finally went down on thirteen years of socialist tyranny, I said that Nick . . .

[The Deputy Prime Minister touched his forehead in an informal salute to the Press.]

The Prime Minister: . . . and I wanted to put aside party differences and work together like the absolute bloody clappers in the national interest. Both parties have now given their full backing to this Liberal Democrat–Conservative Government, the first Coalition Government in Britain for sixty-five years. It will be an administration united behind what Nick and I are calling the Three Fs: Freedom, Fairness and a Five-Year Lockdown.

The Deputy Prime Minister: Yeah. So Fuck Off.

The Prime Minister: Hey, maybe that should be the FOUR Fs!

Hon. Members of the Press: *[sycophantic laughter, phone-tapping]*

The Prime Minister: Nick and I have just come *[the Deputy Prime Minister sniggered]* from inside 10 Downing Street. I have to say no Government in modern times has ever been left with such a terrible economic inheritance, or such genuinely ghastly furniture and fittings. I am pleased therefore to report that my wife Samantha and her interior-designer friends have formulated some exciting ideas for a 'makeover'. Earlier this year they all jetted off for a mini-break in Dubai, laughing through the shopping malls, swinging designer shopping bags, ogling men . . .

Hon. Members of the Press: *[sycophantic puzzlement, inter-journalistic sexting]*

The Prime Minister: Oh, oh, correction. My mistake. What an idiot I am. Ha ha, that was *Sex and the City 2*!

Hon. Members of the Press: *[sycophantic metrosexuality, shrieking]*

The Prime Minister: No, but if I may be serious for a moment, the redecoration of Number 10 will actually be quite straightforward. Our reform will be bold and decisive. For a start, let's chuck out all that awful fucking Quaker furniture. Mrs. Cameron is very keen on what she calls 'organic-y, Milan-y' soft furnishings. The task is huge, but we must once again strive to encourage aspiration in this proud nation's Prime Minister's house. There is no time to lose. That is why I have today instructed Mrs. Cameron to procure, at no cost to the Treasury during this fiscal year, some little touches of glamour from various Notting Hill boutiques run by her sassy girlfriends – who incidentally actually HAVE just returned from a Dubai mini-break!

The Deputy Prime Minister: Of course – sorry to interrupt, David . . .

[The Prime Minister shook his fist in comical retribution, giving the Deputy Prime Minister a stare possibly signalling caution.]

The Deputy Prime Minister: . . . but I think we're both aware of the big risks involved in this enterprise.

The Prime Minister: Yes. Yes, quite. But if I may say this: we are witnessing a historic and seismic shift in British politics. Not, obviously, like an earthquake or anything shaking British politics to fucking bits. Obviously, not that at all. The people of Britain will be perfectly safe during the coming massive tectonic upheaval, united as we are in our demand for strong and stable leadership. Of course, some structural damage cannot be ruled out. But rest assured this nation's leadership, and their most trusted friends, will remain strong and stable.

The Deputy Prime Minister: I agree with David. A new progressive partnership. Believing in enterprise. Believing in markets. Believing in having a bloody good laugh.

The Prime Minister: Mm. New Politics. Where reasonable, civilised, grown-up behaviour is not a sign of weakness . . .

The Deputy Prime Minister: *[inaudible, possibly 'Your mum shat herself in Waitrose']*

The Prime Minister: . . . building a Big Society with Big Citizens . . .

The Deputy Prime Minister: *[inaudible, possibly 'With Big Tits, no returns']* Thank you, David. Yesterday we were rivals. Today we are colleagues. That says a bloody lot actually about how brilliant our new kind of Government is going to be. This is a Government that will last. Not because of our policies, important though they will be when we have thought of them, but because of our Five-Year Plan, which removes the possibility of a General Election in the next five years. That is what the people of Britain would want, if – and these are not my words, but the words of a cab driver I chatted to last night – 'if the people of Britain could be bothered to take their fucking heads out of their multicultural fucking arses for five fucking minutes'.

The Prime Minister: OK, we'll take questions now. Gary.

The Deputy Prime Minister: No, we bloody won't, you total cock. *[addressing the Sky News camera]* Ladies and gentlemen, you can call it 'fairness'. You can call it 'responsibility'. You can call it 'liberalism'. It makes absolutely no difference to us. Honestly, whatever, yeah? They're all totally brilliant. OK, we'll take questions NOW. Gary.

Mr. Gary Gibbon (Channel 4 News & Ting): Prime Minister,

Deputy Prime Minister. First of all, congratulations. And thanks a million, guys, for letting me ask the first question. I'm afraid it will have to be a difficult one: do you think coalitions are a good thing? Will this coalition, you know, last?

The Deputy Prime Minister: *[inaudible, possibly 'Unbelievable, what an oily fucking tit']*

The Prime Minister: Look. This coalition will last five years from today, May 12th 2010, OK? That is why we have agreed on a five-year term: because that is how long we have bloody well decided it will last. Five years, five years, five years. You know, the other night Nick and I looked at each other . . .

[The Prime Minister and the Deputy Prime Minister looked at one another.]

The Prime Minister: . . . and thought, yes, we could do a one-off thing, no strings, no recriminations, just two straight guys exploring one another's politicuality. We just sort of thought, God, that's so not inspiring or exciting or anything. Let's commit.

[The Prime Minister and the Deputy Prime Minister ceased looking at one another.]

Mr. Nick Robinson (BBC News for Now): Nick Robinson, BBC News for Now . . .

The Deputy Prime Minister: Did you say 'Nick Bobbington' or 'Nick Monitor'? It's just, you look a bit like a monitor lizard.

The Prime Minister: Yes, yes, with the liddy eyes and the little lizardy face.

Mr. Nick Robinson: Oh, really. You two can fucking talk: Mr.

Potato Head and his new best mate, the Human Fucking Aubergine.

The Prime Minister: Ha ha. *[inaudible, possibly 'I hope you've got an Oyster Card, fuckface, because we're coming down on the BBC like a massive cube of iced piss ejected from a Boeing 747']* Look, Nick. Of course there will be scepticism. But you'll just have to trust us. This will be utter dog-bollocky brilliance, I promise. Coalition. Five years. So much more than two competing teams trying to occupy the same space at the same time.

[The Prime Minister and the Deputy Prime Minister looked at one another.]

Mr. Adam Boulton (Sky News & Greggs): Yeah, two-part question for you, gents. Firstly, why the fuck didn't I get to ask the first question? I am certainly the heaviest political heavyweight here. Don't think you've heard the last of this, either. Mr. Murdoch likes things to be in order. Secondly, you both keep mincing on and on about political reform, but you're basically just talking shit. Are you going to reform Prime Minister's Questions, for instance?

The Deputy Prime Minister: Yeah, yeah, I mean, I mean, you ask what will change, what will change. Blah blah blah, whatever, you know? Everything. Everything will change.

The Prime Minister: If I'm not there, Nick will be answering. I'm, ha ha, looking forward to a lot of foreign travel!

Hon. Members of the Press: *[sycophantic giggling, synchronised wriggling]*

The Prime Minister: No, no. I really am.

Mr. Jon Snow (Hauteurcue): Bah! Where will Mr. Clegg live? In a cupboard under the stairs at Number 10? Bah!

The Deputy Prime Minister: I'm not quite sure where my office is, though I have been there and I'm told that it's connected to David's via a back passage.

[The Prime Minister and the Deputy Prime Minister looked at one another.]

The Prime Minister: OK, we need to wrap this up now as I have a Government to run.

The Deputy Prime Minister: We. WE have a Government to run.

The Prime Minister: A Government, ladies and gentlemen, that will succeed through its success. Now, who's asking the light-hearted press-conference closer?

Mr. A. Scorchmark (Syndicated Free Press): Prime Minister, do you now regret, when you were pissed and somebody asked you what your favourite political joke was, saying, 'Nick Clegg . . .'

The Deputy Prime Minister: *[mock outrage]* Right, fuck this. I'm off. I'm off.

The Prime Minister: *[mock embarrassment]* Come back, come back.

Mr. A. Scorchmark: . . . saying, 'Nick Clegg walks into a gay brothel to get sucked off by a big black sissy in a frock who says don't I know your face, and Nick Clegg says ha ha which one, and the big black sissy in the frock says you must be that duplicitous cunt Nick Clegg, can I buy some crack off you, and Nick Clegg says sorry I've SOLD OUT, ha ha, now hurry up and suck me off, I'm already late for lunch with that shithead Vince Cable.'

[Birdsong, faint traffic noise, a distant aeroplane.]

The Deputy Prime Minister: *[genuine outrage]* You said that, you smirking COCKFUNNEL?

[The Deputy Prime Minister departed in attitude most flounceful towards the Tradesmen's Entrance of Number 10, Downing Street.]

The Prime Minister: Thank you, ladies and gentlemen, that is all.

[The Prime Minister hurried off and caught up with the Deputy Prime Minister.]

The Prime Minister: Look, dude, I'm sorry shitake. But you know what the fucking press are like. Lesbian. Lesbian. Twisted my words. I'd never say anything like that. You're my bro, dude. Fam. Bredren. Et cetera stroganoff.

The Deputy Prime Minister: Fuck you. Fuck you up the euro with a loofah. It's over. Shitake stroganoff.

[The Prime Minister took the Deputy Prime Minister's arm, in gesture conciliatory.]

The Prime Minister: Look, come back to mine. I'll organise some tea and crumpets and lesbians. And shitake stroganoff. Fuck it, come on.

The Deputy Prime Minister: Bollocks. Stroganoff.

The Prime Minister: Shitake, come on. We could Skype Liz Hurley. She fancies you.

The Deputy Prime Minister: Fuck off, she doesn't. Does she?

The Prime Minister: Mm. She said if you take your top off, she'll take hers off.

The Deputy Prime Minister: Well . . . Lesbian. Shitake.

The Prime Minister: Marvellous. Honestly, dude. You were fantastic back there. We're a team, yeah? We're Eric and Ernie. We're fucking BERT and Ernie. We're fucking . . .

The Deputy Prime Minister: Iggle Piggle and Andy Pandy.

The Prime Minister: Ha ha ha, you're brilliant, lesbian. Shitake stroganoff.

[The Prime Minister and Deputy Prime Minister fistbumped.]

Moment of Disappearance.

FUCTUM EST DE REPUBLICA

House of Commons

Upon the Feast of St. Corgus, the 25th of May 2010

PRAYERS AND THOUGHTS

[A Hot-Water Bottle and Diverse Boiled Sweets
in the Demountable Throne]

Message to Attend Her Majesty

*[A Message of Most Urgent Imperative and Apostrophic Import to
attend Her Majesty, delivered by the Sequinned Yeoman Ushermaster-
Within-Ye-Wardrobe of Black Rod via the Ancient Forked Twig of
Offa, Rex Anglorum, and via Email.*

*The Speaker, with the House, went up to attend Her Majesty,
finding her to be lolled most Regally within the Royal Pantry. Some
Members of Her Majesty's Cabinet attended within the Pantry; the
remainder thronging most densely the adjoining Royal Kitchenette and
also, without, the Royal Smoking Garden. Her Majesty indicated the
Ceremonial Chalice of the Opening of Her Most Loyal Parliament,
which being empty she refilled before asking her Loyal Parliament if
they fancied a Ribena.*

*Pleasantries having been understood to have been deemed to
have been exchanged, the Speaker and the House then returned to*

Parliament, save for Black Rod, the Spangled Bailiffs of Agincourt, the Haughty Swan-Numberers of the Garter and the Sturdygeezers of the Secret Service, who severally attended Her Majesty unto the Conclusion of the Ribena.

Upon their return, the Speaker suspended the Sitting. Her Majesty's Government and Most Loyal Opposition then did fall to Diverse Entertainments, including Sudokus, Crosswords, Phone Sex, Insider Trading, Nude Wrestling, Clandestine Outlawries and Burping Contests.

Her Majesty and her Retinue did then approach the House, Black Rod banging thrice upon the Door.]

Black Rod: Yo ho ho! Upon this day, ye 25th of May in the Year of Our Lord Two Thousand and Ten, I beseech ye without delay to open this Door, for we do bring Her Majesty forthwith!

The Bouncer of the House: Who goes there, Friend or Foe?

Black Rod: Friend, obviously. I have literally just told you we're here with the fucking Queen.

The Bouncer of the House: And your name?

Black Rod: Are you dicking me about? This is the State Opening of Shitting Parliament. Open the bastard Door!

The Bouncer of the House: Getting aggressive is not a good idea, Sir. I can get aggressive too. I need your name. And don't blame me. It's a legal requirement by The Management. House Security is now delivered through a Private Finance Initiative and . . .

Black Rod: Kiss my cock, you SHITPUMP! I've got Queen Elizabeth the Second here. Waiting to State-Open her own fucking Parliament. I'm warning you, she'll have to sit down soon, I think she's a bit pissed.

The Bouncer of the House: What's your name?

Black Rod: *[sighing]* Black. Rod. *[inaudible, possibly 'You fucking loaf of human spam']*

The Bouncer of the House: Mr. Black, Mr. Black . . . first name Rod, you say? No . . . no, sorry, not on the list.

[Mr. Stephen Fry approached via High Dudgeon, live-tweeting the situation on his iPhone.]

Black Rod: Ah, Mr. Fry, perhaps you could have a word with *[indicated Door]* this cunt.

Mr. Stephen Fry on Twitter: Unbelievable! Am at lovely State Opening of Parl filming docu for Beeb with gorgeous Queen. But they're not letting us in! Bum!

Black Rod: *[replying via Osfoora for Blackberry]* Aagh! Poor you! And poor Queen! Surely something can be done? A hashtag? *#letFryin*

The Bouncer of the House: *[via Twitter for Android]* It's not my fucking fault. I have strict instructions. It's the insurance.

Mr. Fry on Twitter: Door still shut. Very tiresome & depressing. With much sadness, I must now say goodbye forever to all public life. *Ave atque vale.* *sadface*

[Mr. Fry walked slowly away, reflecting upon the capricious and melancholic nature of Celebrity, and did sync his gadget.]

Black Rod: *[consulting mobile telephone]* Oh look. Look at Twitter Trending Topics. *#letFryin* is Number 2 already, just behind *#myfavoritesextoy* . . .

[Mr. Fry paused. The sound of the Fearsome Cultural Machinery of the State, at first imperceptible, grew into an Angry Roar of Outrage, shaking the walls of the House and causing tumult and tantrum to reverberate most fearsomely throughout Westminster, as if all were in a Harry Potter film. The Door to the House opened. Inside, the Assembled Company discovered the Remains of the Bouncer of the House still a-smoulder. Much urgent whispering and laughter.]

Mr. Fry on Twitter: Bother. In the words of another Queen: 'Mama, just killed a man.' Oops. Soz. But – huzzah – we're in!

[Her Majesty, singing an old Music-Hall Song, entered the House accompanied by her Retinue and His Royal Highness Prince Philip.]

HRH Prince Philip: Sorry, the old girl's had one too many Ribenas. We'll have to get that big pansy bugger to do it.
Black Rod: *[hushed]* Sire, one cannot talk of Mr. Fry in such terms. The very Fabric of the State would be imperilled.

[The Assembled Company heard an ominous Noise. Some plaster fell from the ceiling of the House.]

HRH Prince Philip: *[hushed]* Well, he IS wearing a bloody frock. And a crown. Touch of make-up too. If I were a bit younger I'd have a go, eh? Eh? Remember having a go on some pansy bugger in Paphos, just after the war. Up the arse, eh? Eh? Any port in a storm, eh? You a navy man?

Mr. Fry on Twitter: Thx sooo much, Prince Philip. Yes, AM dressed as the Queen. Was supposed to be a REVEAL once I'd 'entered House'. NB NOT lovely Hugh Laurie!

[Her Majesty became unwell on the carpet. Mr. Fry was prevailed

upon to read the Queen's Speech and took his place in the Demountable Throne. The House arranged itself into formal quietude. Mr. Fry, having adjusted the Crown of Sovereign Dominions and the Royal Frock of the Commonwealth, took up the Mitre of the Subjugated Wogosphere and the Orb of Magical Entitlement and delivered the Queen's Speech, finally.]

Mr. Fry: My Lords and Members of the House of Commons. My Government's legislative programme will be based upon the principles of freedom, fairness and responsibility. Oh, dear Lord, how much more of this widdle IS there? Reduce deficit . . . restore economic growth . . . well, quite, bravo, I mean . . . *[unintelligible, possibly 'Meh-hehhhhhh'].* Perhaps . . . no, it's a silly idea . . .

[There was an uncomfortable silence, followed by an awareness among the Assembled Company of an expectation to press Mr. Fry further on the matter.]

Assembled Company: Oh please carry on, Mr. Fry. Do it any way you want. Oh do carry on Mr. Fry, oh please fucking do.

Mr. Fry: Oh very well, you sillies. I'll attempt, essay perhaps is a more apposite and elegant . . . where was I, what a dunderhead, goodness me, beh. Yes, let's see, shall we, if it's possible to render the Queen's Speech – perhaps in the interest of brevity and economy . . .

Assembled Company: Wanker! Hurrah! What do you know about fucking brevity? Could I get a picture of me next to you on the Throne? And what the fuck do you know about the economy? Call yourself a national treasure? You're only over here two days a month! And one of those is spent pratting around in the fucking Apple Store! Woof!

[The hon. Member for Sheffield Masturbeighton cautioned Cheryl, his assistance dog, to be silent, reminding her of the Ancient Sanction, to wit the Putting Down of Insolent Beasts During the Queen's Speech.]

Cheryl: *[keen whimpering]*

Black Rod: Oyez, oyez! Be it known by all in this Assembled Company – an Insolence has occurred! First verbal warning, oyez!

HRH Prince Philip: *[hushed]* I'll tell you what: pop suspenders, stockings and a bra on the Labrador I would, if I were younger, eh?

Mr. Fry: Your Majesty, my Majesty, Lords, Ladies, Gentlemen, folk of every hue, class, religious persuasion and sexual destiny . . .

HRH Prince Philip: *[hushed]* I would, eh? Ha ha ha.

Mr. Fry: I give you the Twitter version of the Queen's Speech. The Queen's 'Tweech' . . .

Assembled Company: Oh, how clever! Jesus Christ, 'Tweech'? Show us your tits!

> **Mr. Fry's Tweetstream: High-speed broadband. High-speed railway network. Pish and posh. I prefer good conversation, and walking. *#queenstweech***

Cheryl: Woof! Woof!

Mr. David Blunkett (Sheffield Masturbeighton): Be quiet, girl. *[to Assembled Company]* Sorry, she probably needs a piss. We've been here two hours. You have to get in early or some bastard's nicked your spot. Never mind that I'm registered fucking blind!

Black Rod: Oyez, oyez! Be it known by all in this Assembled Company that an Insolence has occurred! This being the Second and Final Warning! Further Insolence will occasion *[indicated the hon. Member for Sheffield Masturbeighton]*

a Smiting With the Crosier and/or *[indicated Cheryl]* a
Slaughtering With the Mace. Oyez, as you were.

Mr. Fry's Tweetstream: Oh, we'll 'modernise the Royal Mail', will
we? Modernise as in sodomise, I presume. (I am not 'agin' moder-
nity or sodomy per se.) *#queenstweech*

Voice of patients and role of donors to be strengthened in the NHS.
Oops, my mistake: 'doctors'. *#mehhh #queenstweech*

More Academies and Free Schools. Hello, Mr. Chips! *#queenstweech*

Devolve greater powers to councils and neighbourhoods through
systematic indifference. *#queenstweech*

Parliamentary and political reform to rebalance the relationship
between the state and its citizens, who have got heavier recently.
#queenstweech

Fixed-term Parliaments of five years. So save all your sarcas-
tic remarks and hurtful slander until 2015, we'll still be here.
#queenstweech

A referendum on the Alternative Vote system for the House
of Commons and sustained rhetoric about change until then.
#queenstweech

A reformed* second House 'wholly, mainly or sort of' elected on
the basis of proportional representation. **non-recidivist #mehhh
#queenstweech*

Freedoms and civil liberties restored through the abolition
of Identity Cards. Sir, I have nothing to declare but my 'QI'.
#queenstweech

'A referendum on additional powers for the National Assembly of Wales?' *#mehhh #behhh #soundslikeasheep #queenstweech*

The Duke of Edinburgh and I look forward to our visit to Canada in June . . .

[HRH Prince Philip placed a hand tenderly in Mr. Fry's lap; inaudible, possibly 'Big pansy bugger, up the arse, eh?' occasioning a glance, in aspect stern, from Black Rod.]

Mr. Fry's Tweetstream: . . . and to receiving His Holiness Pope Benedict the 16th in September. *#closetbummer #queenstweech*

My Government will seek effective global collaboration for serious discussion of climate change, possibly somewhere warm. *#queenstweech*

Cheryl: Woof woof! Sausages!

Mr. David Blunkett: Shut your gash, you dozy bitch! I'll 'take you tinkles' when the Queen's finished her . . .

Cheryl: Ruff! Ruff! Ruff!

[Black Rod approached the Benches and presented the Crosier to the hon. Member for Sheffield Masturbeighton's beard, smiting him most soundly. Then calling before the Assembled Company for the Mace, which, having been brought by the Bailiff, was then presented by Black Rod to Cheryl, most decisively.]

Mr. Fry's Tweetstream: My Lords & Members of the House of Commons, I pray that the ✠ of Almighty God may rest upon your counsels. Byee! *#queenstweech*

Mr. David Blunkett: I'll fucking have you! What, nobody

intervenes to stop a registered blind man getting battered by some cunt in fancy dress? What is this, Broken Fucking Britain? *[to Cheryl]* Come on, girl, let's go for a piss. Oh, nice one. *[to Assembled Company]* I hope you're happy. *[held hand aloft]* She's had an accident.

Assembled Company: Blood! Blood and hair!

Mr. Stephen Fry: I don't suppose *[summoning the iPlayer to appear upon his iPad]* anyone saw my Wagner thing on iPlayer? One has to immerse oneself completely, not just of course in the music itself . . .

Moment of Signal Loss.

House of Commons

Upon the Feast of St. Latin Bumjoke, the 31st of May 2010

PRAYERS WITH DRINKS AND NIBBLES

[Mr. Speaker on the Booster Seat within the Chair]

Prime Minister's Coalestion Time

Mr. Speaker: Order! Personal statement from the hon. Member for Outer Yeovil.

Hon. Members: *[murmurings of disapproval and indigestion]*

Mr. David Laws (Outer Yeovil): Mr. Speaker, I am sure hon. Members have been following the stories about me in the *Daily Telegraph* concerning my sexuality and expenses. *[produced Daily Telegraph]* Yet today I have again been woefully mis-represented in an editorial piece entitled *[reading]* 'Laws: Sorry for Being Gay, It Was an Accident'. If the House will indulge me, I'd like to quote an extract from it:

Mr. Laws is an admirable politician with rugged good looks. This newspaper acknowledges the important and necessary work that Mr. Laws has carried out. Whether in his capacity as a reforming Orange Book Liberal, or as an able negotiator in the cross-party negotiations to form a Coalition Government, or as a virile and attractive gayer juggling several properties and a boyfriend, his performance has been both tender and athletic.

This newspaper has no feelings about homosexual men one way or the other, suppressed or otherwank. It gave us no thrill at all to 'out' Mr. Laws. We have never had the slightest interest in what he and his boyfriend get up to behind closed doors, or who is 'the lady', or what it must feel like to have well-lubricated sex with someone who understands exactly what you want. No. No.

Now Mr. Laws has apologised, and as we only listened to the first bit, we must assume he has apologised not for his 'genuine error' in managing his Parliamentary expenses but for his 'genuine error' in being gay. We extend ourselves to Mr. Laws and assure him that we have no interest in his 'going straight' except in the strictest innuendo . . .

Hon. Members: *[asleep]*

Mr. David Laws: It is with great regret therefore that I have tendered my resignation as Chief Secretary to the Treasury. I would like to thank everyone who has offered their support. The consensus is very much that it is nobody's fucking business how one claims expenses, and to suggest that in 2010 there is any social stigma attached to one's personal income is utterly disgraceful. To my erstwhile Cabinet colleagues I bid farewell until 2012, when all this has blown over. Thank you.

[The hon. Member for Outer Yeovil then quit the Chamber, slamming the Door and awakening hon. Members.]

Mr. Speaker: Order! In the name of our Most Glorious Sovereign Her Majesty Queen Elizabeth, I command the House to acknowledge this mighty and ancient Chair, and Booster Seat, which signify the Power of the Speaker. Behold the Mace . . .

Hon. Members: *[chatter, phone-checking, masturbation]*

Mr. Speaker: Order, I say! The Mace, signifying democratic justice or something. I can't remember, there's a lot of small print . . .

The Prime Minister (Mr. David Cameron): You'll love it, honestly. There's a little bakery down the road, the locals are brilliant. That peasanty French stuff they all wear, brilliant. Women have tits out to here, blood, I'm telling you. *[indicated curtilage of giant imaginary breasts]* Like fucking traffic cones. Scenery's totally gorgeous . . .

Mr. Speaker: Order!

The Deputy Prime Minister (Mr. Nick Clegg): If you're sure. Sounds fab. Have to check with the missus. Maybe come for a long weekend . . .

The Prime Minister: Let us know, seriously. Any time. Sam's got caterers organised for the fucking whole five weeks, dude.

Mr. Speaker: Order! Prime Minister, we're ready to start! Please, I crave your indulgence.

The Prime Minister: Oh God. Comprehensive Twig's making that awful bloody whining noise again. Better keep calm and carry on, I suppose.

The Deputy Prime Minister: Oh, the Twig? Bum the Twig.

The Prime Minister and the Deputy Prime Minister: 'Bum the Twig, Bum the Twig, all the way to the tuck shop!'

Hon. Members who attended public school: 'Bum the Twig!' Ha ha ha! Brilliant!

Hon. Members who didn't attend public school: *[simulated* *cognition, seeking the approval of those hon. Members who attended public school]*

The Deputy Prime Minister: Hold on.

[The Deputy Prime Minister rose to address Mr. Speaker.]

The Deputy Prime Minister: Mr. Speaker, may I summarise the feelings of this entire House when I say you are an absolutely insufferable little clitwart? I am TRYING to have a conversation with my hon. Friend the Prime Minister of Great Britain, Northern Ireland and whatever suburban dystopia you sprang from. Look at you, man, with your fucking chav haircut and inadequate fucking height. Keep your state-educated fucking townie trap SHUT, you arse-plunging cloud of cum, or I'll come over there and violate you with a fire hose, yes? Anyone else?

[The House fell silent.]

The Deputy Prime Minister: Excellent. Ha ha ha! *[to the Prime Minister]* Boom. Green grow the rushes-o.

The Prime Minister: Boom. Green grow the rushes-o, mummyfucker.

Hon. Members: Hear, hear! Well nang!

[The Prime Minister and Deputy Prime Minister performed an 'Eton–Westminster Fistbump–Handshake' and kissed.]

Mr. Speaker: Yes, good. Don't forget I'm still in the Chair here. Right, who's . . .

Mr. Justin Office (Vaguely Cotswolds): Would the Prime Minister list his engagements for the day? And look, while I'm on my feet can I just say I think the Coalition is doing a terrific job, it really is, and I can tell him as a very able and ambitious backbencher I am more than willing to do anything really . . .

Hon. Members: Kiss his arse! Kiss his arse!

The Prime Minister: Well, fag? WOULD you kiss my arse?

Mr. Justin Office: I . . . loyalty, of course, is very important in these . . . these difficult times.

Hon. Members: Kiss his arse! Kiss his arse!

Mr. Speaker: Order, order! For goodness sake, this is all very rude indeed.

The Prime Minister: It's just that there IS a vacancy arising soon in the Treasury for the right sort of chap. What would my hon. Friend do for THAT? Suck my cock?

Hon. Members: Suck his cock! Suck his cock!

Mr. Speaker: Order, order. Right, that's it. Balls. I'm ignoring the lot of you now. I hope you're pleased with yourselves. I'm just going to do my jumbo crossword.

Mr. Justin Office: Mr. Speaker, I can assure my right hon. Friend that I will suck cock for anything in the Treasury above £130,000 p.a.

Hon. Members: *[rising laughter, mental calculation, moral adjustment, dying laughter]*

The Prime Minister: Mr. Speaker, this morning I had meetings with ministerial colleagues and others . . .

[The Prime Minister was tickled by the Deputy Prime Minister.]

The Prime Minister: . . . ministerial colleagues and ha ha ha . . .

The Chancellor of the Exchequer (Mr. George Osborne): Medes and Persians!

Hon. Members who attended public school: Medes and
  Persians! Who? Who?
Hon. Members who did not attend public school: Mm. Yes! Ha
  ha!
Mr. George Osborne: Blunkett! Do Blunkett!

*[Hon. Members converged on the hon. Member for Sheffield
Masturbeighton.]*

Mr. Speaker: Oh yeah. Order. Whatever. Just mind the dog, we're
  not insured.
Mr. David Blunkett (Sheffield Masturbeighton): Get . . . what
  . . . get off, you cunts, I am registered blind!

*[Hon. Members piled on top of the hon. Member for Sheffield
Masturbeighton, giggling in Latin. The hon. Member's assistance dog,
Dusky Lady, sought refuge by Mr. Speaker's Chair, where she was dou-
bly incontinent.]*

Mr. David Blunkett: *[inaudible]*
Ms. Harriet Harman (Camberwick Betspread): Mr. Speaker,
  if the Prime Minister could stop showing his tiny weeny little
  penis to the Deputy Prime Minister for two fucking minutes,
  maybe he could answer a Parliamentary Question. So far he
  has dodged the issues of Afghanistan, Sure Start centres, police
  numbers and public-sector job losses. Let him give a straight
  answer to this, Mr. Speaker. Why . . .
Hon. Members: Wanker!
Mr. Speaker: Shh.
Ms. Harriet Harman: Why . . .
Hon. Members: Wanker!

Mr. Speaker: Oh, do be quiet.

Ms. Harriet Harman: Why, Mr. Speaker, if the Prime Minister has been so busy with the affairs of State, which are traditionally conducted indoors, is he so tanned?

Mr. David Miliband (South Shields Ocado): Mr. Speaker, they say one cannot polish a turd. Yet the Prime Minister's burnished appearance would suggest otherwise. He is a glistening extruded slithery arsenugget. A big posh human gherkin of shit. Apologies, Mr. Speaker. A human gherkin of poo.

The Prime Minister: Point of Order, Mr. Speaker. The hon. Lady has a face like a fucking cat's anus. Squeezed tightly shut. Fearful, perhaps, of inquisitive fingers. The inquisitive fingers of certain Labour backbenchers . . .

Hon. Members: Wanker!

The Prime Minister: . . . certain Labour backbenchers, Mr. Speaker, who know only too well what the inside of a domesticated animal feels like.

Mr. David Blunkett: *[inaudible]*

The Home Secretary (Ms. Theresa May): Mr. Speaker, I wonder if the hon. Lady opposite is perhaps just a tiny bit envious? Of course, *FHM* didn't describe HER as 'The hottest cock-vixen we've seen prowling the Front Bench since Squirting Maggie Thatcher in that hilarious porn spoof Jonathan Ross keeps talking about,' did it? SHE isn't plastered across two pages of the *Daily Star* as a 'PILF' is she? No wonder. The hon. Lady is about as fucking glamorous as a road sweeper with thrush.

The Jazz Chancellor (Mr. Kenneth Clarke): Mm, what? Tss tss tss, Mr. Speaker, wabbeda wabbeda wabbeda pish pish ga-dap jazz, you say? Mm. Bap bap ba-diddly widdly bap. Tish pish ba-pish. Blap.

Ms. Harriet Harman: Mr. Speaker, is the hon. Lady joking? She is about as sexy as a fucking Eccles cake.

[The Home Secretary removed her outer garments to reveal fetish underwear.]

Hon. Members: Hear, hear!

The Home Secretary: Perhaps the hon. Lady opposite would care to comment on THIS, Mr. Speaker. *[to the hon. Member for Camberwick Betspread]* I don't think the hon. Lady is ready for this jelly. I don't think the hon. Lady is ready for this jelly. I don't think the hon. Lady is ready for this, 'cos my body's too Coalicious for the hon. Ladybabe.

Mr. Ed Balls (Burly & Shitwad): Mr. Speaker, I would like to report the so-called Secretary of State for Education. He's pulling faces. Oh, wait. It's his own. Ha ha ha. He looks like a fucking veal calf in a suit.

The Secretary of State for Education (Mr. Michael Gove): Mr. Speaker, the hon. Gentleman is not only guilty of using un-Parliamentary language. He is also a hypocrite. *[adjusted hair]* Look at him, Mr. Speaker. It's as if someone, humorously and suavely, had inserted a tractor-tyre inflator into his arse and just kept going until the gauge said, '120 per cent normal size' *[adjusted tie]*.

Mr. Speaker: Done, excellent. I'm going for a sandwich. Just talk among yourselves.

Mr. David Miliband: May I also draw the attention of the House to the hon. Gentleman, the Foreign Secretary? I don't wish to be too unpleasant, I must say, but he looks like a blanking kiddie fiddler. If there'd been an eighth dwarf, he would have been it and his name, I might add, would have been 'Paedy' and he . . .

Hon. Members: Wanker!

Mr. Speaker: *[absent, browsing sandwiches in Canteen]*

The Foreign Secretary (Mr. William Hague): Fuck you, monkey boy! You've got a shitting nerve, calling ME weird. Sanctimonious fucking COCKLUMP.

Mr. Kenneth Clarke: Point of squee-bop fuddler duddler pish pish ba-tish, Mr. Speaker, daddio! Mm bubba bubba. Mm bubba bubba bubba fudubba blap blap tish tish ka-pish necessary amendments ga-dish ga-bosh ga-wabbeda wabbeda tss tss drr-ap!

Moment of Syncopation.

House of Commons

Upon the Feast of St. Simon Templar, the 9th of June 2010

PRAYERS AND DIRECT MESSAGES

[Mr. Speaker on an Inflatable Cushion upon the
Booster Seat within the Chair]

Mr. Speaker's Authority Questioned Time

Mr. Speaker: Order, please. I'm in no mood for your mucking about today – I have just had a vasectomy on the NHS. While I still could. Oh, and I should point out that in the interests of impartiality I have had no political influence in any decision-making process whatsoever, whether it be the vasectomy OR the imminent destruction of the NHS.

The Secretary of State for Health (Mr. Andrew Lansley):
[inaudible, possibly 'Fucking shut up, Dopey, you cunt!']
Mr. Speaker: Shit, sorry.

[The Secretary of State for Health became aware of a fixed stare from the Prime Minister and arose to address the House 'ad hoc interruptus'.]

Mr. Andrew Lansley: On a Point of Order relating to the previous speaker, Mr. Speaker *[indicated Mr. Speaker]*, I would just like to 110 per cent assure the House that this Government will, as we said on our tin, cut the deficit, NOT the NHS. I swear on my gran's life, if at any point I stand before this House and announce hastily assembled plans to totally restructure the NHS, even if ALL THE EVIDENCE IT WAS POSSIBLE TO IMAGINE pointed to the need for a major reorganisation in the interests of health and efficiency – I mean, cost and efficiency, I mean, private healthcare providers . . .

Hon. Members: Sweaty wanker!

Mr. Speaker: Oh God. Just . . . shut up, everybody, will you? I don't want to 'come undone' or anything down there *[indicated genital area]*. Prime Minister, whenever you're ready.

The Prime Minister (Mr. David Cameron): My engagements, Mr. Speaker. This morning I had meetings with ministerial colleagues and others. Quite worrying meetings, I should add. Every day as we delve further into the legacy of shit bequeathed upon the nation by the party opposite . . .

Opposition Benches: Piss off, you slithery fucking bumcrammer!

Mr. Speaker: Shhh.

The Prime Minister: . . . by the party opposite, Mr. Speaker, the more we discover just how monumental our task is. I would just like to remind the House that if anything ends up seriously fucked over the next five years, it is their fault . . .

Ms. Nadine Dorries (Double Bedfordshire): On a Point of Order, Mr. Speaker, I would like to show the House something. Honestly, I am not making them up. These *[removed jacket and blouse]* are not my blogs. They are my tits, Mr. Speaker.

Mr. Speaker: Mm.

The Prime Minister: . . . later, I had a lengthy video conference with President Obama, although I'm afraid the subject matter must remain confidential as he realised after five minutes that he wasn't in fact talking to Piers Fucking Morgan . . .

Ms. Nadine Dorries: Some hon. Members may be wondering why there is a fifty-pound note tucked into my bra.

Hon. Members: *[private speculations]*

The Prime Minister: . . . then I did some comfort calls to Saudi Arabia, Egypt and Libya, assuring their ambassadors that despite the recession, Britain remained a dependable business partner, particularly in the aerospace-related sectors. Gaddafi, ugh. I wonder, Mr. Speaker, if hon. Members remember those 'Grass Heads' one used to get for Christmas from distant relatives? Sort of a squashy brown ball full of sawdust and grass seed, with plastic eyes on the front? You watered them and grass grew up from the head like hair and it looked fucking mental? That's what Gaddafi looks like.

Ms. Nadine Dorries: Mr. Speaker . . .

The Prime Minister: No, wait. I'm thinking of Peter Mandelson. Gaddafi is the one with the hat, isn't he?

Ms. Nadine Dorries: Mr. Speaker, let me solve the mystery of the fifty-pound note in my bra. It is a humorous-type reference to my appearance on a Channel 4 reality-TV programme in which I was alleged to have smuggled money into a council flat which I was staying in as part of a social experiment to see how successful people like yours truly, who grew up in a council flat which was eventually liberated from socialist greed through the Right to Buy initiative . . .

Hon. Members: *[nodding off, fidgeting, surreptitious drinking]*

Ms. Nadine Dorries: . . . someone, as I say, like myself, who has done well for myself and is a proper working-class Tory, as I say, with money in her underwear, how someone like myself would get on these days living in a council flat like some *Shameless*-type Labour voter. According to one blog – mine, as it happens, though I may have denied writing it, I can't remember – I

popped £50 where any self-respecting female who knows how to get what she wants would – down my top!

This, Mr. Speaker *[indicated bra]*, is my way of reminding the media that (a) I am still available for Home Secretary, and (b) you can't believe everything you read or hear. Or see. *[indicated ringing mobile telephone]* Sorry, I have to take this. It's my lawyer.

The Prime Minister: Lunch today, Mr. Speaker, was spent in the company of representatives from the PFI contracting industry. We agreed that speedy action to reduce the deficit was necessary and that more could be done in the public sector to help PFI contractors . . .

Ms. Nadine Dorries: *[re-robing]* Sorry, Mr. Speaker. My lawyer has advised me to get dressed in case I incriminate myself through speculation. Mr. Speaker? Mr. Speaker!

Mr. Speaker: *[waking with a start]* Bah! No! I will NOT wear the Robes in bed! You got KY jelly all over them the last time and they cost a fucking fortune to dry clean . . . What? Oh yes, I see where I am. Hon. Members must forgive me. I fear I am still suffering some after-effects from the anaesthetic.

Ms. Nadine Dorries: Mr. Speaker, while you were unconscious we all had a secret ballot and decided to get rid of you. You're a complete bloody liability. Ha ha, the look on your face.

Mr. Speaker: *[shook fist]* Why, you . . .

The Prime Minister: Oh, you know what? Fuck this for a game of marbles, I'm going. My future engagements this evening, Mr. Speaker, you dwarfish buggerfuck, will include a cursory look at some Boxes, a light supper alone in the kitchen, banging one out in the en-suite and a bloody good night's sleep. Nick, you're on.

[The Prime Minister quit the Chamber, other hon. Members following. The Deputy Prime Minister removed his headphones and caused the quietude of his iPod.]

The Deputy Prime Minister (Mr. Nick Clegg): Right. What's occurring? You! Fag! *[indicated the hon. Member for Inverness & Arseache]* Bring me a crumpet! And be quick about it, or there'll be a fireside flogging in the Senior Common Room. Again.

Mr. Danny Alexander (Inverness & Arseache): Woof!

[The hon. Member for Inverness & Arseache quit the Chamber, followed by a number of hon. Members.]

Ms. Nadine Dorries: Mr. Deputy Prime Minister. As the Speaker has fallen asleep again perhaps I should direct my remarks, and my tits, to you. As you may know, there is a plot among senior Tories to get rid of the present Speaker, who is rubbish, and have him replaced by someone who knows what's what. Mr. Deputy Prime Minister, I am more than happy to associate myself with this plot. Not because I feel any malice or whatever towards that snoozing bloody useless tosser, but because I wish to be regarded as a senior Tory.

The Deputy Prime Minister: Oh, blah blah blah, I'm so interested, fuck. *[expiration: imperceptible, possibly 'sigh']* Very well. Let's actually take a vote then, shall we? All those in favour of retaining Mr. Speaker . . . *[counted the Ayes]* two. All those in favour of sacking the little toerag . . . *[counted the Noes]* four, including me and the hard-faced chavvy blonde.

Ms. Nadine Dorries: Yes! *[pumped fist]* Yes!

Mr. Speaker: *[asleep]*

The Deputy Prime Minister: Right, we'll sort out the details in due course. Might have a word with Andrew Lloyd Webber. Maybe we could find a new Speaker on BBC1, Saturday nights, call it *Any Cunt Will Do*. Fag! Where's my fucking crumpet?

[The Deputy Prime Minister and remaining hon. Members quit the Chamber. After an interlude of some minutes, Mr. Speaker regained consciousness, surveyed the empty Chamber and adjusted his Robes.]

Mr. Speaker: Order, order! Or I'll send you all to the fucking Tower, ha ha!

[The Speaker descended from the Chair, taking up the Mace of the House, then manipulating it, uttering lightsaber noises, then dropping it, then reseating it carefully upon the Cradle of the Mace, then returning to the Inflatable Cushion upon the Booster Seat within the Chair.]

Mr. Speaker: *[to imaginary hon. Member]* Are you addressin' me? Are you addressin' me? Then who the hell else are you addressin'? You addressin' me? Well, I'm the only one here. Who the fuck do you think you're addressin'?

[Mr. Speaker drew an imaginary gun and shot the imaginary hon. Member. Mr. Speaker then made a noise of satisfaction, collected his papers and left the Chamber, remembering to switch off all the lights as he departed.]

Moment of Extinguishment.

House of Commons
Upon the Feast of St. Cutlet, the 14th of June 2010
PRAYERS AND REGISTER
[A Guest Speaker in the Chair]

Education, Re-Education and Free Education

The Bailiff of the House: Oyez, oyez! Be it aforeknown that the Speaker of the House is indisposed, due to a Tummy Upset. Concomitantly be it then afterknown in the jurisprudence of *[inaudible, possibly 'Something something I can't fucking remember, I hate this gig, I wish I was still doing shifts down the London Dungeon']* that the Deputy Speaker of the House is *atque in absentia*, being on a *[consulted Absence Form]* 'Family Overseas Parliamentary Business Holiday Conference'. Be it known that he seems to have ticked all the boxes. *Honi soit qui mal y pense,* will the House please welcome back as Guest Speaker for Education Questions – Mr. Bercow's predecessor, the Baron Martin of Hartburn.

[Baron Martin, wearing the Black Robes of State, entered the

Chamber via High Dudgeon, carelessly swinging the Mace of Order, taking his seat upon the Chair.]

Mr. David Miliband (South Shields Ocado): Fucking ouch! Apologies. I meant blanking flip. Mr. Speaker, on a Point of Order, you deliberately hit me in the face. It was an assault – an unprovoked assault, I might add. With, I might add, quite a few witnesses . . .

Hon. Members: Hear, hear. Has he put on weight? He looks a bit unsteady on his feet. Where have you travelled down from, mate? Scotch Corner?

Mr. Miliband: . . . witnesses, as I say, Mr. Speaker. And, I might add, under Parliamentary Rules you are now required to expunge yourself from the Chamber for committing a Gross Breach of Parliamentary Decorum Occasioning Actual Bodily Harm. My cheek will be livid tomorrow morning, I might add.

[Mr. Speaker nodded most gravely to the Officers of the House and rose from the Chair. Mr. Speaker then most forcefully presented the Mace unto the face of the hon. Member for South Shields Ocado, then likewise unto the faces of diverse hon. Members near by.]

Hon. Members: *[commotion, wailing, laughter]*

Mr. Speaker (Fat Scottish): Bailiff, escort yon sorry cunts to the Infirmary. And give the carpet a wee sponge doon, eh?

[The hon. Member for South Shields Ocado and others were helped from the Chamber. Mr. Speaker returning to the Chair, in possession of the Mace.]

Mr. Speaker: Oh aye, ye insufferable tubs o' minge, I know ye all conspired to get me oot. Motion o' No Confidence, ye

Sassenach cockpieces? Fuck ye. But my associate *[indicated Mace]* and I are back, for noo anyway, so if any of ye fucking dribbling bladders o' shite have anything to say . . . No?

Hon. Members: *[studied Order Papers]*

Mr. Speaker: Ye wee cowerin' timorous fucking pasties, I thought no. Lassie in the trooser suit there with the designer glasses and the hint of a moustache, aye.

Miss Patsy Clone (Ealing & Acton with Halloumi): Mr. Speaker, will the House join me in applauding the very lovely Secretary of State for Education? And may I breathlessly commend his brilliant plan to end the bloody awful Marxist tyranny of the State by transferring the financial control of schools from local authorities to his own Department? He is frightfully clever *[inaudible, possibly 'and pretty dishy!'].*

The Secretary of State for Education (Mr. Michael Gove): Mr. Speaker, I thank the learned and hon. Lady most suavely for her commendation. *[adjusted tie]* I have recently been in consultation with some pretty eminent dinner-party guests, who have confirmed my own persuasions. *[adjusted trousers]* Mr. Speaker, it is essential that we liberate schools from the ideological burden of dependable funding. It makes much more sense for school budgets to be co-ordinated in the future by my Department, which as you know abhors State control. And of course it is, conveniently, just down the road from here *[adjusted hair].*

Mr. Ed Balls (Burly & Shitwad): Mr. Speaker, is the hon. Gentleman aware that he has a face like one of the incidental characters in fucking *Peppa Pig*?

Hon. Members: *[pig noises, catcalls, barking, tooting]*

Mr. Speaker: Order in the fucking Hoose, ye scabs, ye jabbering apes!

Mr. Michael Gove: Well, Mr. Speaker, he can talk. The hon. Gentleman looks like the result of a *[adjusted hair]* bizarre gene-splicing experiment, in which human DNA has been microbiologically combined with the plasma from a DONER KEBAB.

Hon. Members: *[singing]* 'Ballsy is a doner kebab, doner kebab, doner kebab . . .'

Mr. Michael Gove: I will take no lectures, Mr. Speaker, from anyone whose materiality, let me again remind the House . . .

Hon. Members: Wanker!

Mr. Speaker: Silence, ye fucking cackworms!

Hon. Members: Wanker! Wanker!

Mr. Speaker: Fucking order! The next cunt that speaks oot o' turn will be beaten into fucking Summer Pudding. By me and *[indicated Mace]* 'Mr. Murdoch' here.

Mr. Michael Gove: . . . whose materiality, Mr. Speaker, is biologically based upon fucking kebab plasma. A rumpled, sixteen-stone duvet of glistening plasmatised kebab, squeezed into a grey two-piece suit from Marks and Spencer. Yes, let the hon. Member put THAT in his pipe. Indeed, Mr. Speaker, he is most welcome to light the pipe and then shove it up his fat flapping doner kebab of an *[adjusted cufflinks]* arse.

Mrs. Olivia Vida-Loca (Buxton with a Hint of Cranberry): Could the Secretary of State confirm that his Department is to be 'rebadged'? Also, could he acknowledge that I am physically here, for the purposes of expenses?

Mr. Michael Gove: Mr. Speaker, I am happy to acknowledge the presence of my hon. Friend and thank her for her important question. I can confirm that we have done away with the ridiculous title devised by Labour – the Department for Children, Families, Feelings, Schools, People, Relationships and Learning to Live. It is now to be known simply as the Department for Education.

Ms. Sarah Teather (Brent Non-Gluten): Mr. Speaker, the hon. Gentleman makes me, a Liberal Democrat, absolutely sick to my vulva. Is this so-called 'rebadge' not typical of the Tories and their crypto-fascist dog whistles? We are all aware that 'Department for Education' is exactly what it was called in Nazi Fucking Germany *[consulted notes]* and, OK, I've just remembered we're in the Coalition. No further questions, Mr. Speaker.

Mrs. Olivia Vida-Loca: I would just like to say to the Secretary of State: keep up the good work. As the Beatles nearly said: 'All You Need Is Gove'.

Mr. Speaker: Order, order! The hon. Lady kens full well that was no a question. She must either ask a fucking question or piss off.

Mrs. Olivia Vida-Loca: I apologise unreservedly to the House, Mr. Speaker. Would the Secretary of State care to *[manipulated breasts]* visit my constituency? He will discover a rosy-fingered dawn for education, and exciting new horizons.

Mr. Michael Gove: Mr. Speaker, I acknowledge the hon. Lady's impassioned advocacy. I can assure her that I will *[adjusted trousers]* weigh all the evidence most carefully.

Ms. Sarah Teather: It's just that . . . does the introduction of so-called 'free schools' not effectively invert the status quo, Mr. Speaker? Here we have groups of pushy parents who will be given public funds – and public buildings – in order to set up their little hothouses for spoiled children, while those marooned in the public sector must seek money and buildings from the private sector? Is it not the case that these 'free schools' are simply a cheap and convenient way for so-called 'yummy mummies' and 'faddy daddies' to secure a private education for their little darlings at the expense of fucking taxpayers?

Hon. Members: *[clamour, alarums]*

Mr. Speaker: Order, order. I'm warning ye, some fucker's going to get a Mace in the face any minute noo.

Mr. Michael Gove: Mr. Speaker, the hon. Lady may complain about free schools as loudly as she likes. We all know what the Liberal Democrats favour: a socialised kibbutz network teaching nature studies and fucking Woody Guthrie songs. *[consulted notes]* However, I am reminded that the hon. Lady is actually in Government. She is a valued and most diligent colleague. I see my mistake, I gladly confirm that free schools will allow Liberal Democrat parents *[adjusted face]* to secure Latin and history lessons in Georgian buildings vacated by community groups who no longer receive adequate funding from local authorities . . .

Mr. Ed Balls: And whose fucking fault is THAT, you mimsy ponce?

[The Chamber fell silent. Mr. Speaker took up the Mace and presented it with force unto the guts of the hon. Member for Burly & Shitwad.]

Mr. Speaker: Bailiff! Have that sack o' fucking offal removed from the Hoose! Lassie with the shit-eating grin, pray continue.

Mr. Ed Balls: *[exiting the Chamber, inaudible, possibly 'You cunt,*

Gove, you just nicked all our ideas but fucking explained them better. Excuse my grammar – I went to a private school']

Ms. Sarah Teather: Mr. Speaker, I am grateful to the hon. Gentleman for acknowledging our meeting of minds on this matter. I was indeed commending his proposals to create 'middle classrooms' in converted buildings across the country. The only way to encourage fairness in the system, as he knows, is to have boutique schools popping up here and there at the behest of the bourgeoisie. May I suggest he goes further, by scrapping Labour's preposterous League Table of Schools and replacing it with a League Table of Parents, who should be required to show their aspirational fitness to receive the very best education for their children that public money can buy.

Hon. Members: *[waved Order Papers and body parts]*

Mr. Alfie Noakes (Dudley Moor): Eh up, Mr. Speaker, you all right? As a Comical Northerner elected by Comical Northerners to be Comically Northern in this 'Ouse, can I pull this reet funny face? *[gurned]* I think we all know why t' Secretary of State has dumped t' recipe book for schools that t' previous Government produced, which as you will recall, Mr. Speaker, included recipes for reet proper English food, e.g. Lancashire shitpot, battered rural-cottage pie, foonky choonky chips and puddens. Aye, but t' right hon. hoity-toity shitty-twatty Gentleman might not have heard of those, because I understand from *T' Times* this morning that his favourite meal is summat called 'scaloppini wi' parmentier potatoes'. Well, we don't get fancy foreign muck like that up north because we are hard and dead scared someone will call us 'omosexual. If northern kiddies are now going to be force-fed fucking scaloppini wi' parmentier potatoes in school canteens . . .

Mr. Speaker: Shut up, you cunt. Next.

Mr. Phil Space (Breafton Askingham): Can the Secretary of State not find a post within the Government for the brilliant Toby Young, whose inspiring struggle through months of white wine and olives and cultured conversation with like-minded parents gathered round an antique kitchen table looked fucking brilliant on the television? He was also very good on *Celebrity Come Dine with Me*, Mr. Speaker.

Mr. Michael Gove: The gentleman whom my hon. Friend mentioned, Mr Toby Young, is one of the most fluent advocates of scaloppini with parmentier potatoes in West London *[adjusted hair]*. I am pleased to be able to report that he has accepted a post within my Department as senior adviser on hosting free-school explorative dinner parties. He will . . .

Mr. Alfie Noakes: Fuck Toby Young in t' face with his own bloody fancy Beef Wellington! T' people of t' North . . .

Moment of Interruption with Mace.

House of Commons

Held upon the ███ *of* ███████████

ONGOING AND PERMANENT SESSION
OF THE PUBLIC ADMINISTRATION
SELECT COMMITTEE

THE IRAQ INQUIRY

Redacted in the Interests of ███████ ████████

Appearance by Mr. Tony Blair

Lord ████████████: Is your name Tony Blair?

Mr. Blair: Yep, yep, sure. That's my name. Don't wear it out!

Lord ████████████: And you were Prime Minister at the time of the Iraq War?

Mr. Blair: Look, the Iraq War happened to occur during my tenure as Prime Minister, yes. I mean, I can't deny that. I can't fucking change history, can I? Not any more!

[The Inquiry was suspended for a short while to allow Mr. Blair ██████████████████████████████████ *]*

Lord ████████: If I may turn now to the period in the run-up to war. Your religious and moral convictions led you to believe . . .

Mr. Blair: Yeah, if I can just stop you there. Enquiries of this nature should be directed to the Tony Blair Faith Foundation. They're dealing with all the 'what I genuinely believe' stuff these days.

Sir ████████████████: We HAVE tried to contact them, Mr. Blair. We were on hold for twenty-five minutes listening to some bloody awful gospel-rock music.

Mr. Blair: Well, of course God's BUSY. He's GOD. Duh.

Lord ████████: Mr. Blair, Sir ████████████████ described you as having a 'gleam in your ████' as war approached. Is that true?

Mr. Blair: I fail to see what the condition of my ████ has to do with anything. Both President Bush and I agreed that these were dangerous times. We all had to keep our ████s peeled . . .

Sir ████████: Is that someone's mobile phone? There is a very strict rule . . .

Mr. Blair: Yeah, hi. Bit awk, to be honest. I'm in the inquiry. IN THE INQUIRY! Oh fuck, hang on, I think we're about to go into a tunnel . . .

Lord ████████: Is it nearly lunchtime?

Sir ████████████: It's certainly after ten . . .

Moment of Suspension.

House of Commons
Upon the Eve of the Sacred Reduction, the 17th of June 2010
PRAYERS AND WIND
[The Chair unoccupied]

Deficit Attention Hyperactivity Disorder

Ye Bailiff of ye House: Oyez, oyez! Be it known in abidement and department, along and abroad, that the Speaker of the House is this day indisposed. I have a note here *[produced note]*:

Dear House of Commons, I'm afraid John (Mr. Speaker) will not be in today. I am keeping him at home. John tells me he is being systematically bullied by hon. Members. This is unacceptable. I am extremely cross and have now referred the matter to the Whips Office (cc: the Privy Council, *Newsnight*, Buckingham Palace, *Watchdog*, Facebook). What I need from you is (1) an assurance that the bullying will be tackled and subsequently enforced on a zero-tolerance basis, and (2) an official apology from the House of Commons. Until then, John will be at home, studying on the Internet, doing educational jigsaws, etc. Yours, Mrs. Bercow kiss kiss.

Oyez, thereuntowithstanding the aforementioned, will the House please welcome, at very short notice, in his new robes, straight from The Place We Dare Not Name: Baron Prescott of Kingston upon Hull!

[Baron Prescott entered the Chamber via Old Pie Corner, enclad in finest robes of ermine, badger, red squirrel and lynx. Also a black velvet hat most commodious in volume, bearing the Playboy emblem. Then before the Table of the House, nodding most gravely to Officials and hon. Members. Then recognising an hon. Member on the Back Benches, pointing and shouting.]

Mr. After-Dinner Speaker (Baron Prescott of Kingston upon Hull): Ozzie! Oz! Oz, lad! Do us a favour, son, wake up that fat prick at the end. Cheers. Ozzie! John! You all right? Aye, in Chair today! *[indicated Opposition Front Bench]* Bloody hell, Government Front Bench look like a right fucking shower of jessies, eh? What are you doing on Tory side, you dozy get?

[The Clerk of the House in remindment to Baron Prescott, viz. inasmuch that Government and Opposition hon. Members had exchanged sides of the Chamber following the General Election. Baron Prescott then indicated an Old Penny dropping and did take his seat upon the Chair, exhaling most diversely.]

Mr. After-Dinner Speaker: Ladies, gents, may I take this opportunity to say how truly great it is to be back here in this House. Which reminds me of a story. When I was a steward in Merchant Navy we had Sir Anthony Eden on board, and I used to bring him his drinks. If anyone wants a proper after-dinner speaker for whatever function or event, I've got a million stories like that one. The time I tried to have a piss with boxing gloves on. The time I tried to play piano with boxing gloves on. The time I was your proper working-class heart and soul of Labour Party, aye, before Lord 'Ooh Matron the Curtains' Mandelson became our manager and turned a raw northern R&B band in leather jackets and jeans, over in Germany a lot of the time, Cold War then, tuneful pop, we all had to wear suits, though I may be confusing meself with one of that Fab Four as it happens, probably John Lennon, a poet of the people I have always admired for his honesty, like mine. Irregardless, what you see is what you get. Take me as I am. I hope by the end of me after-dinner speech which I am prepared to offer anyone here a discount if they have a function or event coming up and they wish to add a bit of meat and potatoes to their steamed green vegetables, that's fine with me. Seriously, put yourself and your company or organisation in my hands for forty-five minutes, I will show you that there is more to me than croquet, bulimia, that famous 'chipolata cock' and punching the face of some cunt with a mullet.

[Baron Prescott laughed most heartily, his reading spectacles then losing purchase and falling to the floor.]

Ms. Trimmy Ladygarden (Portsmouth Entryfoam): Will the Chancellor of the Exchequer tell us how he plans to reduce the deficit? A scandalous deficit created by the party opposite and then just dumped in our laps like an aborted lamb?

Hon. Members: Wankers! Deficit deniers! Deficit confirmers! Do you do weddings?

Mr. After-Dinner Speaker: Eh eh eh eh eh eh, order now. Shit! Missed call. Keep fucking noise down, show a bit of respect, eh? Tranny with that silly wig on, aye, you. Sorry, love *[replaced spectacles]*. I should have gone to Specsavers, I'm doing one for them next week. Pray continue, love.

Ms. Trimmy Ladygarden: Dumped in our laps like a steaming heap of aborted lamb, as I say, with a scrawled note attached from the former Chief Secretary to the Treasury – yes, Mr. After-Dinner Speaker, *[indicated]* the giggling hon. Member for Birmingham Souplunch there – that simply said:

Ha ha ha, I'm afraid to tell you there's no money left, we've shoved fish fingers under the floorboards and blocked up all the toilets in the Gents with shredded accounts, fuck you.

Perhaps the manly and, if I may say so, dashing Chancellor of the Exchequer could fill me with love – I mean, us in.

[The Chancellor of the Exchequer (Mr. George Osborne) gave a slight cackle and stroked a bullwhip.]

Hon. Members: *[kissing noises both exaggerated and perfunctory, idle scratchings, gurning]*

Mr. Liam Byrne (Birmingham Souplunch): Mr. After-Dinner Speaker, the hon. Lady may think what she likes. She reminds me of one of those very, very slow girls you get sometimes in a charity shop, who smell of TCP . . .

[Mr. After-Dinner Speaker, having made his way to the Opposition Benches, did then punch the hon. Member for Birmingham Souplunch in the face, twice. Then occurred an overbalancing and a catching of the Robes, Mr. After-Dinner Speaker toppling most unpropitiously upon the hon. Member for Doncaster Awkwood, who then did cry out in self-censored expressions of outrage.]

71

Mr. Ed Miliband (Doncaster Awkwood): Blank you, you blank-ing blank of blank! Mr. After-Dinner Speaker, I'm not blanking joking, I think you've burst my blanking pancreas!

Mr. After-Dinner Speaker: Fuck, fuck. Never mind your bloody pantyhose, son, I think I've done me back. Bailiff, get me off this twerp and back on me feet, eh?

[The Bailiff of the House then retrieving Mr. After-Dinner Speaker and calling for the Paramedics of the House, who having been summoned did most expeditiously remove the injured from the Chamber via stretchers.]

Hon. Members: *[cheering, sneering, jeering, peering, leering, questioning]*

Mr. After-Dinner Speaker: Me poor bloody back. I've got twinges now. Hasn't felt like this since I gave me secretary one over the desk for a laugh and I slipped on a fax and broke the desk and hospitalised me secretary and put me fucking back into spasm. I hadn't even got it in! As I say, any do, any function, I'll tell me little anecdotes without *[mimed 'punching']* compunction. Sneery bastard. Aye, you, son. Let's have it then. Spit it out, you smarmy fucking bugger.

The Chancellor of the Exchequer (Mr. George Osborne): Mr. After-Dinner Speaker, I most cruelly invite the House to commend our Emergency Budget. Now, I won't deny that it will hurt. But through the pain, the people of Britain will thank me and, ha ha, beg for more because they love it really. I can see it in their frightened, excited eyes. It pleases and arouses me.

Mr. Alan Johnson (Long Division & Baffle): On a Point of Order, Mr. After-Dinner Speaker, I have got a copy of the

Emergency Budget here *[produced copy of Select Committee Report on 'The Sanctioned Torture of British Citizens at Guantanamo Bay']* and as Shadow Chancellor I can tell the hon. Gentleman he is demonstrably incorrect about everything. *[consulted report]* OK, I seem to have brought the wrong document with me to the House, but I can definitely remember the important bits.

Hon. Members: Wanker! You couldn't shadow a fucking snowman! Fuck off back to your old job, Postman Cunt!

Mr. George Osborne: Mr. After-Dinner Speaker, I note the hon. Gentleman has a report on *[purred]* torture there. Well, I can assure the House that I know more about economics AND torture than the stumbling cocklump opposite. Look at him, Mr. After-Dinner Speaker, he's shambolic. He's got fucking toast crumbs on his tie and shaving foam behind his ear. And I am supposed to take criticism from this vulgar human wreck? *[thrashed Dispatch Box with cane]* No, Mr. After-Dinner Speaker, I am not. I intend to show the House why it is necessary to penetrate this country's fiscal rectitude with a deep thrusting motion, administering the cruel but very necessary arse-fucking the nation requires again and *[cane thrash]* again and again. Bring in the Players!

[Then entered the Chamber a troupe of actors from the Community Theatre of Crouch End, in Matinee Performance costumes celebrating the Golden Era of Rock and Roll: the Gentlemen in pomaded hair, dressed as hon. Members of the Labouring Classes with disposable income; the Ladies attired in gingham or leather. Music having been caused to issue from a CD player, the Assembled Players then singing and dancing the musical number 'You're the

73

One that I Want'; the Chancellor of the Exchequer delivering a
meta-narrative.]

Mr. George Osborne: *[shouting]* I commend to the House the
lessons of *Grease*! We must not allow this to happen here! Mr.
After-Dinner Speaker, observe the smiling musical players as
they cavort so extravagantly in a world of plenty, without a
care in the fucking world! *Grease*! Kept going for years with the
hard-earned money of ordinary people throughout the world,
bankrolling an absurd and irritating world of make-believe! Ha!
But observe how the apparently financially secure *Grease* falls
apart, most cruelly, *[purring]* ha ha ha!

[One by one, the Assembled Players stopped smiling, and in aspect dif-
fident did appear to forget their lines, fall over, etc.]

Hon. Members: I like the sulky one with the big tits! Olivia
Newton-John, phwoar, I used to wish she'd take me up
her Country Road! Didn't that little one used to be on the
television?

Mr. After-Dinner Speaker: *[singing]* 'You're a wobbly dog, whoo
hoo hoo!' Belter.

Mr. George Osborne: *[shouting]* The House will observe the
nightmare that *Grease* has now become. Confidence falling!
Amiable mood dissipated! Interest rates rising! Mannered theat-
ricality giving way to maudlin introspection! Costumes torn and
dirty! Jobs lost! Strikes! *[the Assembled Players sitting on the Floor*
of the House] Violence! *[then hitting one another]* Riots!

[A Running Amok in the House, Mr. After-Dinner Speaker then
confronting and punching several of the Players, the Bailiff and Royal

Cudgellers then driving them from the Chamber, some alarums with cudgels and small arms, the House then being suspended for twenty minutes.]

Mr. George Osborne: My point is this: *Grease* delayed deficit reduction and is now 'the word' for 'fuck-up on a massive scale'. Mr. After-Dinner Speaker, *Grease* faces in the end not fewer but MORE drastic spending cuts than if they'd acted properly in the first place! *[consulting with the Prime Minister]* As I say, not fewer but MORE 'sensible budget savings'. This country is now back on the path of fiscal responsibility. We are out of the Danger Zone. The world has backed us. Our credit rating – the mark of trust in our economy – has been preserved. The International Monetary Fund, the G20, yes, even the EU. Deficit reduction, *[cane thrash]* deficit reduction, *[cane thrash]* deficit reduction *[cane thrash]*. Everyone in the fucking world supports our course of action. Why won't the pussies and bitches opposite do the same?

Hon. Members: Bollocks! Quim-diddlers! Fuckshafts!

Mr. After-Dinner Speaker: Oy oy, now then, let's have a bit of order in House, eh? All this disruption and commotion reminds me of Trades Union Congress, in old days. Bloody hell. Smoke-filled rooms. Beer and sandwiches. Quick knee-trembler with some little poppet from *Manchester Guardian*, up against cubicle door, aye, I've got hundreds of stories like that from 'Politics's Age of Innocence'. See me after if you're interested in me anecdotes, not me knee-tremblers; as I say, me fucking back's gone.

Mr. Alan Johnson: Could the Chancellor of the Exchequer explain to the House how it is, in the figures he *[consulted* *memory]* gave us, how those figures even add up? Because buried in the small print for all this is a rise in National Insurance contributions of 5,000 per cent! Income tax makes even less sense when you try to do the sums. I have tried to fathom how his calculations for corporation tax have been made. It's a total fucking mystery to me, Mr. After-Dinner Speaker. The hon. Gentleman should therefore resign.

Mr. George Osborne: I wonder if the hon. Gentleman could tell the House whether in his 'calculations' he has remembered to subtract the escalating integers from all cross-quantified virements?

Mr. Alan Johnson: *[consulted memory for some time]* I would remind the hon. Gentleman, Mr. After-Dinner Speaker, that he is the one who's supposed to be answering the questions here, not me.

Mr. George Osborne: Has he subtracted the escalating integers or not? It's a perfectly straightforward question for someone standing there with a fucking straight face pretending to be Shadow Chancellor.

Hon. Members: Answer! Aye or No? Escalating integers – Aye or No? You useless dollop of sex gunge!

Mr. After-Dinner Speaker: Order, order. This level of debate is nothing like it used to be in the 1970s. I once punched all four members of Slade, you know, in Blackpool. Hon. Member with face like a fucking death mask.

Mr. Alan Johnson: Mr. After-Dinner Speaker, yes, I did remember to subtract the . . . those things referred to by the hon. Member. Now perhaps we can move on to the much more important issue of . . .

Mr. George Osborne: Aha! I made it up, Mr. After-Dinner Speaker! I just fucking made it up! The hon. Gentleman's fallen right into my trap! I will be back later to poke him with a sharpened stick. Ha ha ha!

Mr. Alan Johnson: I have been informed, Mr. After-Dinner Speaker, that there is a chimney fire at one of my houses. I'm sorry, I'll have to go. But the House hasn't heard the last of this, or me. I know how many beans make five, don't you worry about that!

[The hon. Member for Long Division & Baffle quit the Chamber, shouting, 'Five!' then stumbling on his way out and neglecting to nod to Mr. After-Dinner Speaker, who then summoned him back to the Chamber for a punching, then allowed him to leave, to the delight of the House.]

Mr. George Osborne: If I may turn to the subject of our proposed pension upgrade. We now have a triple lock in place to make sure that nobody wanders out into the road. They're really pretty easy to subdue, to be honest. Frail. *[purred]*

[The House then disrupted by the re-entry of the cast of Grease, *in rioting synchronous, further demonstrating the Errors of Fiscal Impropriety with criminal damage and a medley. Mr. After-Dinner Speaker then punching all within his reach and further promoting his services as an anecdotalist.]*

Moment of Constitutional Suction.

FUCTUM EST DE REPUBLICA

Justice Select Committee

Time held: 5/2, going into 6/4 for the middle eight

PRAYERS AND RIMSHOTS

[The Jazz Chancellor and Secretary of State
for Justice on the Stool]

Fullsome Prison Blues

[The Jazz Chancellor shuffled in on the off-beat, extinguished his pan-atella and took his place upon the Stool. Hon. Members of the Select Committee then arranging themselves loosely on improvised seating.]

The Jazz Chancellor (Mr. Kenneth Clarke): Welcome to this wap bap brrr-dap pish exploratory session, where I hope we might lay down some initial bap bap wabbeda wabbeda wabbeda pish pish ga-doof doof guidelines and parameters. If everybody's ready, I'll count us in. A one, a two, a three, a bap bap . . .

Ms. Connie Mingus (Scatford): Jazz Chancellor, nobody supports the notion of a strong and independent judiciary more than mm ba ba be-diddly mm bah boo I. Never the skiddly bap less, there really do seem to be some tss-tss irreconcilable

78

issues here, Jazz Chancellor. Not least your hoo mm hoo wah mm bap bap views on short-term sentencing. Surely the political momentum is with the n'dooden-dooden-doo bah idea be-doo n'doo ba-boo that a FIRMER line should be taken with these repeat offender toerags. Or have I wap bap ba-fiddly barp be-ba n'doo bip missed some essential jive background briefing, daddio?

Committee Members: Hear, wap bap ba-glap tish doof doof ba-squiddly hear!

Mr. Kenneth Clarke: Wabbeda wabbeda look, I'm not going to sit uncomfortably on this stool and tell you boom bap bap scriddly beep that clang I have all the squee squee hubbeda pish pish answers. Yes, we have to be tough on crime, but let's fuggeda fuggeda face facts. The prison population now stands at an astonishing 85,000, sister! Short tss tss blap prison sentences are hopeless, frankly. You can't rehab-a-bab-babbeda-babbeda-ilitate anyone in less than twelve months. Ba parp parp duddler there's barely enough time for a drum solo.

Committee Members: Tss-tt-tt-tss-tt-tt-tss blap boodler boodler wap wap! Hiddler diddler diddler diddler doof! Smack bap ga-blap blap fa-diddler buddler hoodler mummener pish gack ba gack!

Mr. Ronnie Scotsman (Easy & Mellow): Mm, if I may, Jazz Chancellor, mm bubba bubba hm, isn't there a very real danger of the Coalition Government being mm seen mm seen mm seen to be soft and chilled-out on crime mer-mm mm hm mm?

Mr. Kenneth Clarke: Oh, tish tish. That's utterly pre-Pappa-You-Done-Yo-Sugar-Mama-Wrong-posterous. *[general laughter]* Oh, I see. Ka-boom tish. A joke. Very good, splap splap but seriously, wabbeda wabbeda look. All the political cats and catesses know me. I'm a moderate. I'm not from the hanging and flog bog ga-dogging wing of the party. I'm not going to delight the shit fuck bollocka bollacka *Mail on Sunday*. 'Soft', 'tough' on crime, glap? EVERY sensible jazzer's tough on crime. But huggela huggela blap bap ga-pish we had twenty-one criminal-justice bills in thirteen years under Labour. We have got to be-bup drap-wap ba diddly tss repeal some of that hoo-doo they fiddler buddler babbler wabbler done, take it away.

Mrs. Minny Minstrels (South-West Dixieland): Bah bah boo let's be honest, these young offender pwee peeply peep peep peep shitbags have absolutely no respect for property, or jazz. And a one and a two and since when can the European Convention on Human whee tss-blap blap Rights force us to give fucking paedophiles the vote?

Mr. Kenneth Clarke: It's really not as hap da-pap pap blang hap ba dap-dap fuddler widdly bap-bap wabbeda wabbeda wabbeda straightforward as that . . .

Mr. Perry Mentalshit (Baritone Saxmundham): It barp is, though. What next? Paedophile MPs, kiddie-fiddler ga-blap bap widdler diddling their expenses all the way to respecta-bap-ga-dap-ga-dish-ga-dap-ga-doof-ability? Paedophile ministers parp? Is that what the bish bish parp Jazz Chancellor wants? A bum bum ba-fiddler diddler pss-pss ba-bum fiddler nonce in Number 10?

Committee Members: Huggeda huggeda bap dap ba-tss tss tss! Solid gone! Sorry, I'm lost, can we take it from the top again?

Mr. Kenneth Clarke: Wabbeda wabbeda look: drugs, alcohol, a feckless disregard for others. These tss-tss things have always been brilliant for producing great jazz. But blap bap ba-diddly boo hoo tss it is a sad fact that only a tiny minority of alcoholic junkies go on to be fucking amazing on the flugelhorn. Or to drr-blap drr-blap produce seminal works that push back the theoretical boundaries of free-form music. In fuggeda fuggeda fact, quite a few druggy pissheads end up taking the Underclass A-Train to prison and back, bap ba-diddly diddly bap, prison and back, bap ba-diddly diddly bap. We need to tackle this in two tss-tss ways. In the 'trad' way, with firmness. Ba-dom ba-doom glap glap ba-BUT also in the 'post-bebop' way. Syncopated rehab-de-bab-ilitation. Pastoral jazz tss-tss support. A more intuitive, jamming kind of ooh woo wah wah brap dap puddleduck puddleduck puddleduck bap da-glap tss-tss pit pat paddle pat hubbler bubbler pish pish ka-bosh Probation Service.

Mr. Eddy Choplicks (Newcastle Coltrane): I don't wish to fweep boop play devil's advocate, but does the Jazz Chancellor think he might actually just be on the tss-tss Front Bench as some kind of drr-glap mascot? You know, like an elderly, wrinkly, amiable, harmless, dozy tss-tss fucking dog? To make the Coalition seem friendlier, more 'weekend'? Bap bap huddler doof doof ba-diddly widdly widdly biddly pish?

Mr. Kenneth Clarke: Wabbeda habbeda bubbeda brap brap pish ba-tish tish boom sorry, what was the wabbeda wabbeda question?

Moment of Hamlet.

House of Commons

Upon the Feast of St. Culpababel, the 24th of June 2010

PRAYERS AND RECRIMINATIONS

[Mr. Speaker upon the Booster Seat within the Chair]

The Big Family

Mr. Jonty de Meanour (Toad-in-the-Wold): Will the Prime Minister be so good as to tell us what he had for breakfast this morning? I for one am dying to know.

Hon. Members: *[wriggling, giggling, absence, sanctimony]*

The Prime Minister (Mr. David Cameron): Mr. Speaker, I am happy to inform the House that I had a poached egg on Marmite toast, black coffee, my special vitamin drink and a handjob . . .

[The Prime Minister fistbumped diverse Ministers of the Crown and mimed a golf swing.]

Hon. Members: *[mimed 'handjob']*

Mr. Speaker: Order. I apologise for interrupting the Prime Minister's golf swing, but this level of uncoordinated pretend cock-bashing is unacceptable, and I can tell the House that it is detested by the Electorate. It must stop.

Hon. Members: *[mimed 'handjob', 'cocksuck', 'arsefist', 'quimgush', 'titwank', 'regional waterboard']*

Ms. Harriet Harman (Camberwick Betspread): Can I ask the Prime Minister about families with children? Families with children, because that is what I want people to think about for a moment. But what sort of families with children am I going to talk about? I wonder. *[consulted notes]*

Hon. Members: Asian ones! Fat ones! Those weird ones near Norwich with the incest and the webbed feet!

Mr. Speaker: Oh God, just shut up! Just shut up!

Ms. Harriet Harman: Families with an income of less than £40,000. Well, Mr. Speaker, they may be breathing a well-earned, hard-working sigh of relief that they still have their tax credits, as that was on the news last night. But is it right? Was the news correct? Can he confirm that, as he promised in the Election mini-series on the television well before that, that families on less than £40,000 will not forfeit that tax credit? Because I have to tell him that those of us on this side of the House have had a good look at his economic plans, and this is apparently the best we can fucking come up with.

The Prime Minister: What we are doing is this, Mr. Speaker. We are making sure that the less well-off families get the most money. It's that deceptively simple. Deceptive, Mr. Speaker, because it is true. And what a contrast again. Since 2004, child poverty went up by *[consulted watch]* 100,000 per cent under a Labour Government. In this Budget, child poverty does not go up by a single family. On the contrary, it goes down by the same family and by the same amount. Real policies, real families, and the hon. Lady looks like some sort of woodland creature caught in the headlights of a Land Rover. No offence. Or a fucking witch.

Hon. Members: Hubble bubble! Sorry, it's the prescription drugs! Look, magic – I'm waving my wand!

Mr. Speaker: Order. It was intolerable five minutes ago, it is still intolerable now. Hon. Members have exhausted my patience. I hope you're happy with yourselves. I am going to the toilet, I expect to see everyone on their best behaviour when I get back. Shame on you. Mr. Bailiff, you're in charge.

The Bailiff of the House: Yo ho, Mr. Speaker!

[Mr. Speaker then quit the Chamber, the Bailiff taking up the Mace and considering hon. Members with an expression most fearsome.]

Ms. Harriet Harman: Once again, the Prime Minister is not answering the question. The actual truth is that, despite the Chancellor's promise, the Budget SMALL print shows BIG cuts in eligibility for tax credit in the MEDIUM term. The Prime Minister promised that no family on less than £40,000 a year would lose child tax credit. Will he admit that that is not the case? Will he admit that there are families on a joint income of £30,000 who will lose all their tax credits? Really, Prime Minister? Tax-credit eligibility? Families with children on the news last night? Somewhere between £30,000 and £40,000? *[checked notes]* Would hon. Members not agree that these are the sort of sentences I should be saying?

Hon. Members: *[asleep or caught up in private and silent despair]*

The Prime Minister: The questions the right hon. and learned Lady has to ask herself are these. Who left us a budget deficit of £155 billion? Who then promised £50 billion of cuts

84

without specifying any details whatsoever? And who *[consulted conscience]* dreamed of building a platoon of lethal unionised robots disguised as NHS doctors whose sole task was to massacre innocent elderly people living in the countryside? Labour. Incredible. Mr. Bailiff, the whole country can see what is happening here: one party shoved us right up the arse of tribulation. Into what the Archbishop of Canterbury – the Archbishop of Shitting Canterbury! – described as:

a diseased sphincter of calamity wankety blankety fuck.

Mr. Bailiff, two parties are working together to get us out of that diseased sphincter. I will take no lessons in moral proctology from the hon. Lady opposite.

Mr. Peter Hain (Tancab & Supplements): *[waking with a start]* What? Who dares impugn the sphincter of the Acting Leader of the Opposition, and a Lady? What? Grr! *[indicated 'fisticuffs']*

[The Bailiff of the House then frowned upon the hon. Member for Tancab & Supplements, indicating the Mace.]

Ms. Harriet Harman: And I will take no lessons, Mr. Bailiff, either from the hon. Gentleman opposite or from Teddy, the performance coach I am supposed to train with every day, according to those smug teenage bastards at Party Headquarters. It is all very well, Teddy, saying, 'Oh no no no, Harriet, you must PROJECT! Aim your point at their hearts, like a DAGGER. Come, come, let us try it again.' The fact is, Teddy, that I have FUCKING SHIT MATERIAL. I would remind the House that as a senior Labour politician and a woman I have a serious job to do, i.e. stand here and soak up all this piss for a few weeks while the party decides which bloke it wants as Leader. I'm sorry, Mr. Bailiff, but they're all fucking chumps.

Hon. Members: Hear, hear! What? Wait, I've forgotten whose side I'm on. Well, you tell me – what sex are you? Not half, I've got the use of a flat upstairs. Doesn't bother me, I don't like 'em too 'chesty'.

The Prime Minister: Oh, the right hon. and learned Lady is promising the extinction of the Labour Party now, is she? She should think carefully before she makes any more promises. We remember Gordon Brown telling us there would be 'no more bum and bust'. Yet look at the hon. Lady herself. Bum and bust is all she is, with a squeaky stupid little mouth somewhere in the middle of it, ho ho!

[The Prime Minister exchanging fistbumps with Ministers. The hon. Member for Camberwick Betspread conferring with the Bailiff of the House, who then acceding did vouchsafe to her the Mace, the hon. Member then delivering a mighty blow unto the Prime Minister with it. Mr. Speaker then returning from the Toilet.]

Mr. Speaker: What in the blazes is going on here? You know, I thought about having a Number Two, then thought, no, I'll be away from the House for too long, Lord knows what chaos would ensue. Mr. Bailiff, take the Prime Minister to the Infirmary. The hon. Lady will return the Mace to me immediately.

[The Prime Minister was helped from the Chamber by the Bailiff of the House, to cheering from hon. Members. The hon. Member for Camberwick Betspread then throwing down the Mace at the feet of Mr. Speaker.]

Mr. Speaker: Ah! Ah! That landed on my fucking foot! The hon. Lady will apologise at once!

Ms. Harriet Harman: *[inaudible, possibly 'Oh, I'm so sorry, I'm sure']*

Mr. Speaker: This is utterly unacceptable, again. The hon. Lady had better watch her step . . .

Mr. Peter Hain: *[waking with a start]* What? How dare you threaten my mother – I mean, Leader? I'll knock your bloody block off!

[The hon. Member for Tancab & Supplements indicated readiness for combat, in carriage pugilistic and in facial tone magenta, approaching Mr. Speaker.]

Mr. Speaker: Royal Cudgellers, ahoy!

[The Royal Cudgellers then entered the Chamber, their Quelches drawn.]

Mr. Speaker: There he is! Quelch him! I don't know how he got past Security! He's an anarchist, and he's about to dig up the floor of the House in some sort of mad protest! Careful, he may have a bomb!

Interruption by Cudgellers with Quelches.

The Telephonic Ether

Date unknown; the Metropolitan Police regret
they can find no record at this time
BEEPS AND CRACKLING
[Mrs. Sharon McEnenery in the Vaguely
Ergonomic Swivel-Chair]

Interception Proves the Rule

Mrs. Sharon McEnenery (Customer Services): Hello, ye're through to Vodaphone, my name's Sharon McEnenery, how may I help you noo anyway, aye, are ye all right today?

Mr. Billy Williams (World of Journalism): Ooh helloo, yes. This is Sienna Miller. Woould it be at all poossible too change a PIN number? Oonly I've foorgotten the one oon my moobile phoone and I need too access my vooicemail?

Mrs. Sharon McEnenery: Sienna Miller? The wumman? Only ye soond a wee bit like a fella doing a high voice, nae offence, son.

Mr. Billy Williams: Noo, I'm definitely Sienna Miller. Plus, hoow dare yoou? I coould list all the films I've been in, if that woould help establish my identity. Helloo, are yoou still there?

Mrs. Sharon McEnenery: Aye, could ye do that for us, aye.

Mr. Billy Williams: *Layer Cake. Alfie. Factoory Girl. The Edge of Loove* . . .

Mrs. Sharon McEnenery: Och, that's ma mind set at rest right there, ye must be Sienna Miller, aye.

Mr. Billy Williams: Ooh, and *G.I. Jooe: The Rise of Coobra* . . .

Mrs. Sharon McEnenery: Lovely, aye. Noo, if I could just take ye through the security procedure. Could I have the second letter from your password?

Mr. Billy Williams: Ooh, my passwoord. I think I've foorgootten that too. It's all these films, they make yoou foorget things so easily. My head's full oof scripts all the time, see, learning lines, eck cetera. Coould yoou email me my passwoord noow, while we're dooing this?

Mrs. Sharon McEnenery: Ach, no problem, I'll sort that oot for ye noo. *[inaudible, possibly 'Ye dozy fucking bag o' shite']*

Mr. Billy Williams: Ah. Ah. Oonly, I've changed my email address. It's a new one. Froom tooday.

Mrs. Sharon McEnenery: Really.

Mr. Billy Williams: Mm. It's . . . wait a sec, it's 'glennthelovemachine', all loower case, '@hotmail.com'.

Mrs. Sharon McEnenery: Could ye just bear with me, Sienna. I'm putting ye on hold for a wee moment.

[The first sixteen bars of an electronic samba version of 'Light My Fire' were repeated several times, causing a corrosive resonance in the inner ear and teeth of Mr. Williams.]

Mrs. Sharon McEnenery: Hi, Sienna. Sorry tae keep ye waiting.

Mr. Billy Williams: That's OoK. Is everything in oorder?

Mrs. Sharon McEnenery: That address you give me? Aye,

it's come up on our Suspicious Calls and Emails Alert List. According tae a trace report, it's the personal email address of a private detective supplying confidential information to the *News o' the Wurrold*. S'a shocker, eh?

Mr. Billy Williams: But that . . . that's ridiculoous! Ooh, ah, I see what I've doone. I've given yoou the wroong email address. I . . . yeah, I had that email handy because I was actually gooing to email that persoon myself and tell him to stoop eavesdroopping oon my coonversations. Blooody *News of the Woorld*. Althoough I have to say their poolitical cooverage is very impressive. Hoonestly, I think I may technically be asleep at the mooment. The relentless partying is taking its tooll. I am so exhausted, it's poossible I've fallen asleep and yes, that's what's happened, I'm talkin to yoou in my sleep. Look, I tell yoou what. Let's foorget it foor now, I'll just use my oother phone . . .

Mrs. Sharon McEnenery: Aye, wait up, Sienna. I'm afraid this is a reportable incident anyway. We had some guy on yesterday pretending tae be that lassie wi' the wee chipmunk face and the sensible shoes. What was her name, Isla? *[inaudible, possibly 'Harriet Harman']* I cannae remember. Kirsty Wark? From noo on, we're obliged to notify the police, and I must caution ye . . .

Mr. Billy Williams: The police? Get IN! I mean, the poolice, excellent. They will I'm sure take the approopriate actioon. That is after all what they are being paid – handsoomely – to doo. *[inaudible, possibly 'In your fucking face, Vanessa Fucking Feltz! We are The Murdoch, we are The Murdoch, dah da-da-dah! Phil, mate, chop 'em out!']*

Moment of Disinterception.

House of Commons

Held upon the Feast of the Advent of the
Parasites, the 12th of July 2010

AMENDED PRAYERS AND SUPERSTITIONS

[Mr. Speaker upon the Inflatable Doughnut within the Chair]

Oral and Anal Questions to Ministers

Mr. Speaker: Order. Before I take Community Questions, I would like to draw my Inflatable Doughnut to the attention of the House. *[arose, indicated Inflatable Doughnut within the Chair]* It is part of my ongoing quest for sensible and measured reform of This Place. I hope it will afford me a clearer overview of our Proceedings. Questions to the Secretary of State for Communities and Local Government!

Hon. Members: *[derision, quacking, self-medication]*

Mr. Simon Burns (Chelmsford Half-Timbered): *[inaudible, possibly 'Stupid sanctimonious dwarf, ha ha ha']*

Mr. Speaker: Order. I apologise for interrupting the Minister, but there was an interruption from the hon. Member for Chelmsford Half-Timbered.

Mr. Simon Burns: I didn't say anything. It was a burp.

Mr. Andy Burnham (Mersey & Emotional Side): Mr. Speaker, he did say something, dough, I heard him. He said you were a stupid sanctimonious dwarf.

Mr. Simon Burns: Bollocks. I said he was a . . .

Hon. Members: Wanker!

Mr. Speaker: Order, order, you unruly blooming rabble!

Mr. Simon Burns: I said he was an astute . . . magnanimous . . .

Mr. Andy Burnham: He never, Mr. Speaker. He said, 'Stupid sanctimonious dwarf.' And he's looking daggers at us now, dough.

Hon. Members: Hit him! Fuck him! Wankers! Spunkfrothers! Chumquivers! BBC3! What are you fucking talking about? I'm being hostile!

Mr. Speaker: Mr. Bailiff, escort the hon. Gentleman into the Corridor and make sure he takes his place upon the Naughty Step, there to purge his contempt and compose an Apology. I seek this Apology *[indicated self]* not for myself, not for *[indicated Inflatable Doughnut]* the Chair of Authority and its Inflatable Doughnut, but for *[indicated 'everything']* the House, and for *[indicated hon. Members]* Democracy. If there's any trouble, Mr. Bailiff, have him Cudgelled.

The Bailiff of the House: Yo ho! *[escorted the hon. Member for Chelmsford Half-Timbered from the Chamber for the Extraction of Contrition with Cudgelling]*

Mr. David Miliband (South Shields Ocado): Mr. Speaker, may I ask what the blanking hon. Member for Chelmsford Half-Timbered was even doing here? Is he not a blanking Health Minister? And why, Mr. Speaker, is every blank remotely connected to the Health Department in this Chamber at the moment? Is there to be a Statement on the NHS or some such blank? I smell a blank here.

Hon. Members: Blanker!

Mr. Speaker: Order, order! Or I shall get really cross. And believe me, the House does NOT want to see me in a cross mood. Questions to the Minister!

Mr. Billy Bugginsturn (Whippingham): Would the Secretary of State list his engagements for today? And may I say what an inspiration he is, leading the Big Society by example?

Hon. Members: Yeah, he must weigh thirty fucking stone! Whoa, his features are all clustered in the middle of his face, like they're being sucked into some sort of very slow whirlpool of fat! Shit, it looks like a fucking airbag's gone off inside his head!

Mr. Speaker: Order, please. There is really no need for this level of unpleasantness. Minister, pray turn round and continue . . . I see my mistake, you are facing us, very good, thank you. Order.

The Secretary of State for Communities and Local Government (Mr. Eric Pickles): Thank you, Mr. Speaker. Now I often joke that I *[indicated guts]* have 'a lot on my plate' *[consumed sandwich]*, and today was no *[inaudible]*. I started off the day with a Full English as per usual, four slices, extra black pudding. Then I had a so-called 'working breakfast' with ministerial colleagues and others – I say breakfast, it was just bits of pastry and fucking FRUIT. *[consumed sandwich]* So, as you can imagine, I was keen to tackle brunch – battered cod, chips, mushy peas, four slices, twice – before dozing off on a power nap with my advisers, who have been with me on this roller coaster of a political journey from the beginning and who are now all the same shape. I woke up twelve minutes later, fucking starving to be fair, so had a *[consumed sandwich]* box of Quality Street to keep me going until my pizzas arrived – Four Seasons, one for each pizza – *[inaudible]* lemon curd tart, two-litre bottle of Um Bongo, crisps, a dozen eclairs and a roast suckling pig, then a few 'working' pre-lunch pints with my key advisers – Stotty, Harry, Gutsy, Barmy, Shitty and Benno – then lunch at 11.30. Now, I WAS going to have the roast chicken, but then I saw the . . .

Mr. Andy Burnham: On a Point of Order, Mr. Speaker, the Secretary of State is just talking about what he's eaten, not what his ministerial duties have been, dough. He is not being ministerial, and I think you should tell him off. I bet he wishes he was like me: all lithe and laddish and talking about the footie, dough at the same time in touch with me sensitive side, eh?

Mr. Eric Pickles: *[inaudible]* Mr. Speaker, sorry, those sausage rolls go on for longer than you think. Mr. Speaker, Labour are analogue politicians in a digital age! What do I mean by this? I will tell you what I mean by this *[consulted notes]*. I mean that the typical old-fashioned, stubborn, reactionary Labour councillor – let's just imagine what he looks like – wants to stop ordinary folk from doing their citizen journalism by blogging and tweeting, etc.! Well, I say . . . *[turned page, swallowed bap]* I say no, we need to open up *[some bap dislodgement]* local councils to greater democratic scrutiny. *[inaudible]* their spending online. Let's have it out in the open! *[appearance of toasted-cheese plasma]* Details of every pay packet! *[consumed Kit-Kat]* Every perk! *[consumed samosa]* Every pie! *[consumed pie]* Let these be our clutchwords: pay packet! *[Kit-Kat]* Perk! *[samosa]* Pie! *[pie]*

Pay packet! *[Kit-Kat]* Perk! *[samosa]* Sorry, Mr. Speaker, I've come over all queer, I'll have to have a sit down. *[inaudible]*

[The Secretary of State stumbling unto the Dispatch Box, losing purchase, then falling towards Mr. Speaker, who, moving quickly from the Chair, did witness the Secretary of State fall in great confusion and imburstment upon the Inflatable Cushion.]

Mr. Speaker: Bloody hell, is nothing safe in this blooming House any more? Where *[indicated scene]* is the dignity of the House now? Mr. Bailiff, summon the Cudgellers! Have them bring a very large tarpaulin! And some sort of traction engine!

The Bailiff of the House: *[exiting the Chamber]* Yo ho ho and up she rises, Mr. Speaker!

The Secretary of State for Health (Mr. Andrew Lansley): Mr. Speaker, may I heartily commend my *[indicated resting form of the Secretary of State for Communities and Local Government]* hon. Friend's work in helping to build sustainable, life-choice-accurate communities? Unfortunately, Mr. Speaker, I have to dash off now. But as I mentioned, I just wanted to be here to be able to say, 'Well done, Eric, you're a great big guy doing a great big job. Thanks.' *[inaudible, possibly 'Oh, and we've published a Health White Paper, a copy of which has been deposited in the Library of the House']*

[The Secretary of State for Health gathered together his Order Papers and took up a Cardboard Box. Then nodding most gravely to Mr. Speaker was in approachment of the Door of the House, when the hon. Member for South Shields Ocado did then invoke the Ancient Right of Cherchez Dynamitey.]

Mr. David Miliband: By *[consulted Parliamentary Rules app]* the Defracted Power of Her Majesty and the Sanction of Her Nobility I do hereby challenge the hon. Member to declare if he be a Vile Papist or No. And to ask, with all the House . . .

Hon. Members: What's in the Box – is it Dynamite?

Mr. Speaker: Oh, Secretary of State, you know it's just a bit of fun. Cherchez Dynamitey – you have to show us what's in the box. Otherwise *[inviting the House to share his mirth]* we might think you're a Vile Papist come to blow us all to Kingdom Come with your Vile Papist Dynamite! So, ha ha, please, what's in the Box – is it Dynamite?

[The Secretary of State for Health then in manner nonchalant did reveal the contents of the Box, to wit a number of copies of a White Paper, these then being seized by hon. Members in a frenzy of entitlement and rage.]

Mr. David Miliband: What the blankety blanking blank, Mr. Speaker? This is a White Paper! Did the Secretary of State think he could simply slip this through with nobody blanking noticing? Does he take us all for cunts – correction, blanks – Mr. Speaker? I must say . . .

Hon. Members: You shitsquirting lump of cockphlegm! Correction – cunt! Blank! Double blank! What's a White Paper? The *Westmorland Gazette*?

Mr. Speaker: Order, order, this is all most trying. Well, Secretary of State? IS it a White Paper? I was certainly not informed there was to be a White Paper. Most irregular. Irregular and insulting.

Mr. Andrew Lansley: *[in attitude of most emphatic innocence]* What, Mr. Speaker? I said earlier. I told the House. We've published a White Paper, no big deal, *[coughed]* as I say. If anyone wants to slip along to the Library, I've *[studied Order Papers]* left a copy in there, so . . . Look, I've got to shoot off, but . . .

Mr. David Miliband: Mr. Speaker, I know for a blanking fact that the Secretary of State did NOT leave a copy in the Library. Look at his eyes, Mr. Speaker. The eyes of a liar.

Hon. Members: Outrageous! Retract! Let's do Cherchez Dynamitey again!

Mr. David Miliband: Mr. Speaker, I apologise for my un-Parliamentary language. The Secretary of State does not have the eyes of a liar. He has exactly the sort of artificially wide-open eyes you get with one of those Mr. Potato Heads. How very appropriate, Mr. Speaker. How very blanking appropriate.

Mr. Speaker: Well, Secretary of State? IS there a copy of *[consulting White Paper]* 'Equity & Excellence – Liberating the NHS' in the Library?

Mr. Andrew Lansley: *[indicating wounded integrity]* Yes, there fucking is. I left it on the Periodicals Desk, under the *New Statesman*.

Mr. David Miliband: Oh, this is blanking hypocrisy of the blankest kind, Mr. Speaker. Under the blanking *New Statesman*? Why did he not put it with the porn, where everybody can see it?

Mr. Andy Burnham: On a Point of Order, Mr. Speaker, it's not fair. You keep letting my hon. Friend here have a go at the Secretary of State, when it's me who's actually Shadow Fucking Health, dough. I should . . .

Hon. Members: Wanker! You're not Health! They moved you last week to Football, don't you remember?

Mr. Andy Burnham: The Footie? I'm Secretary of State for the Footie? That's safe, that is. *[a look most sceptical]* Am I really, dough?

Ms. Harriet Harman (Camberwick Betspread): Mr. Speaker, I would remind my hon. Friend that he is Health this week, then Education next week. He asked us to keep things flexible as he expects to be Leader of the Labour Party quite soon! Ha ha ha!

Mr. Ed Balls (Burly & Shitwad): Aha ha ha indeed, you maudlin Scouse wanker! You couldn't head a fucking BUS QUEUE, no offence.

Mr. David Miliband: Hee hee hee, you cheeky blanky fuck-blanker, I might add. Correction, blankfucker.

Ms. Diane Abbott (Stoke Newington Greenroom): Mr. Speaker, I am more than happy to confirm my candidacy for the Labour Party leadership. In my view, speaking as a woman, I think the time has come for us to have a woman in the top job, ideally a black woman. Not just because they're black and female, but still. Someone who's sassy, media-savvy and massively popular. *[performed Showbiz Stance with Jazzhands, fell over]*

Mr. Ed Miliband (Doncaster Awkwood): Brerk.

Mr. David Blunkett (Sheffield Masturbeighton): Mr. Speaker, someone's fallen on my fucking dog again!

Mr. Blunkett's Assistance Dog Jolly Kate: *[muffled whimpering, demonstrable support for the hon. Member for Stoke Newington Greenroom]*

Mr. Speaker: Order, order! As diverting as it is for the House to hear members of the Labour Party debate which of them *[exchanged glances with the hon. Member for South Shields Ocado]* is to be Leader, I want to hear more about this White

Paper that I wasn't blooming well told about. Secretary of State!

Mr. Andrew Lansley: Look, Mr. Speaker, no, all it is, it's just giving folk – ordinary, decent, hard-working people, let me insert – more choice. Of course, the PHS or, no, NHS as it is now and always has been for more than sixty years, could be time for an overhaul, the NHS, let me be clear, will remain free at the point of delivery, of course it will. But why should health customers not be able to pay that little bit extra to spoil themselves once in a while on the NHS with professional services at competitive rates, or wait a bit longer for their biopsy results, it's entirely up to them, it's their choice. Equity and excellence, liberating the NHS, simple as that.

Hon. Members: What does 'equity' mean? What does 'excellence' mean? What does 'liberating' mean? Who does your hair, the fucking Jehovah's Witnesses?

Mr. Speaker: Order *[distracted by signs of movement within the suit of the Secretary of State for Communities and Local Government]*, order.

Mr. Andrew Lansley: Well, to be honest, Mr. Speaker, I'm not entirely sure myself. I think the Rebadge Team went well into the early hours. The missus and I like to be in bed by 22.30, so I left them to it. 'Equity' as in 'holding shares in', I would have thought? 'Excellence' as in 'private'? We're trying to liberate the NHS from this very narrowly focused idea of itself, in order to take it out of itself, perhaps to an independent sanitarium or something in Bournemouth or somewhere. As I say, Mr. Speaker *[gesture of impotence]*, I was asleep.

Mr. Billy Bugginsturn: Would the Secretary of State agree with me that a thorough overhaul of our beloved NHS, though not strictly speaking in our Election Manifesto, is actually a lovely surprise and should be welcomed by everyone?

Mr. Speaker: Secretary of State?

Mr. Andrew Lansley: Apologies, Mr. Speaker, I was miles away, just reading it myself . . .

Mr. Simon Hughes (Bermondsey Metrosexual): Hang on, it says here you want to transfer control of £80 billion of NHS spending to GPs and create a Market in Healthcare open to 'any willing provider'! Are the Tories so completely demented, so utterly obsessed with this two-dimensional idea of theirs – 'Let's turn everything into one big fucking market' – that they would really dare to do something this mental *[consulted memory]* unless they were assured of an uninterrupted five-year term thanks to Coalition Partners who are all in it together, I remember, oh God, is that the time? Mr. Speaker, I give way.

Interruption with Tarpaulin.

House of Commons

Upon the Eve of the Rising Member, the 27th of July 2010
BAR WITH PEANUTS
[Mr. Speaker in the Sedan Chair]

End-of-Term Assembly

[Mr. Speaker entered the Chamber within a Sedan Chair portered by members of the popular dance act Tru Shit, who, having settled the Sedan Chair before the Dispatch Box, did then perform a physical allegory upon the theme of Urban Life, exuberant in mode and gymnastic in execution, to a medley of light-classical favourites played by the Band of the Coldstream Guards. The performance concluded by the youngest hon. Member of Tru Shit, Mr. Nex Flo, who to most clamorous applause did ascend a Human Pyramid composed of Tru Shit colleagues, executing a Trademark Double Backflip and landing most precisely upon Mr. Speaker's Booster Seat within the Chair.]

Hon. Members: *[applause, braying, honking]*

Mr. Nex Flo (Tru Shit): Order in the House, yo! *[giggled]* I be hereby in charge of like the whole Parliament and that, you feeling me? And I do hereby give like a big-up to all you Tru Shit fans out there. *[intimated emoticon, possibly 'winking yellow globe with thumbs up']* And I do also be hereby giving an OBE to my mum, who does like the best roast dinner in the world, trust. Nah, scratch that. I be hereby giving her a 'YO' BE! *[intimated emoticon, possibly 'yellow globe, self-hugging, eyes closed']* LOL.

Mr. Speaker: *[from within the Sedan-Chair]* Ha ha, order . . .

Hon. Members: *[fistbumps, gun fingers, complicated handshakes]*

Mr. Speaker: OK, you've had your fun. Marvellous display. Now if I could just have my Chair back . . .

Ms. Harriet Harman (Camberwick Betspread): Mr. Speaker – I mean, of course, our new 'cool' Mr. Speaker with the spectacles and the Afro – just look at all these lovely young men here, still breathless from their exertions. Would the House agree with me that street dance is not just a very useful tool in the social-justice toolbox, but also an economic generator that may yet lead this country out of recession and into my labial maze – I mean, sustainable growth.

Mr. Guest Speaker: Just like follow your dream, yo. If you want something – or, ting – bad enough, it'll happen. Trust. *[intimated emoticon, possibly 'yellow globe with winky smile']*

Hon. Members: Ha ha! Winker! Wanker!

Ms. Harriet Harman: Exactly, Mr. Guest Speaker at the Start of His Sexual Journey of Discovery. As an older woman and experienced lover, I commend your remarks. Perhaps the Secretary of State responsible could tell us why funding for street dance has been savagely cut, along with all the other marvellous expressions of Hormonal Britain which define this nation's cultural booty.

Mr. Guest Speaker: *[indicating contents of the Chamber]* Yo, which one of you saggy-ass motherfuckers be being the like Secretary of Street Dance? *[intimated emoticon, possibly 'yellow globe with grotesque frown']*

Hon. Members: Statement! This is a fucking disgrace! Yes, I really liked Dick van Dyke and those chimney sweeps in *Mary Poppins*!

Mr. Speaker: *[from within the Sedan Chair]* Prime Minister, I insist. Order in the House! Order, you disrespectful *[inaudible, possibly 'buggers']*. Order, I say! Right! That is it! I am not coming out of this Sedan Chair until I have the House's assurance that I will get my Chair back. *[inaudible, possibly 'Hmmph']*

Mr. Guest Speaker: Yo, in terms of popular culture? Street dance be the popu-LEST. I'm a show you what I'm a talk about LOL.

[Old-School Break Beats did then issue from the Band of the Coldstream Guards, prompting hon. Members of Tru Shit to liberate diverse moves. Mr. Speaker peeping from the Sedan Chair to see if his Chair be vacant, finding it to be still engaged, then some moments of ponderment, then quitting the Sedan Chair and most solemnly confronting the House with the Dignity of his Office.]

Mr. Speaker: I have just about blooming well had enough of this. You will all respect the Office of Speaker. I command you! And YOU *[indicating Mr. Flo, avoiding the peripheral flails of hon. dancing Members of Tru Shit]*, get out of my bloody Booster Seat! I want an end to this blooming nonsense, now!

Hon. Members: Through the Chair! Address the House through the Chair!

Mr. Speaker: *[rending his garments]* This is intolerable, I say!

Mr. Guest Speaker: Through the motherfucking Chair, yo.

[Hon. Members became aware of Mr. Speaker's deteriorating mental state and, realising that their unseemly and riotous hubbub might provoke a Snapping of the Mind, did most assiduously increase their commotion.]

Mr. Guest Speaker: Order in da House, order in Tru Shit, yo. *[intimated emoticon, possibly 'yellow globe rolling on floor laughing, minus global buttocks']*

[The Remaining Members of Diversity then did reconstitute their Human Pyramid. The Band of the Coldstream Guards produced a drum roll, Mr. Speaker performing a Fevered Mime (unclear: possibly 'Actions speak louder than words') and in vest and pants then ascending unto the summit of the Human Pyramid, where he did steady himself. Mr. Speaker then attempting a Non-Trademark Rising Double-Turn Backflip into the Public Gallery, which, having recently been befitted with Bulletproof Glass, did offer most stout resistance to Mr. Speaker's face. A moment of purchase, yielding to a sliding fall of sudden perpendicularity and an arrival with great force upon the hon. Member for Sheffield Masturbeighton's assistance dog, Black Betty.]

Mr. David Blunkett (Sheffield Masturbeighton): Steady, girl. What was that? Oh dear. Oh fuck. Who's done this? Who's done this? I'm registered fucking blind, you cunts! I'd only just got this one trained up as well. Removable canine dentures. Changed my life, Mr. Speaker.

Mr. Speaker: *[inaudible, possibly 'Oh God, oh God, the blood']*

[Mr. Flo, having been pressed by the House to remain as Guest Speaker for the duration of the Debate, ordered the removal of Mr. Speaker and the Remains of Black Betty, then asking hon. Members

of Tru Shit to wait for him in the Green Room, who did tumble and moonwalk from the Chamber, to warm acclamation.]

Mr. Guest Speaker: Prime Minister, pray like continue to be doing that thing you like be doing, yo. *[intimated emoticon, possibly 'yellow globe of haughty demeanour']*

The Prime Minister (Mr. David Cameron): Mr. Guest Speaker, I will take no lessons from the hon. Lady opposite in street dance and its value to communities up and down the country. My wife and I have seen *Billy* Fucking *Elliot*. Twice.

Ms. Harriet Harman: Perhaps the Prime Minister could explain then why the following Street Dance Pathfinder Projects have been cancelled due to the complete lack of shit-giving so wantonly displayed by this *[indicated Government Front Bench]* fucking Nazi Supper Club . . .

[A list of imperilled street-dance projects was then passed to the hon. Member for Camberwick Betspread by the Clerk of the House, who having received it from the Guest Speaker did then exchange fistbumps with both sender and recipient.]

Ms. Harriet Harman: 'Bitch Jointz, Haringey. Glee Street, Doncaster. Strickly Come Movin, Lewisham. Bombsquat, Maidstone. Hip Hop Pussydiss, Birmingham. Mash Bang Wallop, Shropshire. Pubic Obsexion, Windermere. Dantsunami, Nottingham. Breakin Legz, Ipswich. Hot Bovril, Godalming. Pengversity, Penge. Succulent Chickenz, Bristol. *Trus in Urbe*, Eton. Steptoe & Hoes, Tottenham . . .'

The Prime Minister: Yes, Mr. Guest Speaker, if I may interrupt the hon. Lady. She may read out a list of ludicrous names until her fellow cows come home . . .

Hon. Members: *[howling, mooing, cackling, barking]*

Mr. Guest Speaker: Order, order, yo! *[intimated emoticon, possibly 'wrathful yellow globe, steam issuing from ears']*

The Prime Minister: The fact remains that under Labour's own Plan for Deficit Reduction *[brandished copy of 'A Measured Slashing']* street-dance funding was to be reduced by 12 per cent! We are reducing it by 20 per cent, which leaves Labour's legitimate level of indignation at just fucking 8 per cent! The House will be aware of the inter-Departmental character of street-dance funding. I'm sure my ministerial colleagues will have lots to say on the matter. I'm afraid I have to pop off to Washington now to see Hillary Clinton, perhaps you've ha ha heard of HER!

Hon. Members: *[cries of 'Ooh', much extruded in their execution]*

Mr. Guest Speaker: Order. Could you get Mr. Obama to sign my *[searched pockets, produced document]* Asbo? I would owe you big time, bruv. *[intimated emoticon, possibly 'auto-fellating yellow globe']*

[The Prime Minister nodded most gravely to the Guest Speaker, assuring him that he would do his best. Then taking his leave of the House while directing an elaborate Mime at the hon. Member for Camberwick Betspread – enigmatic, possibly 'Go and thoroughly milk yourself, you fucking heifer, oh yes, then make a milky tea with your milk, you big milky fucking cow loser.']

The Secretary of State for Education (Mr. Michael Gove): Unlike the previous administration, Mr. Guest Speaker, this Government will not *[adjusted hair]* be blown off course by the capricious winds of populism. That is why I have today committed my Department to a new initiative, the, the *[adjusted* *trousers]* Free-School Street-Dance Initiative. I propose the introduction of a, a Synchronised Movement Baccalaureate, as well as *[adjusted cuffs]*, as, as Visiting Street-Dance Fellowships and many other things that when taken together very quickly will completely eclipse the summary suspension of capital works on 715 schools, and yes, OK, we are going to reduce the *[adjusted belt]* money spent on Sure Start centres but only through identifying inefficiencies in the system, so nobody will notice at all *[adjusted flies]*. If there ARE any complaints about our cancelling Labour's school-rebuilding plan, let them be directed to the party opposite, who, let's remember, started all this fucking nonsense in the first place *[adjusted tie]*, Mr. Guest Speaker.

Mr. Ed Balls (Burly & Shitwad): Mr. Guest Speaker, this is absolutely appalling. A Street-Dance Initiative for free schools, while kids in the run-down local shithole have to make do with old Steps videos and the fucking hokey-cokey? Today is a black day for our country's schools, as most of them now won't have access to a world-class street-dance act as part of their whatever – curriculum.

Mr. Guest Speaker: Yo yo yo, what you saying – 'black day'?

Hon. Members: Racist! Danceist! Wanker!

Mr. Ed Balls: Oh, Mr. Guest Speaker, I meant 'blank day', as in, 'These poor kids have drawn a blank in terms of . . .'

Mr. Guest Speaker: Be silent! Mr. Dude with the Funny Wig and the Like Shakespeare Garments, how do I have someone 'done' here? *[intimated emoticon, possibly 'yellow globe with bandanna and AK-47']*

[The Clerk of the Court then outlining to the Guest Speaker the full

spectrum of retribution, including Administration of the Mace, Royal
Cudgelment, etc. The Guest Speaker then taking up the Mace, testing
its heft and reach, thereby accidentally and most grievously hitting the
face of the Secretary of State for Education.]

Mr. Michael Gove: Buggering bollocking shitflapping ouch,
   what the FUCK! I'll knock your block off, you comprehensive
   scumbag.

Hon. Members: Fight! Fight! Wow, this is like one of those alle-
   gorical plays they sometimes do on Radio 4, and you can't be
   arsed to get out of the bath to turn it off!

Mr. Guest Speaker: Order, yo. The hon. Tosser will chill the fuck
   out. Firstly, yeah: *[intimated emoticon, possibly 'mortified yellow
   globe apologising, but with a winky smile'].* Also, secondly: the
   hon. Tosser cannot be dissing me like that. He may think he's
   a bad motherfucker, but he ain't bad enough, yo. He ain't no
   motherfucker, yo. He a AUNTIEJUMPER!

Hon. Members: Ha ha! Not a motherfucker but an auntiejumper!
   Wanker! Piss off, you trembling fucking skein of cock plasma!

*[The Secretary of State for Education then quit the Chamber via High
Dudgeon to seek medical assistance, hon. Members jeering and laughing, and quaffing ale and calling one another 'gay'.]*

The Home Secretary (Ms. Theresa May): Mr. Guest Speaker,
   I would like to assure the House that street dance will be a
   key feature of this Government's package *[indicated the Guest
   Speaker from the waist downwards]* of prison reforms. Urban-
   dance classes, rigorously enforced by trained dance warders,
   can offer prisoners a way of avoiding a life of crime, and also a
   way to achieve something meaningful – for example, a video on

YouTube. This initiative I am sure will be seen in the fullness of time as being much more significant than privatising prisons, which is just something we are thinking about and not planning to do at all.

The Secretary of State for Communities and Local Government (Mr. Eric Pickles): Mr. Guest Speaker *[consumed hard-boiled egg]*, my Department is keen to harness the *[consumed fajita]* power of street dance as part of our complete overhaul of the community system in this country. At the moment *[consumed pastry]* members of the community are poorly organised into expensive little *[inaudible, gagging, consumed pickled cucumber]*. We need to get members of what we're calling the 'community community' out of those buildings – highly desirable and *[consumed turkey drumstick]* disposable properties, some of them – and back onto the streets, where they can dance, as we have seen, Mr. Guest Speaker *[consumed savoury flan]*. Bringing real community back to the community community. I for one can still do the conga *[burped]*.

The Secretary of State for Culture, Olympics, Media and Sport (Mr. Jeremy Hunt): Mr. Guest Speaker, I am happy to inform the House that, excitingly, we are about to 'roundtable' and 'roadshow' street dance under the, the auspices of a new taskforce. The – oh, what shall we call it – Street-Dance Liaison Unit will lay down the framework upon which we may explore the whole area in value-for-money terms in order to create a viable and happy medium . . .

Hon. Members: Cunt! Cunt! Jeremy Hunt! Derek Acorah, he's one!

Mr. Guest Speaker: Yo, silence in court or I be like clearing the public gallery and . . . *[addressing the Clerk of the House]* yeah

yeah, and also like silence in Parliament too, yo. *[intimated emoticon, possibly 'winking yellow globe with ball gag']*

Mr. Jeremy Hunt: Yes, Mr. Guest Speaker. One can only hope that this bright new future for street dance may inspire local arts groups to get off their fat backsides and do some Olympic-style sports, fun runs, etc. To any arts body that has been liquidated, to any arts group waiting to find out if they have funding still, I say this: there is more to Culture, Olympics, Media and Sport than fucking Culture. And I should fucking know, I am the Secretary of Fucking State for the whole lot!

Mr. Guest Speaker: Yo, I know you. That Lord Coe, yeah? On the telly about the Olympics all the time? Got into trouble years ago for shagging that bird?

Mr. Jeremy Hunt: On a Point of Order, Mr. Guest Speaker, I AM on the telly all the time about the Olympics, although I am not Lord Coe. Still, the ladies do tell me I'm pretty trim *[executed pelvic 'cha-cha-cha'].*

[Mr. Nu Brrap, hon. Member of Tru Shit, then calling through the Door of the House.]

Mr. Nu Brrap: Yo, bumbaclaat! Car's here! Fucking move, we got some peak PA at the Adam Smith Institute in fifteen!

[The Guest Speaker then without ceremony did street-dance from the Chamber, hon. Members applauding, collecting their Order Papers, etc.]

Moment of Holiday.

House of Commons

Being in Recession, upon the 6th of August 2010

FEARS AND TREPIDATIONS

[Mr. Sheen in the Air]

An Unscheduled Debate

[The Chamber silent and in darkness, the House having risen for Summer Recess. A sudden Illumination, several Cleaners then entering with professional gear, tackle and apparatuses. Following on swiftly, the Master of the Cleaners.]

The Master of the Cleaners: Right, pay attention. We've got tourists in tomorrow, fucking loads of them. This place has to look mint. Quick reminder: all food and perishables, anything organic, however gross, in here *[indicated wheelie bin].* All wigs, hairpieces, extensions, teeth, prosthetic items, surgical equipment, sexual appliances, rings, watches, wallets, pens, coinage, spectacles, phones, gadgets, trinkets, weapons, clothing, dirty diamonds, etc. in here *[indicated jute sack].* All discarded Order Papers, White Papers, Green Papers, briefing notes, reports, communiqués, paper planes, improvised paper missiles, paper cricket balls, etc. in here *[indicated cardboard boxes]*. The Scrutineers of the Rubbish will be along later to dispose of it all.

Mrs. Rachel Brannigan (Southwark Shitend): On a Point of Order, can I just check that we're not going to get blamed like last year if anything Top Secret ends up in the papers?

The Master of the Cleaners: Don't worry, they've now introduced a system of checks and balances. It's a bit like WikiLeaks but without the sinister campness, burst condoms and fucking tantrums. Also, a certain Newspaper Proprietor will underwrite any thorough police investigation that may be required following the leak of sensitive material. *[consulted watch]* Look, just collect the fucking shit and give the place a proper going-over, or I'll put you all on Toilets, OK?

Hon. Cleaners: *[thoughtful consideration, crestfallen solemnity]*

Mrs. Rachel Brannigan: Yeah, it's just . . .

The Master of the Cleaners: The Toilets in the House of Lords.

Hon. Cleaners: *[studied mops]*

The Master of the Cleaners: Right. Good. Fuck me, what is that smell? Like a dog's . . . oh God . . .

[The hon. Cleaner from Waiting upon Maintenance then indicated the corpse of a black Labrador, clothed in human underwear and a Bullingdon Club hat, upon a Back Bench.]

Ms. Justyna Lechniak (Waiting upon Maintenance): It is dead.

The Master of the Cleaners: *[dialling]* You don't say. Hi, yeah, is that Retrieval? Mm. We've got another. Yep, it'll be outside in five.

[The Assembled Company did then enbag the Remains of Mr. Woofer and drag them unto the Corridor, the Master of the Cleaners

remaining there to greet the Yeomen of the Retrieval, who did then
altogether quit the House with great haste and in furtive demeanour.
The hon. Cleaners returning to the Chamber, there causing Radio 1
to utter from a small wireless and thenceforth attending to their duties
until the Calling of the Tea Break with Flasks and Biscuits, the hon.
Cleaner from Southwark Shitend taking up an ironic position upon
the Chair of the House.]

Mrs. Rachel Brannigan: Order, order. *[indicated document]* You'll
like this. Mr. Cameron says he's worried about social mobility.

Ms. Fatiah Ibrahim (Edmonton Leftover): I must take two buses
and the Tube to get here.

Ms. Justyna Lechniak: Perhaps Mr. Cameron will give us all cars.
Perhaps he will give us all wings.

Miss Salome Kyere (Watford Paygap): Which one is Mr.
Cameron? Is he the one with the face of a crying child, who is
telling people they must get out of their wheelchairs and go to
work?

Mrs. Rachel Brannigan: No, that's Duncan Smith. Mr. Cameron
is only the bloody Prime Minister, that's all.

Miss Salome Kyere: What does he look like, this Mr. Cameron?

Mrs. Rachel Brannigan: Sort of . . . plasticky. Very smart with
all his hair. Looks like the busy, grumpy bastard you always see
at the bank when they call you in and tell you they've stopped
your fucking overdraft.

[The Assembled Company did then agree that the entire Cabinet, the
entire Shadow Cabinet and indeed All Politicians looked like this.]

Mrs. Rachel Brannigan: Anyway, *[indicated document]* the idea is
to lift all the poor people into the middle classes.

Ms. Justyna Lechniak: Hooray. Perhaps Mr. Cameron will give us all hats. Perhaps he will give us loud voices. 'Oh rather. Jolly good. Who's in charge here, I have a complaint!'

Ms. Fatiah Ibrahim: Yes. 'I have indigestion! Summon an ambulance! A pink one!'

Mrs. Rachel Brannigan: *[reading]* 'Not everyone will support our plan to get Lie-In Britain out from under the duvet, showered, downstairs for a bowl of porridge and off to work. Well, I say to them: please yourself, but when you finally DO haul your fucking constipated arse out of bed just before lunchtime and come downstairs for a fried breakfast you'll find there IS no kitchen. Outraged, you will go back upstairs so you can log on to Twitter and tell everybody about your missing kitchen, only to discover that upstairs has disappeared too. You will find yourself in some sort of eerie limbo, standing in your pants in a bleak featureless landscape with a cello playing something tragic by Shostafuckingkovich or someone, and wherever you go there will be a big target shining down on you . . .'

Ms. Justyna Lechniak: Oh, mother of God, no. I think I saw a trailer for this on television, one of the BBC High Numbers. I do not wish to be middle-class. I wish to watch Sky and ITV. I do not wish to be in limbo with just my pants on.

[The Assembled Company concurred.]

Mrs. Rachel Brannigan: *[reading]* 'Yes, we will cut housing benefit. Yes, we will means-test disability claimants. Oh yes, we are coming down like a ton of fucking bricks to get rid of these and all the other perks of being working-class. These handouts are squeezing society's middle, and the effects are now grotesque.

Society has a waspish waist but horrible ballooned-out legs and a massive head. It is unacceptable. Why should hard-working citizens who are doing the right thing, eating the right breakfast, choosing the cleaner who's right for them . . .'

Miss Salome Kyere: Now we are going to lose our jobs to all the middle-class cleaners who will come to Britain and take our jobs.

Ms. Fatiah Ibrahim: Yes, with their fancy hats and muesli bars and drop earrings and the impractical shoes of whores.

Mrs. Rachel Brannigan: *[reading]* '. . . choosing the cleaner who's right for them, why should Ordinary People subsidise these obscene bonuses to social-security fat cats? What have they done to earn these bonuses? Let us not forget what caused this global recession: the greed . . .'

Ms. Justyna Lechniak: The bankers! *[shook fist, presented 'war face']* Grr!

Mrs. Rachel Brannigan: *[reading]* '. . . the greed of people who borrowed more than they could pay back, squandering it all on sub-prime mortgages and plasma televisions. The global economy was stretched to its very limits by the fat feral-cat poor, buying shit they didn't need with money they couldn't afford to pay back. Do they think that money grows on fucking trees? That it magically appears on the end of cocktail sticks, like those ghastly cheese-and-pineapple nibbles they have in working-class homes on special occasions?'

Miss Salome Kyere: He is a very rude man. Although I do feel guilty and ashamed for my part in the global economic meltdown. I bought my son a bicycle on instalments. Although it was stolen before I made the last payment, so maybe I will still get a hat at least.

Mrs. Rachel Brannigan: *[indicating document]* Oh, this is good, look. He's scribbled little notes for himself on the other side. 'Difficult questions and how to answer them. (1) How will restricting local-authority and housing-association accommodation to short lets improve social mobility? Answer: by reminding the poor that unless they find a job in the private sector sharpish they won't have anywhere to fucking live . . .'

Ms. Justyna Lechniak: I had a letter from the council. They asked, have I considered moving to the North, where housing is cheaper and everyone is happy?

Ms. Fatiah Ibrahim: I have seen the North on television. The people are very fat and not at all happy. When the police investigate a murder in the North, it is difficult because everyone seems guilty.

Miss Salome Kyere: But if we are socially mobilised with our hats and shoes and private-sector jobs and lah-di-dah and *[improvised minuet]* not part of the swollen legs of society any longer but part of the middle, which is no longer being squeezed because we are all in the tummy together, we could go to the Lake District. It looks lovely there.

Mrs. Rachel Brannigan: '(2) You said Sure Start centres would not shut, yet in my constituency they are shutting all over the fucking place. Now you want to get rid of that brilliant scheme that gives books to poor kids and close children's libraries, when your own fucking research clearly shows that the early-years literacy gap determines the destiny of every child passing through the education system! Why do you hate my children, Mr. Cameron? Why?'

Miss Salome Kyere: Yes, why does he hate my children?

Mrs. Rachel Brannigan: 'Answer: that is ridiculous. How can I hate your children? I don't even fucking know them. I mean, where am I supposed to bump into them? At a Sure Start centre, when I drop by to pick up Sam and the toddler? Ha ha, idiot. It's the local authorities shutting everything down. It's not our fault we're giving them less money, is it? If they choose to reduce front-line services and shut shit down, essential shit that helps our poorest families, that is a terrible indictment of our local authorities. Imagine doing something horrible just like that to make a political point, to try to twist the moral lessons of this nation's Deficit to suit their own ends. PS As well as local authorities, don't forget to blame the last Government, who fucking caused everything.'

Ms. Justyna Lechniak: Mr. Cameron sounds depressed and angry. Perhaps we have all been too negative about the cost of child care and less money coming in and the advice centre shutting down and still no money from the father of my children. Perhaps if we have nothing good to say about Mr. Cameron we should say nothing at all.

Ms. Fatiah Ibrahim: I for one feel bad about this. We are fortunate *[indicated Chamber]* to be working in such a place. To be sitting *[occupied the Prime Minister's position before the Dispatch Box]* where the Prime Minister himself sits. Maybe if I do this *[wriggled]* I will absorb some of his middle class through my tabard.

Mrs. Rachel Brannigan: '(3) What makes you think that private landlords will lower rents in line with cuts to housing benefit? Are you 'on' something? Answer: let me be clear. We all do things when we're young that we later regret. That's all in the past. I'm surprised you brought it up at all, unless this is another of Mr. Murdoch's practical jokes, but I can assure you I am definitely not off my face at the moment. And yes, I am confident that landlords will cut their rents in line with housing-benefit reductions. What is the alternative? That they put UP rents in line with the demand for rented property, fuck their existing tenants, they can go and live in a skip, who gives a shit, I can get a childless young professional in here like that, oh, and wave goodbye to your deposit, this carpet shows signs of wear? Is THAT what the critics think is going to happen? It's a disgrace. Landlords have been the backbone of this country since Magna Fucking Carta! They know they're all in it together with the rest of us. Leave private landlords, and me, out of this.'

Miss Salome Kyere: This has put my mind at rest. Finally, someone is prepared to stand up for landlords.

[The Master of the Cleaners entered the Chamber 'in mobile', the Assembled Company then most diligently returning to their tasks.]

The Master of the Cleaners: Don't fuck me about. Well, what's that doing in the Members' Dining Room in the first fucking place? What? No, mate, it's not my job to sort this one out. You need Special Branch. *[terminated call]* Right, gather round. I've got exciting news: this cleaning team is now officially part of the Big Society.

Mrs. Rachel Brannigan: Will we get hats?

The Master of the Cleaners: My budget's been cut by 25 per cent. One of you will have to go. The other three will have to share the extra work, fairly.

Moment of Traffic News on Radio 1.

Annual Conference of the Green Party

Held simultaneously in Birmingham and Narnia
upon the 10th of September 2010
APPLAUSE AND HUMMING
[Ms. Caroline Lucas upon the Zero-Carbon Stage]

Keynote Speech with Polite Interruptions

[Delegates having taken their place upon the Conference Beanbags, in a flat above Whole Earth Co-Operative Pulses, a hidden hand caused the solo flute work Syrinx *by Debussy to occur via cassette player. Ms. Caroline Lucas then appeared from behind a curtain dressed as an Elfin Sprite and performed an interpretative dance (unfathomable, possibly 'expressing the passion of Nature and the need to conserve Earth's Precious Resources').]*

The Elfin Sprite: Friends. Sisters, brothers. Cyclists, vegetarians and in-betweeners. Welcome. Before we start, let us all join together in curbing harmful carbon-dioxide emissions by holding our breath for one minute. Starting from . . . now!

[The Delegates held their breath, prompting diverse hues and vary-ing levels of panic. At the conclusion of Syrinx *a loud karaoke version of 'Dressed for Success' by Roxette, featuring the voice of Ms. Lucas, uttered from the cassette player. Ms. Lucas, in some alarm, disap-peared behind the curtain. The cassette player fell silent. Ms. Lucas took advantage of her invisibility by exhaling and inhaling as quietly as possible, the Delegates doing this also before she reappeared.]*

The Elfin Sprite: Marvellous. Well, this is lovely. First, I have to make a couple of housekeeping announcements. Fire safety: no joss sticks, I'm afraid. Car parking: if you have a car parked anywhere at all, shame on you. Four wheels bad, two wheels good. Wheelchairs are exempt. Buggies are OK, I suppose, but I would urge any parents to be aware of the lifetime energy impli-cations of babies and toddlers and to carbon-offset their chil-dren with sustainable forestry capture. I have some leaflets here.

Delegate: If I could just intervene? I hope they're not made from paper, because that would be hypocrisy of the most disgraceful kind.

The Elfin Sprite: *[cocking her ear to the 'wind']* The Spirits say, 'Don't be paperist, there is no fucking room in the Green Party for intolerance. All things must pass, amen.' Now, our member-ship has grown significantly over the last year, up by nearly a third . . .

[Some Delegates ruefully considering their torsos, and one another's.]

The Elfin Sprite: It's such a pleasure to see so many people I don't recognise! I feel as though I know you already! Not intimately perhaps, but I could definitely pick one or two of you out of a police line-up!

Delegate: Sorry to interrupt, but I thought you'd be interested to know that I have taken up ecologically sound pottery in my retirement. I have made a ceramic 'dreamcatcher' for the kitchen and, if I say so myself, a rather special wormery in the back garden. It's a perfectly accurate scale model of the London Gherkin.

The Elfin Sprite: Ah, thank you. Oh, *[listening]* the Spirits, however, say, 'Shut your wobbly gash, old weirdo fuck with the plaited beard. However energy-efficient the Gherkin is, it remains a symbol of wealth and power, plus who gives an actual shit about your fucking wormery?' Oh, that does seem a bit harsh, but don't shoot the messenger, comrades, I'm simply a policy conduit. Now, let us remind ourselves what a Green Party stands for. Fairness. Justice. Sustainability. Bicycles. Laughter. Tears. Make-up sex. Yummy Fairtrade chocolates. Sustainable bikes. Fair sex. Just chocolate. Make-up tears. List endless. Wait . . . Shared bag of chips at the bus stop, you're fifteen . . .

Delegates: Yay! All hail the Elfin Sprite! Sorry, where's the toilet?

The Elfin Sprite: For years our critics said, OK, if you're a serious political party, why haven't you got any MPs in Parliament? Well, they can eat their fucking polysaturated words now, ladies and gentlemen, because *[indicated self]* you're looking at Brighton's newest MP! Me! Ha ha ha! Amaze!

Delegate: When are we going to stop all travel through the skies?

The Elfin Sprite: I cannot tell you what a privilege it was to stand on that Stage and represent this wonderful movement of ours . . .

Delegate: I embroider jute bags and sell them on Etsy! No way, me too! I'm talking to myself again, aren't you? We are. Nice bag. Thanks.

The Elfin Sprite: . . . tireless work by so many thousands of people, over so many years. Believing against all the odds, I totally
HEART *Glee*, I don't know about you. Ignored or even at times
[shuddered] ridiculed by the mainstream . . .

Delegates: No meat for oil! No meat for oil!

The Elfin Sprite: Yet we stuck to our *[adjusted costume]* principles.
Reducing our footprint. Our footprints. Our feetprint. As you
were, actually, reducing our footprint. And our active verbs. For
a better way, a better world. The idea that politics can be different in a fun way. Simple, powerful, the right time, our future,
forward, the Critical Mass cycle rides, pause and reflect. Hope.

Delegates: Would anyone like to see my allotment? Semi-
skimmed is still half wrong! Turf over the M6!

The Elfin Sprite: Young people are brilliant, aren't they? Those
aged between sixteen and eighteen can be particularly brilliant,
as this is the age when they're most likely to go vegetarian, get
interested in global warming and explore their sexuality in big
jumpers. That's why lowering the voting age to sixteen makes so
much sense, especially for us.

Delegate: The way to reach a teenager is through animals. It could
be a seal pup, or a mummy panda giving birth on the Internet,
say . . .

The Elfin Sprite: Yes, *[listening]* the Spirits are very clearly saying, 'Shut the fuck up, pancake-faced woman with the inhaler.'
Which reminds me, we need more women, everywhere. Why
shouldn't MPs job-share? Mm? Why shouldn't we ALL job-
share? It may seem crazy now . . .

Delegate: I'll share your job! Can I finish your address? I've got a
couple of Jeremy Clarkson jokes!

The Elfin Sprite: Bear with me just a second.

[Ms. Lucas disappeared behind the curtain and then reappeared, strumming an autoharp.]

Delegates: Oh fuck, not this Joan Baez shit again. Do you know any Levellers? Help, I can't get out of this beanbag!

The Elfin Sprite: *[singing]* 'I have done seen misfortune and I have done seen pain. I have had substantial political knockbacks done to me again and again. Westminster have been doing me wrong, allow me to do explain. In voting procedures there are no mechanisms through which I can actually fucking abstain . . .' Thank you, good night, you've been a lovely audience. And remember *[signalled Thumbs Up to an unseen agent on the roof]*, let us tread lightly upon the Earth. Or maybe . . . let us DREAM, and not tread upon the Earth at all!

[It became apparent to Delegates that Ms. Lucas was attached to a flying harness. To the sound of evident physical exertion from beyond the Velux window, Ms. Lucas was hoisted a yard off the floor and made several slow circuits of the room, from time to time gently colliding with those Delegates too infirm to remove themselves from her path.]

Moment of Communal Singing.

Annual Conference of the
Liberal Democrat Party

Held in the Liverpool Sentimentalside Ballroom
upon the 20th of September 2010

CONFLICTED TRIUMPHALISM AND
INTERNAL EXAMINATION

[Mr. Nick Clegg upon the Crucifix]

Keynote Speech with
Whispered Amendments

[The Stage being obscured by a Videowall, the House Lights dimmed
and Delegates hushed. A short film upon the subject of The Passion
of Our Saviour *emitted from the Videowall, depicting the trials of*
the Deputy Prime Minister at the hands of the Squares, the Cynics
and the Media; also his endurance of Great Miseries and Mockings
therefrom. The film concluding with a close-up of the Deputy Prime
Minister in aspect pietistical. A chorale from Bach's St. Matthew
Passion *performed by the LibDem LGBTQ Singers uttered from*
the Public Address System. The Videowall was then raised into the
Proscenium Void by a team of Young Liberal Democrats in orange

tabards, to reveal Mr. Nick Clegg clad only in loincloth and crown of thorns, apparently nailed to The Cross and furnished with a radio microphone.]

Conference Biomass: *[disgust, shock, awe, sexual excitement, secular revulsion, fidgeting]*

Mr. Nick Clegg: The *Guardian* forgive them, for they know not what they do.

[Mr. Clegg mimed his mortal expiry. 'Roll Away the Stone' by Mott the Hoople occurred upon the Public Address System. Mr. Clegg then winking at Conference did alight from The Cross, aided by tabarded volunteers, and performed a Wriggly Dance and an Air Punch.]

Conference Biomass: Blessed is he who comes in the name of the Lord! I know not what we do as well. Look, we're on the fuck-ing monitor, ha ha!

Mr. Nick Clegg: *Ecce homo*, dudes and dudesses. *Ecce homo*. Two and a half years ago, I stood in this very hall. Made my first speech as Leader of our party. Then, I was wearing a light navy suit from Paul Smith. Now *[indicated loincloth]*, I stand before you, suffering tortures on your behalf. And why? So that *[pointing]* you, you, you and you may have eternal life. But what is eternal life if the quality of that eternal life is compromised because 'God' or whoever is still paying back a massive loan on whatever, Paradise, and he's had to lay off front-line . . . angels, for instance? This is mere speculation as I'm an atheist, so relax and just enjoy the rest of your lives, yes? Give yourselves a round of applause, you bloody deserve it.

Conference Biomass: *[self-satisfied applause, looks of sanctimonious self-regard, murmurs of self-approval]*

Mr. Nick Clegg: Oh yes, Conference. You are not like those cold-hearted bastards, the two-faced shits, all the haters out there. Of course they're going to condemn us, me in particular. That's because we are doing the right thing. It's as simple, and believable, as that. Every time we do the right thing, the enemies of reason – their swarthy faces contorted with rage and hatred and envy – say we're wrong. Well, that's easy, isn't it? Anyone can say anyone is wrong. Big deal. THEY'RE wrong. Cynics. Squares. The Media. They question our moral agenda. They shout obscenities at us, even when we're in First Class. Yeah, haters. Where are you going with this? Let me tell you. You are just going on to a late pub lunch with your fucking mates, yes? *[indicated Conference]* I – we – are going on to important roles within Government.

Conference Biomass: Ooh, a late pub lunch. No, no, that's what we DON'T want. It's what I want, Mr. Fucking Combover, or don't I have a say in my own fucking afternoon any more? We ALL have a say in your fucking afternoon, and my say is shut up, you pissed fucking airbag. I agree with Nick.

Mr. Nick Clegg: The Cynics expected us to back away from coalition with a Conservative Government. Why? Because they'd heard what certain Members of the Liberal Democrat Party had publicly said about the Conservatives. Consistently nasty things. I hold my hands up *[held arms out]*. I said some pretty shitty stuff myself about the Tories. When David Cameron told the people of Glasgow East they should 'stop thinking of themselves as unemployed morbidly obese depressives and start thinking of themselves as fat fucks too lazy to get off the cocksucking sofa, even to go to the toilet . . .' this is what I said on *Newsnight* later that evening:

I think there is no excuse in politics for the lucky and the privileged to show such fucking contempt for the poor and the forgotten. David Cameron makes me fucking puke. Not only is he morally repulsive, he's hideous close up. His skin looks like it was made in fucking Westworld.

Conference Biomass: Oh, he was great then, wasn't he, Nick? We hated the Conservatives last year, didn't we? Mm.

Mr. Nick Clegg: So what would the Cynics have done in our position? Refused to form a coalition? What, we should have walked away, cackling, with our integrity and independence intact, allowing a minority Conservative Government to limp on for a while, powerless, unable to tear up every fucking single tenet of the Welfare State because we refused to help them? Is that what the Cynics wanted? And then for another General Election to be called later in the year, allowing us to maintain moral credibility and increase our power base? Get a grip, Cynics, yes? Because the only reason you think we are wrong is not because we are wrong but because we are right. That's why you're the Cynics, Cynics. And why everything, actually, is fucking silk.

Conference Biomass: He does argue very persuasively against cynicism. Yes, although it does feel a bit opportunistic. Yes, and he does sound like . . . who? You know, we're not allowed to say his name. Voldemort? No, you dickpump. *[inaudible, possibly 'Blair']*

Mr. Nick Clegg: I am so, so proud of the quiet courage and determination which you have shown through this momentous period in British political history. Cheers. Hold our nerve and we will have changed British politics for good. Hold our nerve and we will have changed Britain for good. Pensions. A Freedom Bill. Ending the injustices of Christmas. Identity Card Laws gone, bad business with the expenses thing, back next year? Oh sorry, just a note for myself. Bankers stacked like sandbags to plug the financial hole in our floodplain economy. Low earners, yes? A Pupil Premium. Green-Fingered Britain, ladies and gentlemen.

Conference Biomass: I hope the lunch is better than yesterday – puy lentil bake, like lino, horrible. I always bring my own: hummus and rocket batons, beetroot crisps, 200 mg of cubed fruit . . . 'Oh, meh-meh-meh, I always bring my OWN,' shove your fucking baton up your ugly duckling and give my regards to Clapham Common, you knobring. You know what, fuck you AND the rest of your ethnic minority. Oh, I'm telling security, racist. Oh, you called me racist, racist. Racist. Racist.

Mr. Nick Clegg: Some things are different in Government. Some are the same. For example: the catering's a LOT better. But you still get that same smell of pine air freshener, wherever you are in Westminster. Look, we will take risks in Government, but we will never lose our soul. If anyone comes up to me in the next five years and says, 'Nick, we're looking for the soul of the party, we can't seem to find it anywhere,' I will tell them they're *[indicated loincloth]* looking at it. Verily, verily, I say to you I am the life and the soul of the party. I have everything under control and there will be fireworks in due course.

Conference Biomass: Bet he's NOT the life and soul, I bet he's in the kitchen blocking access to the fridge and droning on to some hippy in Dutch about the fucking Oslo Accord. Yeah, or underneath the big pile of coats in the bedroom, crying and

masturbating and telling myself this is absolutely the last time
. . . I'm not being funny or anything, I know you're mayor of
somewhere in the South-West, but would you mind fucking off
back to your own seat?

Mr. Nick Clegg: Remember the four big promises we made in the
Election campaign? Quickly, can you definitely remember if 'no
increase in tuition fees' was one of them?

Conference Biomass: *[struggled to remember, not entirely sure]*

Mr. Nick Clegg: Exactly. That's what I am talking about. Forget
the past – the broken politics, the broken memory, the broken
metaphors – and let's get on with the future, yes? The new politics – collegiate politics, partnership politics, Coalition politics
– is the politics of both singular and plural politics, which is
precisely – precisely – what our nation needs today. The Liberal
Democrats and the Conservatives are and always will be separate parties. They've got nude wrestling, great tailors and those
secret dinners where they eat endangered species. We've got
skiing, diet pills and the occasional game of football with disad-
vantaged kids. Maybe we'll do something clever for Red Nose
Day . . .

Conference Biomass: Emma Freud, she's clever, I wouldn't mind
doing HER for Red Nose Day. Yeah, Emma, kiss my 'red nose'.
Ha ha ha. Excuse me, would you two gentlemen mind keeping your fucking sexist bullshit to yourself? Well, excuse me,
Woman from the Halifax Ad, we're lesbians. Oh. Yeah, what
have you got to say for yourself now? Firstly, I'd like to apologise
. . . Ha ha, got you, you dozy fucking cow, we're not lesbians
at all, we ARE gentlemen and we're in the CABINET. Hey,
Hugo, got any more of those diet pills?

Mr. Nick Clegg: Dudes and dudesses, we are gripped by a crisis. And it's the worst kind: shitty but invisible. You can't actually see the debts mounting up like a peninsula of shit. Walk the high street, go to work, talk to your friends, you won't see the signs of our debts. People are saying, 'Hey, what recession are these guys talking about? I feel great now that we're tackling the deficit at last. I might have another pudding and an armagnac, I'm feeling saucy.' I walked down a high street recently and this is very much more or less the message that filtered back to me: keep up the good work, ignore our grumpiness, we're feeling a bit under the cosh at the moment, it's probably a virus.

Conference Biomass: *[auto-erotic applause]*

Mr. Nick Clegg: Yes, it will be difficult, but it will not be like the '80s. We will not let that happen. I will not let this party be some crappy 'power pop' band playing support on a Tuesday night at the Rock Garden then getting pissed on bottles of weak beer with bits of lime stuck in the neck and swigs of Jack, then doing coke and talking shit all night and trying to bag some German bird doing a PhD in . . . No. This time it will be different. We will be headlining at the Rock Garden and someone from the *NME* will be there and I will definitely get a blowjob off the German bird, I promise you.

Conference Biomass: It won't actually be like the '80s, will it? They're not going to allow smoking indoors again, are they? Oh God, weren't there Dangerous Dogs in the '80s? Yes, and 'Argies'. What are Argies? I think they were some sort of hairy toy.

Mr. Nick Clegg: It's not smaller Government I believe in. It's a different kind of Government: a liberating Government. This

Government *[mimed adaptation of a 1980s Transformer toy]* will take the state in its hands, reverse generations of centralisation, pull this bit out here and *voilà*: Optimus Prime, the coolest state ever. Power. Sheer fucking power. Local people, local power, local change. Robots in disguise! *[indicated Transformer attack]* Ack-ack-ack-ack-ack – boom!

Conference Biomass: I liked *ThunderCats*. Speed of the puma! Strength of the . . . bear? The day I held aloft my sword and said, 'By the power of Grayskull!' Gang of Four, wasn't Shirley Williams in that? I heard when she was an undergraduate at Oxford she used to cycle round town with a dildo in her front basket. You just made that up. It's OK, I'm a lawyer.

Mr. Nick Clegg: Yes! Let us remember what Labour did to our memories. *SuperTed* videotapes destroyed on an industrial scale and replaced with *Pingu* DVDs. A widening gap between rich and poor. Failure to act on the environment, even though the environment is clearly playing up and needs a proper fucking role model. Let me tell you something, yes? We held a public consultation about the Spending Review. We had a staggering 100,000 ideas from members of the public about how to cut waste and do things more effectively. 100,000 ideas! OK, not all of those 100,000 ideas are the fucking Theory of Relativity, but add them all together and who KNOWS what we've got? We're still working our way through them, but wow. Wow.

Conference Biomass: My idea was colour-coded benefits. My idea was air farms. I proposed a new public holiday, a bit later than Whitsun, to celebrate diversity and to celebrate the diversity of the celebrations of that day themselves, anything goes these diverse days, a multipurpose holiday with no commemoration as such, for everyone be they religious or be they atheious, and I would call it Left Blank for Your Message Day.

Mr. Nick Clegg: *[smiling to self]* Now, it wouldn't be a Liberal Democrat conference if we didn't have a motion that provoked strong passions on both sides. And what is the really bloody great thing that all Liberal Democrats share a passion for?

Conference Biomass: Marijuana. Having a sensible grown-up debate about marijuana. In the kitchen baking bread that looks like it was hacked out of a fucking peat bog and maybe having a cheeky spliff, with Radio 3 on.

Mr. Nick Clegg: Education. When it comes to lasting fairness, education is everything. Now, we all love lasting fairness, yes? It's brilliant. We all want education to be everything to every-one. So I'd really really fucking appreciate a bit of support on this one, OK, because no way – no way – will there be a few schools singled out for preferential treatment. No, because we want all schools – very nearly all – to be Academies. That way, all schools are free to know best about what they want. That's just common sense. Anyway . . . So *[consulted Autocue]* the immediate future will not be easy, but the long-term prize is great. I want you to imagine what you will say to people when you knock on their door at the next General Election. Imagine. Just *[closed eyes]* close your eyes and imagine. Mm . . .

Conference Biomass: 'Look, first of all I'd like to apologise.' 'I like your door.' 'That dog really should be on a lead, you know.'

Mr. Nick Clegg: That's why, my friends, colleagues and ordinary people who have come here on coaches hired by constituency offices to be with me – us – I say: stick with me-stroke-us. Soon, these crazy liberal plural politics will feel as natural as breathing normally after a panic attack. Hold your nerve and stick with us, yes? Look, I know Britain in 2010 is anxious, unsure about the future, a bit down in the mouth *[performed 'facial unhappiness']* . . .

Conference Biomass: Jesus, he looks just like one of the characters from *Lost*. He looks like one of the characters from fucking *Waiting for Godot*.

Mr. Nick Clegg: . . . but Britain in 2015 will be a different country. *[mimed 'strength']* Strong. *[mimed 'Scales of Justice']* Fair. *[removed loincloth]* Free.

Conference Biomass: I say. I like the way he said 'free', then showed us his 'point of delivery'. Bravo. Consummate performance.

Mr. Nick Clegg: This is the goal we must keep firmly fixed in our minds. This is the prize. Oh, and by the way, Conference, just in case you've forgotten, I still think the war in Iraq was illegal *[erection]*. The years ahead will not be easy but they will make the difference our country needs. Stick with us *[indicated self]* while we rebuild the economy with those 100,000 brilliant ideas. Stick with us *[waggled]* while we restore civil liberties, protect our environment and repair our broken politics, all smashed to fucking bits by Labour in a drunken rage. Stick with us *[standing ovation]* and together we will change Britain for good, and then it'll be too late to change it back again, yes?

Moment of Doubt.

Annual Conference of the Labour Party

Held at World of Hogwarts, Greater Manchester,
upon the 28th of September 2010
AUTOMATED RESPONSE
[Mr. Ed Miliband and Imaginary Friend]

Keynote Speech with Whispered Counterpoint

[Mr. Ed Miliband, the newly elected Party Leader, appeared upon the Stage in a state of some agitation, wearing a new suit from which the retailer's labels still depended. He was greeted by Mr. David Miliband, who embraced his younger brother and muttered some words of encouragement: inaudible, possibly 'Good luck, you snake in the fucking grass. Oh, and I told Auntie Mavis it WAS you who smuggled Uncle Brian's porn out of his shed and into our den that time we had to stay with them, when all the rellies were holidaying with the Hobsbawms in Provence, so there, Mr Oh-help-Mummy-I've-wet-the-bed-and-my-Dan-Dare-pyjamas-are-soaked-boo-hoo. Oh, and you've got something on your tie, fucky fucky squirtypants . . .' Mr. Ed Miliband cast his gaze downwards and was flicked upon the nose

by Mr. David Miliband, who then exited the Stage. Mr. Ed Miliband moved with evident trepidation to the Rostrum, accompanied by 'Christopher', his Imaginary Friend, Confidant and Adviser since Secondary School.]

Christopher: Don't look at the front row. Keep saying 'new power generation' and they'll think you're Prince. Don't sweat. And don't do that mad fucking thing with your mouth, it makes you look like a fucking balloon animal.

Mr. Ed Miliband: Conference, I stand here now today ready to lead: a new power generation now leading Labour. I tell you this. Be in no doubt. The new power generation of Labour is different. Different attitudes, different ideas, different ways of talking, new power syntax. Today, I want to tell you who I am, what I believe and how we are going to do the most important to-do thing we have to do: win back the trust of the country. New. I tell you. Brerk.

Christopher: And don't make those stupid noises. Charlie Brooker and his sniggering mates will take the piss, and then that's the student base fucked. Do the Poliakoff stuff.

Mr. Ed Miliband: Conference, I tell you. Each of us has our own individual story, because people are unique. I want to tell you about mine. It starts in 1940, when my grandfather, with my dad, climbed onto one of the last boats out of Belgium. It ends with a young man, endearing smile, getting a Master's at the London School of Economics. All the bits in the middle, brerk, just imagine the back story for every tragic character in a Stephen Poliakoff drama.

[Nodding, applause, conferring upon the subject of Mr. Stephen

Poliakoff. Some in favour of the notion that Mr. Poliakoff is brilliant, some preferring his early work, others confusing him with Mr. Steven Berkoff and imagining a young Mr. Miliband in a profound rage and/or an act of sexual humiliation.]

Christopher: Stop doing the noise, you cunt. Mum, mum. Tell them about your mum.

Mr. Ed Miliband: Conference, I want to tell you about my mum. I know nobody more generous, nobody more kind, nobody more loving and nobody more relieved that this contest is over than my mum. Honestly, Mum, you're the best mum in the world . . .

[Mr. David Miliband surreptitiously flicking rubber bands at Mr. Ed Miliband's face.]

Mr. Ed Miliband: . . . and I know you like me better than David. Not just because I got my grade 8 violin. But because I didn't blooming well agree with the Iraq War. Plus I didn't allow the torture of terrorist suspects. What did you call it, David? 'Extraordinary rendition'? I tell you, Conference, it wasn't as extraordinary as David's rendition of 'Don't Stop Believing' at the Hampstead Fabians fundraiser. Ha ha ha, brerk. Yes, Conference. I tell you, we were wrong to take Britain to war, and we need to be honest about that. This is the new power generation. My name is Ed. And I am funky. Brerk.

[Applause. Mr. David Miliband asked Ms. Harriet Harman why she was applauding, given that she had voted for the Iraq War. She replied that she was demonstrating support for The Leader and that Mr. Miliband was only sulking because he didn't win the Leadership

Contest, and that he should grow up. Mr. Miliband replied that he hated her, that she wasn't his friend any more, and that her face looked like a bum and her mouth looked like the crack in the bum where the poo comes out.]

Christopher: Stop fucking saying 'brerk'. Stop it. Shower them with shit about how well they did in the Election. Say something nice about the way they look.

Mr. Ed Miliband: Conference, can I thank you for the heroic work you did at the Election. I tell you, the reason we denied the Conservative Party a majority was because of the incredible work that is done by Labour and trade-union members the length and breadth and width of our country triangulated, with Northern Ireland more of a lozenge or something. Brerk. From Birmingham Edgbaston to Westminster North and from Edinburgh South to the Vale of Clwyd, these are important new-power-generation lines. We must lay more of these. And I tell you we shall, Conference. Oh, and may I ask you something, Conference? You're looking brerk great. Have you lost weight?

[Applause. Some agreement that the Labour Party did indeed now appear to have less weight.]

Christopher: Mouth! Mouth! You might as well have a trembling 'lady's sex kebab' roaming round your fucking face. It couldn't look any more cartoonish. What is it with Labour leaders? Why do they all have to have shonky cakeholes? Blair: smile like a fucking pterodactyl. Brown: did that spasmic cocksucky thing. Harman: mouth is a cat's arse but OK, only caretaker for a few months. You: never mind your mouth, your whole fucking

137

face looks like it's been CGI'd, you startled mechanical wanker. Right, hold your fucking nervous system still for a minute and do The Journey.

Mr. Ed Miliband: Conference, we had a bad result. We had a very bad result. And we are out of Government. Obviously, you know this. Conference, you are not stupid. Let me tell you, there is nothing good about opposition. Every day that passes without our new power generation being plugged into the national grid of pure funk energy is another day of brerk being off school with glandular fever, unable politically to change our country for the better. We must go on our own journey. This will require *[mimed weightlifting]* strong leadership. It won't always be easy. You might not always understand what I have to say. But now you've elected me Leader and now I tell you, lead you I now will. Come with me on this journey.

Christopher: No, don't do the fucking Community Theatre bollocks. Don't.

[The House Lights dimmed. A CD – Relax: Ambient Sounds of the Rain Forest – occurred. An aide brought Mr. Miliband a pith helmet and blunderbuss, which items having been appropriated, Mr. Miliband then mimed 'exploring' as he spoke.]

Mr. Ed Miliband: I ask you, Conference, where are we going? What will I tell you we will discover? Ooh, look, there's the elephants' graveyard of New Labour. Let's move on, quietly. This IS a jungle, you know. Shh! What's that up ahead? Idealism about the future. No, wait. What was that I saw just now behind me, brerk, no, what's that up ahead? It is humility about our past. I tell you, Indigenous Native Scout, i.e. Conference,

138

we should all be proud of our humility about the past. But we should also be humble about our pride for the future.

[Conference restless or asleep. Some noiseless movement towards the Exit with apologetic toilet-themed miming.]

Mr. Ed Miliband: On we go, Conference. A new power generation thirsting for change. *[swigged from canteen, spat]* Ugh. Alcohol – *nein danke*! This will be a long journey involving hard thinking for our party, I tell you, brerk . . .

Christopher: Yeah, to be honest most of the hard thinking has been about what you look like. It was Wallace out of *Wallace and Gromit* yesterday. Today, they're all Googling 'Barton Fink'.

Mr. Ed Miliband: I tell you, I can see something in a jungle clearing up ahead. It is an economy that works better for working people and a society changed so that it values community and family, not just work, because we understand there is more to life than work, though obviously brerk there must be both work AND non-work for them both to work together, Conference, values, new power politics for a new power generation, my name is Prince. And I am thinky.

Christopher: Fuck the thinking. Nobody cares about the thinking. Tell them about your optimism. Or I will make you tell them about fingering Sylvia from Highgate during the Quakers' camping weekend when you were 'supposed' to be her daughter's boyfriend. I'm warning you, I will.

Mr. Ed Miliband: Shut up, Christopher. Conference, I tell you: optimism. David Cameron. I tell him, come off it. His is a miserable, pessimistic view of what we can achieve. I have an entirely different sort of pessimism, which is optimism. The

optimism to say OK, we did not do enough to address concerns
about some of the consequences of globalisation, including
migration. The optimism to understand people's anger about
immigrants. The optimism to oppose irresponsible strikes. The
optimism to support a tax system for businesses who are on our
side. To these and others too numerous to mention I say: come
on in, the optimism's lovely.

[Applause. Conference signalled its full backing for optimism.]

Christopher: Excellent. Keep saying all that David Cameron shit.
They love it. If only you could write a speech. And you didn't
have a voice like a struggling food mixer. And you didn't look
like the president of the fucking Sixth-Form Debating Society
who's been up all night playing *World of Warcraft*.

Mr. Ed Miliband: But I WAS president of the . . .

Christopher: We. WE were president of the Debating Society.
WE did the Gap Year. YOU fingered poor old Sylvia by the
dying embers of the Quakers' camp fire.

Mr. Ed Miliband: I tell you, Christopher, I will not stand for
this. Either work with me, in my head, or fuck off back to
Imaginaria or wherever it is you come from, certainly outside
the EU. Conference, I notice you are looking at me in some
puzzlement. I was just being a weary explorer talking to himself.
Aha, what's this up ahead?

Christopher: I don't know. Is it Sylvia's vagina?

Mr. Ed Miliband: Conference, I tell you, it is a family on benefits
for whom the system has become a trap and who are frankly
fed up to the back teeth with being stereotyped and patronised
by the Tories, and who look to us to protect them and make

sure they have the help they need to ensure they do not become mere statistics in political point-scoring. Brerk. Ooh, what's this new thing I have spotted on my journey through the spoken jungle? It is an elephant trap. And there's something down there, look. *[cocked blunderbuss]* Perhaps I will have to carry out a mercy killing if it's broken its leg. Oh, I see. Brerk. It IS an elephant. But not an 'elephant in the room', as we are in the jungle. No, Conference, I tell you that this Elephant in the Elephant Trap is a composite elephant consisting of strong families, time with your children, green spaces, community life, love and compassion. *[laid down blunderbuss, mimed helping elephant out of trap]* Come on then, baby composite elephant, let's get you out of there and back into the mainstream agenda . . .

[Conference making elephant noises and wondering what sort of food might entice one out of a trap.]

Christopher: Don't tell me you forgot the fucking buns, shithead.

Mr. Ed Miliband: Shut UP, Christopher. *[addressed offstage: inaudible, possibly 'Buns!' An aide appeared with a bag, which Mr. Miliband seized, his pith helmet becoming dislodged. Mr. Miliband produced a bun]* I tell you, Conference, the new power generation is hungry for change. And justice. *[took a mouthful of bun, mimed elephant-coaxing; inaudible, possibly 'Come on, little elephant']*

Christopher: OK, you can't actually pull that fucking metaphor out, it's too heavy. Do foreign policy now. Wait. Pick up the blunderbuss! Pick up the fucking blunderbuss!

Mr. Ed Miliband: Conference, we'll come back for the elephant later. *[picked up blunderbuss, playfully 'aiming' it at Mr. David*

Miliband. Some nervousness in the Hall] I tell you, in our foreign policy too the new power generation must challenge old thinking. The generation that came of age at the end of the Cold War. Let's not brerk forget 9/11. Or Afghanistan. Or the Middle East.

Christopher: Don't mention Israel. Do not fucking mention Israel. Mention Israel, and I'll make you mention Sylvia.

Mr. Ed Miliband: And let me say this. I will always defend the right of Israel to exist in *shalom* and perpetuity. But Israel must accept and recognise Palestine's right to statehood and its legitimate inclusion in the Eurovision Song Contest. Plus, the attack on the Gaza flotilla was wrong. Plus, the Gaza blockade must be lifted. We must lift the blockade, Conference, and see Sylvia's pants underneath. What is beneath Sylvia's pants, ladies and gentlemen? Sylvia's vagina – shut up, Christopher, it was a one-off, she was a widow, Harriet didn't really like me that much anyway, we split up a few weeks later, plus how am I even the villain here, hello, brerk? Some fucking jobsworth Quaker elder was wandering past on his way to the toilet block and interrupted us before she could give me a handjob, it happened once, Harriet, once, we both regretted it, never made eye contact again, I tell you, fuck you, Christopher . . .

[Conference checking their printed copies of the speech against delivery, looking one to another in some confusion as to the origin and destination of Mr. Miliband's narrative.]

Christopher: You know, they're already trying to work out who your successor will be, and you haven't even finished your first speech as Leader! You fucknugget! Wrap it up. We've got lunch with the Kinnocks in some grisly fucking curry house.

Mr. Ed Miliband: I tell you, brerk, no instant results, no instant votes, no instant popularity, no *X Factor* politics. That's what the focus groups told us: no focus groups. We can't be imprisoned by the focus groups. That, Conference, would be false imprisonment. I will be who I am. When I disagree with the Government I will say so loud and clear. 'Come off it, you brerk Tories,' I'll say. 'Come off it.' I tell you this, Conference, the new power generation must find a new way of conducting new politics. Centre-Left Optimism – it's never been tried before. Well, it has, but sadly many of those people are now dead. We are the optimists now. It's time brerk for a grown-up conversation. Let the message go out: a new power generation has taken charge. Our name is Labour. And we are funky. Our name is Labour. The brerk one and only. We did not come to fuck around. Optimistic about our country. Optimistic about our world. Optimistic about the new power of new politics. We are the optimists and together we will change. Brerk.

Christopher: 'We are the Optimisties, little girls and boys . . .' Come on, Barton. Lamb dansak and Mateus Rosé with the fucking Kinnocks. You can do all the talking.

Moment of Afterthought.

Annual Conference of the
Conservative Party

Held in Birmingham upon the 6th of October 2010

APPLAUSE AND CACKLING

[Mr. David Cameron on the Stage]

Keynote Speech with Mutterings
from Colleagues and Delegates

[The house lights having been dimmed and the song 'Intro' by The xx caused to utter from the public-address system, to the visible dismay of older Delegates, a giant luminous Egg was brought upon the Stage by diverse attendants in costume suggestive of prodigal sexuality. The Prime Minister emerged from the Egg wearing a neon onesie and addressed the Conference.]

The Prime Minister (Mr. David Cameron): Woo! Bless. Fam. In the words of Neil Tennant at the Labour Party Conference in Sheffield 1986: Do you feel all right?

Colleagues and Delegates: Mm.

The Prime Minister: I said, DO YOU MOTHERFUCKERS FEEL ALL RIGHT?

Colleagues and Delegates: Yay! Mm. I just fucking said yes, are you deaf? I hated that shit Kinnock. Me too, he looked like Mussolini. Yeah, but without the tailoring. Yeah, fucking sheep-shagger. Ah, where have the years gone? Shh. Mostly around my middle. Ha ha. Ha ha ha. Shh. Fuck off. Why's Cameron talking like that? To show he's 'street'. Which one, Canal Street? Shh. Bless you. Ha ha. Fuck off. Shh.

The Prime Minister: It is an honour and a privilege to stand here behind the par-TAY like some intrepid explorer or shit, driving a team of centre-right-ass huskies. Conservative Prime Minister of the United Kingdom? Aight.

Colleagues and Delegates: Oh God, not the fucking huskies again. Who wrote this shit? Hilton. Coulson. Hilton, Coulson – fuck, they even SOUND like those *Top Gear* cunts. You watch, it'll be *Monty* Fucking *Python* next.

The Prime Minister: Fam, I want to tell you all where we be being at. Then I want to tell you where we be going. But, whoa. Rewind, motherfuckers. Let us remember where we be coming FROM.

Colleagues and Delegates: Faversham. Bath. Near Chalfont St. Giles. Empingham. Islington. Snape. Seaview, Isle of Wight, marvellous marvellous Latvian girl does everything. Oh, just here on holiday from the Cayman Islands, sorry, I have to take this.

The Prime Minister: Remember what those tinky-ass mother-fuckers say about us? They say we a dead parrot. They say we be ceasing to motherfucking be . . .

Colleagues and Delegates: Told you.

The Prime Minister: . . . well, fuck you, tinky-ass dickjammers, because this is the centre-right-ass RE-UP right here. Do you know what I'm saying? Because what I am saying, like the great Arnold Schwarzenegger before me, is: We Have Come Back.

Colleagues and Delegates: Ha ha. I need your clothes. *Hasta la vista*, Boo Boo. Has he started yet?

The Prime Minister: First, I wish to commend most heartily those who led this par-TAY before me. William Hague got us back on our back, people. But crucially, one foot always remained on the bedroom floor, you know what I'm saying? Iain Duncan Smith helped us channel our emotions and so forth with his passive-aggressive crybaby face and his Henman Fist. Michael Howard made us all feel good about ourselves for the first time in years. How? By not being Iain Duncan Cocking Smith. Hey, guys, I just be fucking with you all. Peace.

Colleagues and Delegates: I liked Thatcher best. Yes, Thatcher and Churchill. Yes, Thatcher and Churchill and that one who reformed local government. Way back. The regime-change one with zero tolerance for insurgents. William the Conqueror. Yeah. Ah, *la belle France*, I mean, fucking Europe. Shh.

The Prime Minister: The voters left us with a *[swivelled hips]* hung Parli-ay-ment. So we took that shit, got Coalicious on the nation's ass, boom shakalaka fuck yeah. And you know why? Because this par-TAY be always putting the country first. Mm-hm. Specially at weekends. *[mimed shooting game bird]* Boom. Trust. Leave the vested interests to others. Old school friends, donors, former business colleagues, the offshore boys and the West End girls . . .

Colleagues and Delegates: Wanker. Why is he doing all those silly fucking hand gestures? He looks like a bookie. Or those

146

coloured boys who do the angry shouty music. Perhaps he's having a fit. It looks like quite a tight one. Ha ha. Shh.

The Prime Minister: Look what we be doing already. We be policy-delivering on your collective ass. Two hundred new academies in just one sentence. Ten thousand university places in another. Fifty thousand motherfucking apprenticeships – that's what I'm saying and I think it jolly well merits another round of applause, collective bitch.

Colleagues and Delegates: *[polite applause, unwrapping of sweets, rectal plosion]*

The Prime Minister: Corporation tax axed. Jobs tax axed. Police targets – whatever they are, consider them well and motherfuckingly truly boom shakalaka smashed motherfuckers. Immigration – squashed into something maybe the size of a processed-cheese slice. Home Information Packs – what the fuck were THEY about, fam? Fat-cat salaries – monitored and frowned upon. ID Cards piled onto a Bonfire of the Insanities, another headline right there, dog. The NHS – and look at me because I do not be shitting you – PROTECTED. We be protecting the shit out of that motherfucker.

Colleagues and Delegates: Marvellous, he should do stand-up. It has to be 'blue' to be really funny, I always think. Cameron's not very 'blue', is he? Tebbit, he was blue. Told the most appalling joke, something about Barbara Castle's 'third vagina'. Shh.

The Prime Minister: Quangos – shit off, man, you fucking rotters. A bank levy – coming right up, watch this space, dog. Cancer drugs fund – three nouns, all vital. Six billion pounds of spending saved this year, we could go somewhere nice, out of season, bitch. For our pensioners – new listening measures and improved visibili-TAY. For our new entrepreneurs – employees' tax reduced, a fistbump and a trip to a lap-dancing club, what happens in Conkers stays in Conkers, dog. Lady entrepreneurs – whatever, a tranny show. Aight.

Colleagues and Delegates: Does he keep burping? Excuse me, would you mind flattening your hair, I can't see properly. It's ALL burping.

The Prime Minister: Check what we did in five months. Imagine what we can do in *[executed a High Five]* five years.

Colleagues and Delegates: *[imagined non-executive director-ships, lobbying opportunities, reciprocal fact-finders/Barbados/The Cricket]*

The Prime Minister: This Government be setting a new direction on the ass of foreign policy. We be talking tough and dealing rough – in accordance, of course, with all legal requirements governing the international trade in security logistics and so forth bada bing and so on, trust.

Colleagues and Delegates: Yes, a foreign policy arm in arm with the arms trade. Yes, a foreign policy with legs. Yes, arms and legs all over the place, I'll drink to that.

The Prime Minister: Anyone else feel like puking they guts when that bitch responsible for the Lockerbie bombing, the biggest motherfucking mass murderer in British history, be getting a Hero's Welcome in Tripoli? No. Uh-uh. Nuh-uh. Libya? Fuckya. This Government be definitely not be propping up no oppressive regimes in the Middle Fucking East, no mo, mofos, ladies and gentlemen. *[inaudible, possibly 'Except Saudi Arabia']*

Colleagues and Delegates: He should have been strung up, cancer or no cancer. If I had my way, he'd be bundled out of an aeroplane without a fucking parachute, see how he likes it, yeah, give my regards to the 'compassionate grounds' when you hit them in ninety seconds at fucking 6,000 mph. But oh no, we're all supposed to be friends with Libya now. Total fucking disgrace. We've got several building projects over there, you know, the planners are a complete joke, though fair play, the margins are good. Gaddafi. Bless you. He may dress like Elton Fucking John, but he bloody well knows how to crack down on crime. Yeah, he should be Home Secretary, instead of that awful hamster-faced woman. Lady Gaga? Hey, are you insulting Baroness Thatcher? Because I will thump you if you are. I don't care if you ARE wearing glasses and holding a Union Jack. Do you mind? I am a member of the fucking Cabinet. Lay one finger on me and I'll have you fucking detained for twenty-eight days. Bollocks, you've let that lapse, you can only bang me up for fourteen now. Fine. How does a fortnight in fucking Islamabad sound?

The Prime Minister: All over the world, Governments be wrestling with the same challenges. Let me break it down for you all. We gots to get. *[checked Autocue]* Yes, that's apparently what I be saying: we gots to get. We gots to get from A to B. Where A equals State Power and B equals People Power. We gots to get from unchecked individualism to national unity and *[thrusted hips]* PURPOSE.

Colleagues and Delegates: Hang on a minute, that's technically the opposite of what I stand for. Yeah, silly bugger, what's he talking about, national unity? What does he want, a fucking General Strike? And could someone please explain to me what the pissing hell 'checked' individualism is. I don't know – golf?

149

The Prime Minister: Yeah. That's what I gots . . . *[consulted Autocue]* I gots to be dropping on you all. A to B, as I be saying. From Big Government to the Big Society. A nation of doers and go-getters. Stepping forward, not sitting back. Standing up, not stepping . . . in some shit. Leaning with us, not on us. Jumping like this *[executed a Royal Canadian Air Force Starjump]*, not like this *[executed The Splits]*. Fuck. Shit. Fuck. Fuck.

Colleagues and Delegates: Ha ha ha, he can't get up. Is this some kind of clever physical metaphor? Oh wait, they've got him back on his feet. Oh my God, is he wearing fucking trainers?

The Prime Minister: Forty-three billion pounds in debt-interest payments alone. Fuck. Just to be standing still. *[stood still]* Not even to *[leaned forward]* move forward *[fell over]*. Fuck. *[helped up]* Know what we could do with that cheese? Only take 11 million people out of paying motherfucking income tax, that's all! *[clutched thorax]* Fuck.

Colleagues and Delegates: You could call them the cheese burglars. Fucking Aldi customers. Have you ever been inside an Aldi? It's like Southend or somewhere ghastly, but in slow motion. Ha ha, look. Ken Clarke's spilled water all over himself. Shall we make a bolt for it, beat the rush? Rather. I've got us a table at that chintzy Italian place. I know a back route, we could knock over some dustbins. Whiff whaff!

The Prime Minister: Bit dizzy, tbh . . . broader shoulders . . . greater load . . . supporting people out of poverty, not trapping them in dependency . . . big citizens . . . a Britain that believes in itself . . . a life more fulfilled and fulfilling for everyone, these are a few of my favourite things . . . new kind of Government . . . realistic, ambitious, believes, trusts, boosts, elderly, love, parents, children, pull, work, together, national, interest, fuck my balls ache. *[consulted Autocue]* Peace out. Boom shakalaka.

Colleagues and Delegates: *[standing ovation, throat-clearing, monitor-monitoring, queuing for the toilet]*

Moment of Luncheon.

House of Commons

Held upon the Feast of St. Titsnars, the 11th of October 2010

PRAYERS AND CURSES

[Mr. Speaker upon the Booster Seat within the Chair]

Work and Pensions Interventions

Mr. Speaker: Questions to the Secretary of State for Work and Pensions!

Hon. Members: Wanker!

Mr. Speaker: Please do NOT try my patience. That isn't a question.

Hon. Members: 'Why is the Secretary of State for Work and Pensions such a fucking wanker?' then.

Mr. Speaker: That's better. Let's have some decorum, thank you. Minister, pray continue.

[The Secretary of State for Work and Pensions arose, his eyes cast downwards in great pity and sadness, his brow pedimented with condolence.]

The Secretary of State for Work and Pensions (Mr. Iain Duncan Smith): Mr. Speaker, the hon. Members opposite may mime 'wanker' until their arms drop off, but it will not alter the fact that vast swathes of the poorest and most unemployed members of our Big Society are trapped in a vicious circle of joblessness and poverty. Shh. Sadly, it is often the benefits system that requires them to be unemployed and poor, and that cannot be right in any equation of fairness. Shh. Can you hear that, Mr. Speaker? It's the quiet sound of Truth. The truth, Mr. Speaker, that the cart of benefits has been put before the horse of unemployment. Do you see what I'm driving at? The need for progressive compassion . . .

Hon. Members: Oh, progressive, progressive, progressive! Fucking dementia, that's 'progressive'! Why don't you shove a garden hose 'progressively' up your arse until the sprinkler emerges from your stupid mannequin face, then fuck off and water my rhubarb?

Mr. Speaker: Order, this is dreadful behaviour. I warn you, if this level of disruption continues, I will have to write a despairing piece in *The Times* about Parliamentary standards. Minister, pray continue.

Mr. Iain Duncan Smith: Thank you, Mr. Speaker. Shh. Reform of the entire social-security system is not, as some critics would argue, simply a cost-cutting exercise. That is a terrible accusation, and I hope those who have made it will – shh! – reflect upon the calumny that has been heaped upon me personally *[dabbed eyes]* and this Coalition Government in general. Reducing the dependence of the incapacitated and the jobless – many of whom have families, let us remember – is at heart a human-rights issue. Shh. Fairness, that is all we seek. Fairness, and justice. Fairness, and justice, and progressive . . .

Mr. Speaker, the hon. Lady opposite may indicate her tits if she wishes, but they are hardly relevant to this debate.

Miss Betty O'Seatsafe (Rebadgerton Teesside): On the contrary, Mr. Speaker, they are most germane. Behold my featureless breasts, with these tiny little faces on the nipples. Do they not remind the House of the Secretary of State for Work and Pensions? He's this one here *[nodded]* on the left, with his Cabinet colleague, the Secretary of State for Defence *[nodded]*, slightly to the right of him.

Hon. Members: *[uproaring, downpiping]*

Mr. Speaker: Oh, for the love of Sinatra, please hush now.

Mr. Iain Duncan Smith: Mr. Speaker, the worst, the unkindest thing we could possibly do is to keep giving people money. Because by doing that you are – shh – taking jobs away from them. The best, the kindest thing would be to wean them off benefits altogether. Not only would it give the unemployed poor a sense of dignity, shh. The measurable social good, in Treasury terms certainly, would increase manyfold.

Hon. Members: 'Manyfold', you fucking gust of whirling batshite? Yeah, you daft git! What's a 'manyfold'? It's what your foreskin goes into at the swimming pool! Like a Walnut Whip! Yes, Walnut Whip Foreskin! Shut up about foreskins, I'm eating fucking dried apricots! Boo hoo, fuck off! Foreskins! Shut up!

Mr. Speaker: Order, order, order, order. Order.

Mr. Douglas Alexander (Paisley & Muesly): Mr. Speaker, as someone with a full head of hair plus Scottish, let me ask the Minister two questions. Firstly, does he have a full head of hair? Secondly, is he Scottish? Because if he cannot be trusted on these basics, Mr. Speaker, how can he expect the hard non-working People of Britain to believe a word he says about fucking anything, the daft wee stookie?

Mr. Iain Duncan Smith: Mr. Speaker, I will take no lessons from the hon. Gentleman, whose party – and SHH HA HA THE MORNING AFTER – got us into this terrible awful ghastly state in the first place. Anyway, what does HE suggest we do to Tackle the Ticking Timebomb of Turpitude, Mr. Speaker?

Mr. Douglas Alexander: Well, I suggest something remarkably similar, Mr. Speaker, but done in a much more slow and compassionate way. And put someone in charge who doesn't look like a fucking boiled egg with features drawn on by some wee lassie anyway.

Mr. Iain Duncan Smith: Mr. Speaker, the hon. Gentleman simply cannot be allowed to get away with this. I fucking SAID 'compassion'. At least twice. If he is now accusing me of not being compassionate, then shame on him. I hope he dies in a rail crash. Shh.

Hon. Members: That is an appalling thing to say! I agree, he absolutely DID mention 'compassionate'. Wanker!

Mr. Charles Kennedy (Codshead Revisited): On a Point of mm ha Order, Mr. Speaker. I can assure the hon. Member for Paisley & Muesly that having a full head of hair and a Scottish accent is no shitting help at all, in my experience. *[made self comfortable, lit cigarette]* See, when I was Leader of the Lib Dems, nobody invited ME to form a fucking mm ha Government . . .

Mr. Speaker: Order. The hon. Gentleman will extinguish that thing at once! This is not some gritty blooming police drama set in the 1970s!

Mr. Charles Kennedy: *[extinguished cigarette, unscrewed bottle* *top]* Mr. Speaker, the Minister will know that some members of the Liberal Democrat Party opposed this Coalition but decided to support it as a matter of principle. Now it seems the Government is going back on its word about mm ha fucking everything. Are we to understand that this principle – of believing one thing and doing the opposite – has been undermined by the duplicity of the Coalition Government?

Mr. Iain Duncan Smith: Mr. Speaker, I am happy to reassure the hon. Gentleman that believing one thing and doing another remains at the core of this Government's commitment to – shh – democratic choice . . .

Ms. Glenda Jackson (Hampstead Madscene): Mr. Speaker! Ha! The Lib Dems are fucking LIARS! I tell you, lovey, they are the Thirty Pieces of Silver Party, oh yes, oh yes! And on a Point of Order, when the hon. Member for Codshead Revisited was Leader of his party – a grotty, yucky ragbag party of conscientious objectors, urine drinkers and allotment holders – I didn't see many ladies' pants flying in HIS direction. He was fucking rubbish, Mr. Speaker lovey. When I was in MY heyday I had all sorts. Tits smeared with coal dust, lovey, pubic hair filling the big screen. The *Sunday Times* said I had the most versatile and articulate arse in period drama they'd ever . . .

Hon. Members: *[panic, commotion, sexual arousal]*

Mr. Speaker: Order! Oh dear, oh dear. The hon. Lady *[consulted small black book]* may have a majority of only forty-two. But she is not above Parliamentary protocol, I think. She knows very well that she used the 'L' word. I insist she retract it immediately.

Ms. Glenda Jackson: 'Lovey' you mean, lovey?

Mr. Speaker: I mean That Word Which May Not Be Uttered Within This Chamber Without Severe and Instant Sanction, Madam. THAT 'L' word.

Ms. Glenda Jackson: Oh, 'liar', you mean, Mr. Speaker lovey. Well, in that case, let me 'apologise', Mr. Speaker. (Aficionados will have detected the subtle modulation of my voice there to suggest quotation marks. And brackets. RADA, lovey. RADA.) The Lib Dems are not merely fucking liars. They are morally bankrupt tosspots who would do anything for ministerial trappings and a comely intern. Furthermore, lovey . . .

Mr. Speaker: Order, enough. The hon. Lady will take no further part in this debate. And if there's any more nonsense, I shall expel her from This Place.

Hon. Members: *[civil unrest, civil rest, snacking, ennui]*

Mr. Speaker: Order. Please, let us conduct ourselves in a manner that befits the House. Minister, pray continue.

Mr. Iain Duncan Smith: Thank you, Mr. Speaker. As I was saying, there can be no reform without compassion. Shh, but let me be clear. By the same token, there can be no compassion . . . oh, very nice, Mr. Speaker. The hon. Member for Hampstead Madscene has exposed her arse, which has a poorly executed likeness of me on it, in black marker pen. It is rubbish, Mr. Speaker, 'I' haven't even got a mouth. Oh, wait a minute . . .

Ms. Glenda Jackson: Gottle of geer. Hello, goys and girls. Hy name is Iain Huncan Shit. I am a harsehole. To the Heofle of Gritain I say – gollocks!

Hon. Members: Marvellous! It's like her arse is alive!

Mr. Speaker: OK, that's it. If the House is more interested in the hon. Lady's anal caricature than in Procedural Correctness, so be it. Fine. I am off. Mrs. Bercow and I are halfway through our *Mad Men* box set, and I could murder a large Sauvignon Blanc. I only live upstairs, I can be home in three minutes to surprise her.

Moment of Speculation.

House of Commons

Held upon the Feast of the Bigask, the 21st of October 2010
PRAYERS AND BOTTOM-LINING
[Lord Sugar upon the Telephone Directories
upon the Booster Seat within the Chair]

The Enterprise Britain Challenge

[The Chamber suffused with a dark blue light, Prokofiev's Dance of the Knights *issuing forth from the English Chamber Orchestra in the Corridor, Baron Sugar of Clapton in the London Borough of Hackney entered and took his place upon the Telephone Directories as Guest Speaker.]*

Mr. Guest Speaker: Good evening.

Hon. Members: Good evening, Lord Sugar.

Mr. Guest Speaker: Now you're probably wondering why I've brought you here, to these very famous Houses of Parliament in Westminster. This is the premier Parliament in probably the whole world. Bah. They've been making politics here since the times of Julius Caesar and Robin Hood. Today's task will stretch you, and me, to our limits. We've got two teams here *[indicated*

Government and Opposition Benches], and this is what you're going to do. You're going to go through those Division Lobbies, you're going to come up with team names for yourselves, the stupider the better to be honest with you, then you're going to decide who's going to be the project manager, then you're going to come back here for further instructions. You'll be selling policies. The team that sells more policies than the other team, simple, that team's the winner. Understood?

Hon. Members: Yes, Lord Sugar.

Mr. Guest Speaker: Any questions?

The Provisional Leader of the Opposition (Mr. Ed Miliband): Point of Order 1.a, Lord Sugar. Brerk. Where is the usual Mr. Speaker? Point of Order 1.b, I have just been elected Project Manager for this team, I don't see why we have to go through the whole flipping rigmarole again. Point of Order 1.c . . .

Mr. Guest Speaker: Right, stop talking. I don't care if you've just been elected bleeding President of the Variety Club of Great Britain. This task is all about innovation, about thinking on your feet. If you don't want to play by the rules, you can piss off home now. I've got my eye on you, you're giving me the right hump already. The usual Mr. Speaker is off doing some charity cancer thing – breast, I think, whatever. I want you all back here in one hour. Mr. Bailiff, lock the bloody Doors. Division!

[The Division Bells then sounding, hon. Members filed through the Division Doors and into the Lobby, where they formed separate project groups of approximately 300 hon. Members each. These then falling most earnestly into the discussion of team names with much brainstorming and argument, the Royal Cudgellers being obliged to suppress sporadic fighting with swords, rapiers, fence posts and Order

Papers. The time allocated for thinking having expired, hon. Members then returned to the Chamber, the Prime Minister and the Leader of the Opposition both entering via High Dudgeon, then taking their seats upon the Back Benches to chamber music most incidental and pizzicato.]

Mr. Guest Speaker: Right. You've got your teams, you've chosen your project managers. Let's have it, my arse hurts and I've got a severe pain in my chest.

Mr. David Miliband (South Shields Ocado): Ahem. I will be leading this *[indicated Opposition Benches, those entering and exiting the Chamber, those lolled in conversation by the Dispatch Box, those absent in the Bar, those absent in the Toilet]* team, Lord Sugar.

Mr. Ed Miliband: It's not fair, Lord Sugar. I came up with all the ideas. Brerk. Then he just sat on me, and everyone was laughing.

Mr. Guest Speaker: Shut your fucking cakehole. I wasn't talking to you. If I want you to bloody say something, I'll point at you like this *[pointed]* and say, 'You. The weirdo. What have you got to say for your bloody self, eh?' Right. The slightly bigger one. Who are you? And what's the name of your bleeding team? And don't come the old Mother Hubbard with me, son, or I'll turn your cock and balls into a fucking mixed grill.

Mr. David Miliband: I am David Miliband, Lord Sugar. David Miliband the brand. And I will be leading 'Aspire'. I am who I am, I might add. I didn't enter this competition to come second. I'm a winner, not a wino. *[consulted notes]* Not a whiner. If I sell a policy, it stays sold, Lord Sugar. *[contorted face, signalling ruthless ambition]* Graaaaagh!

Mr. Guest Speaker: Hm. Pff. My bloody legs ache. And my sinuses are playing up. Bollocks. Other team, what have you got to say for your bleeding selves?

The Chancellor of the Exchequer (Mr. George Osborne): After a spirited debate *[indicated horsewhip]* and a vigorous exchange of views *[several hon. Members flinching from lash wounds]*, the team elected me their cruel but firm Leader. And our name shall be: 'Consignia'. And we shall *[caressed horsewhip]* prevail. Why? Because we are strong and forceful, and we know that some-times cruelty – genuine, passionate cruelty – is the best kindness of all. Leave it with me, Lord Sugar. I know how to persuade people to buy policies. I am The Master, and I will use both stick *[indicated horsewhip]* and *[indicated 'downstairs']* carrot.

Mr. Guest Speaker: Bah. Pff. So. Never mind my toothache, let me tell you what the bleeding task is. Both teams are going to be selling policies. Tomorrow morning there'll be no bloody chauffeur, no bloody limo. Instead, you'll all be catching the bus to the Keir Hardie estate off the Old Kent Road. There'll be two stalls set up there . . .

The Secretary of State for Transport (Mr. Philip Hammond): Sorry to interrupt, Lord Sugar, what's a bus?

Mr. Guest Speaker: Shut up. Two stalls, as I say. One for *[con-sulted notes]* Aspire, one for Consignia. You'll be at these stalls all day, or out and about, knocking on doors, meeting ordinary people of the type of which I was in the old days as a tasty young geezer banging moody gear out of the back of me old dad's Ford Anglia. You'll be selling ordinary punters your poli-cies all bleeding day. At the end of that bleeding day there'll be a mock Election and then the losing team will be dragged back

162

here, you can argue among yourselves about who dropped their plonker in the custard, then I'll point at the person who's clearly been the shittest and fire them, flash bang wallop, sorted. Any questions?

Mr. Nick Clegg (Consignia): Are we allowed to lie at all? I suppose what I mean, Lord Sugar, is, as long as we can sell the policies, it doesn't matter if they don't exist, is that correct?

Mr. Guest Speaker: Do I LOOK like a bleeding philosopher?

Mr. Nick Clegg: You look a bit like Socrates.

Mr. Guest Speaker: Bollocks I do, you dimwit, you're thinking of *Dragons' Den*. Right, now please *[indicated Assembled Company]* do me a favour and piss off.

[The House then being in Suspension for twenty-four hours, the following day's Proceedings filmed and edited to present a summary, as follows, with soundtrack most whimsical performed by a string quartet:

(1) Approximately 625 hon. Members assembling at a bus stop in Parliament Square and awaiting with much excitement and jostling the arrival of the Number 53 to New Cross; the ensuing struggle to board, with menaces and physical violence.

(2) Attempts by Aspire and Consignia project managers to maintain order upon the top decks of separate buses amid rowdy behaviour by hon. Members, to wit wrestling with gouging and heated exchanges of political theorems.

(3) Arrival at the Keir Hardie estate, the two teams then setting out wares upon their stalls. Consignia offering free gourmet sausages to hon. Members of the Public as an inducement, Aspire offering pamphlets upon the Alternative Vote System.

(4) Engagement with hon. Members of the Public, presentation of sausages, attention to the Concerns and Issues raised by residents upon the subjects of the Economy and Civil Order. These being answered with summaries of diverse policies concerning the welfare and social security of residents and upon the subject of Immigration.

Hon. Members then returning to Westminster and taking their places within the Chamber, Lord Sugar taking his seat upon the Telephone Directories.]

Mr. Guest Speaker: Right. Nick?

Mr. Nick Hewer (Chief Herald and Factotum to Baron Sugar): Consignia sold a total of seventeen policies . . .

Hon. Members of the Coalition: *[jubilation, waving of Order Papers]*

Mr. Nick Hewer: Aspire sold nineteen . . .

Hon. Members of the Opposition: *[joyful commotion, line dancing, whooping]*

Mr. Guest Speaker: Order, order, shut your bleeding traps!

Mr. Nick Hewer: However, when the policies were properly examined it transpired that seventeen of Aspire's policies were poorly disguised versions of Consignia's. For example, where Consignia was promising a 'sensible cap' on immigration, Aspire promised 'some sort of novelty sombrero'. In the end, all seventeen copycat policies were disqualified, bringing Aspire's total to just two.

Hon. Members of the Opposition: *[screeching, wailing, ill demeanour]*

Mr. Guest Speaker: For Christ's sake shut up. I've told you once, this is the world-famous House of Commons, the most revered sodding Parliament in the whole bleeding world. Just look at the detailing on them panels. This place is dripping with bloody class. You do know, I suppose, what 'decorum' means, yeah? It's Latin for 'Shut up, you're all giving me fucking dyspepsia.'

Mr. Nick Hewer: I'm afraid there's more bad news for Aspire. Of the two remaining policies, one was just a pizza flyer folded into the shape of a policy.

Mr. Guest Speaker: Bah, gout's playing up. Just out of interest, what WAS the one policy Aspire managed to sell?

Mr. Nick Hewer: It related specifically to the Keir Hardie estate. They promised to tackle gang crime by rounding up all known gang members and gassing them to death.

Mr. David Miliband: Lord Sugar, this policy was just at the exploratory stage. We were merely articulating some . . .

Mr. Guest Speaker: Shut it, son, you're starting to really get on my tits. I've heard enough. Consignia, well done. You'll be spending the evening on a fleet of Thames pleasure barges, drinking champagne, watching fireworks, eating fancy food and feeling each other up. Gertcha.

Mr. George Osborne: Lord Sugar, thank you. I have, however, arranged my own pleasure barge, to which you are most cordially welcome. Just me, some friends and *[surveyed Government Benches]* certain like-minded individuals *[purred]*.

[Hon. Members of the Coalition then quitting the Chamber, gesturing most obscenely at hon. Members of the Opposition, in conga.]

Mr. Guest Speaker: Well, what have you got to say for yourselves?
Mr. David Miliband: Lord Sugar, I . . .
Mr. Guest Speaker: Well. You seem to have right fucked it up,

haven't you, you bleeding muppet? Shut it, I'm doing the talking. Hm. Hm. 'Miliband the Brand'? More like 'Miliband the Bland', eh? Ha ha, you doughnut. You know what I think, 'Dave'? I think I need better bleeding joke writers. Plus, you failed the task in what looks like quite a spectacular bleeding way, didn't you? What went wrong?

Mr. David Miliband: Lord Sugar, our policies were sound, but I was let down by my sales team, and marketing, and the people who did the presentation.

Mr. Guest Speaker: Harumph. *[to Mr. Ed Balls]* Well? Ed? Your job was to sell Aspire's policies. It seems they sold not so much like hot cakes as – are you joking, get me better material next week – cold turkeys.

Mr. Ed Balls (Aspire): Lord Sugar, it wasn't my fault. By the time the creatives finally came up with a pitch it was too late to change anything. I had to try and sell this idea of . . . I don't know, all of us in it together, but NOT THAT, better education for children and more choice for parents, but NOT THAT. All I was supposed to say was that whatever Consignia was selling, we were selling too, but with a 10 per cent discount if you signed up for five years.

Mr. Guest Speaker: I don't know. As sure as there's a hole in my arse, you lot have made a complete fucking right old Horlicks of this whole bleeding thing. You – 'Miliband the Cunt', that's it, I'm writing my own stuff from now on – I want you to piss off out of my sight, *[indicated hon. Members of the Opposition]* and take all your Rag, Tag and Bleeding Bobtails with you. You're going to nominate two people to come back with you into the Chamber, and then we'll sort out who's to blame for this Fiesta. Make no mistake, one of you will be fired.

[The Chamber then in Suspension, Baron Sugar conferring with his Aides.]

Ms. Karren Brady: They were shocking. All over the place. No focus. Completely directionless. Bunch of wankers.

Mr. Nick Hewer: I have to say that of all of them I thought Hugh Gaitskell the most principled in many ways, although of course he did bring in prescription charges in 1951 and unfortunately has been dead for some time.

Mr. Guest Speaker: Gah, I don't know. I think I might have done my shoulder, you know. 'Aspire'? More like 'Expire', I'd say. They're a useless bloody grim collection of jellied eels, if I'm being honest. Jellied eels, boiled beef and carrots, yes, we have no bananas. Bailiff, tell them to come in now.

[Mr. David Miliband returned to the Chamber, accompanied by Lord Mandelson of Guacamole and Sir Alex Ferguson, the Association Football manager.]

Mr. Guest Speaker: Is this one of your oh-so-sophisticated jokes, Dave? Because I don't remember seeing either of these two blokes in your team earlier.

Mr. David Miliband: Lord Sugar, you asked me to bring back two people I blame for losing the task, and here they are. I have brought back Lord Mandelson . . .

Lord Mandelson: Hello, Alan.

Mr. David Miliband: . . . and 'Fergie', because ultimately they both lost us the task.

Sir Alex Ferguson: Aye, you all right?

Mr. Guest Speaker: Both lost us the task, what?

Mr. David Miliband: Sorry, both lost us the task, Lord Sugar. We were finessing a narrative that basically went: 'Labour Party dah-de-dah, Eddie Izzard, under new management, young and sexually active, learning from the past, fit for purpose for a future perfect, share and share alike, *je ne regrets rien mais peut-être quelques regrets*' – is that right? My French is a little rusty – 'we kept the North-East going, footie kickabout, Chekhov, comprehensive education, ordinary people.' But my associates let us down. Lord Mandelson was supposed to be our friend, I might add, however . . .

Lord Mandelson: David, I think you should be awfully circumspect. Don't you?

Mr. David Miliband: Don't care. Don't care, don't care, don't blanking care. *The Third Man*, you overweening blanker? If you were fielding anywhere it was Deep Midwicket! Halfway up Aspire's BOTTOM! Oh yes, of COURSE you were intensely relaxed about people getting filthy rich 'as long as they paid their taxes'. Because you were relaxing WITH them, on a blanking sun lounger, in a tax haven! You alienated our target audience of low-spending Aspire customers, you bugger. Yet nobody knows who you are! We held a focus group, and apparently they all thought you were probably a 'posh baddie in an ITV drama'.

Lord Mandelson: I'll tell you what IS rich: this, coming from someone who couldn't project-manage a toasted sandwich. Aspire's traditional customer base looks at you and thinks, 'No, he doesn't look like the sort of chap I could have a pint with. He looks like the sort of chap I'd find standing on my doorstep with poorly illustrated literature about the end of the world.'

Mr. Guest Speaker: It's your fault, it's his fault, it's your fault, it's his fault again. I don't know. My fucking balls are giving me gyp, I know that. Why have you brought Alex back into the Chamber?

Mr. David Miliband: Lord Sugar, Alex has also helped to create a toxic brand in Aspire. He has alienated our OTHER target audience of educated, high-spending customers who regularly read the review sections of newspapers. One minute Alex is selling Aspire, the next he's at a football match with a face the colour of borscht, screaming spittle-flumed obscenities at the referee. He is vulgar, volatile and a terrible role model for the young, I might add. He certainly wouldn't know which fork to use, unless he was threatening someone at a fundraising dinner . . .

Sir Alex Ferguson: I already apologised for that, ye snivelling fucking trooser press. I was selling Aspire when you were still in fucking nappies, spitting oot your vegetarian quiche. Ach, I do no have to put up with your shite, Judy Fucking Garland. I'm away . . .

[Sir Alex then quitting the Chamber via High Dudgeon.]

Mr. Guest Speaker: Well, what have you got to say for your bleeding self now, Dave? You're supposed to be in here with two candidates for the bleeding chop, and now there's only one.

Mr. David Miliband: On a Point of Order, Lord Sugar. Technically, there are two. It cannot have escaped anyone's attention that you are, in fact, one of Aspire's most celebrated advocates. Your knighthood, your peerage. I might add . . .

Mr. Guest Speaker: You cheeky bastard. I have remained totally inde-bleeding-pendent throughout this whole fuckabout.

Mr. David Miliband: Nevertheless, Lord Sugar, you are indelibly linked in the public imagination to a visceral type of capital-ism . . .

Lord Mandelson: Exactly. If I may interject, Lord Sugar, I would like to say that it is precisely this rebranding of Aspire as a team comfortable with its own entrepreneurial, ruthlessly exploitative nature that has moved us away from old-fashioned notions of socialist . . .

Mr. Guest Speaker: Fuck it, I'm not having language like that in here.

Moment of Firing.

House of Lords

Held upon the Feast of the Easily Digestible Food,
the 2nd of November 2010

PRAYERS AND MUMBLINGS

[The Lady Gaga upon the Woolsack]

Born This Way Although Subject to Change

[The Assembled Company having settled into an Agreeable Mood with
snoozings, medications, fiddlings and amnesia, the Baroness Gaga of
Twitter then entering with great pageantry, regalia, special effects,
hullaballoo, camera crew, hurlicue and curlicue upon a Mechanical
Camel. Then in swirling robes of seeming flame alighting onto the
Floor of the House and with great Majesty taking up her seat upon
the Woolsack, the Mechanical Camel in close attendance, also Bailiffs
with Fire Extinguishers.]

The Lady Gaga: My noble Little Monsters, welcome. Westminster,
do you fancy me?

Noble Lords: *[asleep]*

The Lady Gaga: I said, my noble Little Monsters, do you

MOTHERFUCKING FANCY ME?

Noble Lords: *[awakenings and alarums]*

The Lady Gaga: Because I fancy all of YOU. *[manoeuvred head inside contraption; theme opaque, possibly 'London Gherkin' or 'vaginally intimate cigar end']* Whoi, oi fancy all of youse a roight blooming lot, so oi do, me Little Monsters, Hickory Dickory Dock!

[A Troupe of Cockneys then entered the Chamber, garbed as Pearly Kings and Queens of diverse notional sex kingdoms, then performing a short danced allegory upon Freedom, then withdrawing. Then did the door of the House fly open, Lord Heseltine of Yore entering slowly, clad in body armour, then firing an automatic rifle into the Ceiling.]

Lord Heseltine of Yore: Sorry, my noble Lords. Can't be too careful. I think I got him. Bloody snipers. Keep your eyes peeled, I've got another *[consulted arms cache]* 12,000 rounds or so. Every one with Johnny Taliban's name on, eh? Maybe save a few for any Reds under the bed *[firing into the Floor of the House, some rounds ricocheting most extravagantly, Lord Hattersley of Spudbake being then wounded most grievously in the buttocks]*, eh?

Lord Hattersley of Spudbake: What's that? Apologies, Lord Speaker, I was just having a word with my noble Friend here about the good old days. Hold on, I've been fucking shot! In the arse! *[indicated Lord Heseltine]* You again, Heseltine? You fucking doddery cunt!

The Lady Gaga: My noble Little Monsters, language is a weapon in the hands of the faceless.

Noble Lords: What in Christ's name is Yoko Fucking Ono doing on the Woolsack? Oh bollocks, here we go, good luck, everyone,

I remember when she fucked up The Beatles! Excuse me, you're standing on my catheter bag!

The Lady Gaga: Order! Silence! Lesbonaut, speak! *[then cloaking her mouth with a gloved hand]*

Lesbonaut, the Mechanical Camel [via Vocoder]: Namaste. Thank you for this great opportunity, O Gaga. The wounded one must be taken away for healing and sexual stimulation. The one in battle clothes must be dealt with. Ashanti shalom a bom diddly bom bom.

[Lord Hattersley recovering a little and most anxiously awaiting treatment. A Troupe of Paramedics then entering the Chamber, dressed as Doctors and Nurses in charge of a notional Sex Hospital, then removing the Lord Hattersley upon a fetishistical stretcher, after several attempts.]

Lord Heseltine: My noble Lords, I apologise most profusely. I had a call from an old pal – *[taking seat, accidentally discharging weapon]* no names, no pack drill, let's call him 'Wild Goose' – who told me the bloody place was a vipers' nest of terrorists. I see now *[consulting text]* that it was a practical joke. Nevertheless, a valuable lesson has been learned. It is precisely – precisely – this sort of tough love *[patted then accidentally discharged weapon]* our schools need.

Noble Lords: Hear, hear! Onanist! Bumfiddler!

The Lady Gaga: Order, silence, quiet, it is all the same – the moment of calm in which all energy converges as a bubble. The noble Lord will surrender his weapon without further delay or innuendo. Security!

[A troupe of London Policemen then entering the Chamber with

much cavorting, their truncheons being large dildos and their uni-forms being historically accurate helmets and historically unchronicled leather shorts, then taking the Lord Heseltine's weapon with much licking and suggestiveness, then withdrawing.]

Lord Heseltine: My noble Lords, here is an opportunity to restore proper discipline to our state schools. Recruit retired army offic-ers, guys who know how to dish out a clip round the ear as a warning shot, second one through the fleshy part of the thigh, that sort of thing. Martial law. Give thuggish troublemakers a taste of their own bloody medicine.

Noble Lords: *[cheering, bloodlust, incontinence]*

The Lady Gaga: Guns and violence have no place in the world of Gaga. The fleshy part of the thigh, OK, I like that. Correction: I mean, the thigh has a place in the world of Gaga. *[cloaked face]*

Lesbonaut, the Mechanical Camel: Om nom nom bada bing, ha ha hava nagila. The one called Hasselhof must be gone. Bismillah, salaam a bamma nom nom, O Gaga.

[The Lord Heseltine then quit the Chamber via High Dudgeon. Then a commotion without, concerning the validity of credentials to enter the House. The visitor's name corresponding to one on the Lady Gaga's Guest List, admittance was inferred.]

The Lady Gaga: Who goes there? If it be more flowers, go forth and give them to the poor. If it be my iced energy drink, bring it here forthwith. This dress of flame and hat of gherkin is most hot and motherfucking bothersome, my noble yadda yadda.

Bailiff to the House, Halyard-Keeper and Sergeant-at-Arms to Her Majesty: My Lady, I bring news from the Other Place.

Lord Bumble of Stipe End: *[awakening]* Eh? What Other Place?

The . . . my sister-in-law's house? Because that's been approved as a primary residence.

Bailiff to the House: My Lords, I beg to acquaint the House that a Commission has been issued under Her Majesty's Great Seal, declaring Her Majesty's Approbation of the Cadbury's Celebrations presented to Her Majesty last week by Her Noble Servants in this Place.

Noble Lords: Ahoy!

The Lady Gaga: Twitter Clerk, how many Twitter followers does Her Majesty got?

Twitter Clerk to the House: But an hundred five and twenty thousand, Lady Gaga.

The Lady Gaga: Tell your Queen she is welcome backstage at any time, subject to contract. Lesbonaut will supervise all the protocols and the bluffing with the muffin, etc. Lesbonaut, speak! *[cloaked face]*

Lesbonaut, the Mechanical Camel: O Gaga, waybulloo. It shall be done. All shall come to pay their respects at Gagaham Palace, Geoff deal with this shit, OK, bing bong Amen a-ding dong.

Lord Mounting of Bottlebank: My noble Lords, I am sure I read something in the public prints, possibly years ago now – *Daily Sketch*, I think it was.

[The Bailiff then stepping forward to nudge the Lord Mounting, unpausing his speech.]

Lord Mounting: These reports, as I say, that Her Majesty's Government is intent upon reforming this Place, and that hereditary entitlement is to be replaced by a system of appointments. If this is indeed to be the case, might I take this opportunity to declare myself a loyal servant of Her Majesty's Government?

Baron Plains of Windscale: My noble Lords, if I may be so bold as to interject?

The Lady Gaga: Interject. Be not who they tell you to be, my noble Little Monster, but who you tell them to tell themselves you to be. Not in my direction, however.

Baron Plains: The noble Lord's sense of duty is commendable in the circumstances of his being a senior Opposition spokesman. However, appointments to this House are not in the gift of this Place. The dispensation of such honours lies Elsewhere, and I have to tell the noble Lord that a framework for a system of appointments remains unapproved. A respected member of the judiciary has yet to be invited to oversee its implementation . . .

Noble Lords: *[cultured laughing]*

Lord Benneton of Casual: *[awakening]* Oho, my noble Lords, is there to be war in Rhodesia?

Bishop Bashir: I think, with respect, my noble Lord refers to Arabia, where Native Peoples live under the yoke of the tyrant Saladin.

Lord Benneton: My Lords, if our men are to be sent to Rhodesia, might I suggest that they are properly prepared, with a minimum of three spin bowlers? And must they play in those awful pyjamas?

The Lady Gaga: My most noble and learned Lord, I implore thee most heartily in the name of Fuck You. Yield to common sense, and Lesbonaut here, and be seated. You are blocking my motherfucking camera crew, bless you. *[cloaked face]*

Lesbonaut, the Mechanical Camel: In the name of Gaga, om nom nomine do not obstruct the cameras, halal kumbaya bom de bom.

Bishop Fidler: My noble Lords, members of the Trefoil Guild, Cubs, Brownies, some of you will think me a fanciful old man when I tell you there's a shiny new sixpence in my pocket. Of course, the news is all about whether Austerity Britain can make it, but those among you who remember the dark days of the London Blitz will I am sure be amused to hear this anecdote about the great Donald Bradman, consummate cricketer.

Noble Lords: Hear, hear. Yes, I remember Brownies. I remember sixpences. I remember the war. I remember sixpences. Good Lord, is Bradman still in? I remember sixpences.

Viscount Warehouse of Outlet: My noble Lords, it is not the thought of thousands of troops being sent from this country to quell the Saracens that alarms me so. Rather, it is the thought of thousands of Saracens coming here to 'seek asylum'. Which in my book is just ruddy begging, pardon my French.

Noble Lords: *Honi soit qui mal y pense!*

Baroness Thatcher of Fading: Hnack.

Lord Mandelson of Guacamole: My noble Lords, may I remind you that affairs of State – whether military, commercial, social or just a drop-in and a quick chat – all have a moral dimension, which is covered in part by the Official Secrets Act. The Government is to be commended on its swift course of privatisation. I myself am free for any advisory role that might be deemed appropriate, at slightly depressed rates to reflect my sense of solidarity with the People of Britain.

The Lady Gaga: My most noble Little Monsters, Gaga must away. *[mounting the Mechanical Camel]* May God sex you all!

Lesbonaut, the Mechanical Camel: Halloumi menismus, Galileo Galileo, O Gaga, do not forget there is merchandise on sale in the Corridor, namaste tomato and the Holy Ghost, inshallah.

Lord Molecule of Jar & Swab: My noble and most gracious Lords, I am reminded of a quote attributed to the late Ted Dexter. No, sorry, it's gone.

Moment of Forgetfulness.

Conservative Headquarters, Millbank

An Assembly Impromptu held upon the 10th of November 2010

SHOUTS AND CHANTING

[Jez upon the Sofa from the Foyer dragged
out unto the Pavement]

An Interlude of Televised Revolution

[The Assembled Company in disarray, congregating before bonfires without and running amok within, hon. Building Occupants, hon. Members of the Metropolitan Police, hon. Students and hon. Members of the Media looking on.]

Jez (Anarchist Squatford): Disorder, disorder! Ha ha ha. Here we go then.

Higgsy (Proddigyffan): There YOU go. I don't remember no collective decision about who's on the sofa. Who do you think you are? Adrian Fucking Chiles?

Jez: Come on, you media scum, get a picture! Look, I've got me black bandanna round me face like fucking Jesse James, let's have it!

Hon. Photographers and Journalists: Jez, Jez, flick us the Vs! Great. Could you STAND on the sofa for us? That's lovely. Just look over to the police, nice, do something taunting, sweet. I think he's put on a bit of weight. Definitely. I remember him at Heathrow shinning up that flagpole. Fat chance now, look at that fucking cellulite. I'm going to get a close-up for *Heat*, just in case.

Cody (Blackblocksley Heath): I want a go on the sofa! Shift up!

Hon. Students: *[to the signature tune of* Peppa Pig*]* Clegg is a wanker, Nick Clegg is a wanker!

Hon. Anarchists: Stop the cunts! Smash the window! Dance about!

Hon. Constabulary: Move along now, nothing to see here. Yes, I know about the bonfire. Yes, I can see the broken window and the sofa on the pavement. That's not MUCH to see, is it? Piss off and let us do our jobs.

Hon. Students: Stop rioting! It's counterproductive! This is a peaceful march! I'm going to miss *Doctor Who* at this rate! It's not fair! Yes, next time we'll march against YOU! See how YOU like it!

Hon. Anarchists: Oh diddums! You have your stupid march, with your bobble hats and kiddie rucksacks. We'll have our own march, fuck you very much. A counter-march.

Hon. Students: You're not even marching! How can it be a counter-march? You're just . . . hanging around.

Hon. Anarchists: Mooch, then. We're having a counter-mooch. With anarchist action in your face, Harry Fucking Potter and the Shower of Shit.

Ms. Julie Vagina (Vajazzle Arts Media): I want to sit on the sofa. Or is this fucking Boys Only as usual?

Cody: Sorry, love, just anarchists on this sofa. It's the law.

Ms. Julie Vagina: I AM a fucking anarchist, look *[produced tattoo]*. Plus, I'm sleeping in a disused pub in Bethnal Green. Plus, I know all the words to the Anarchist Anthem.

Jez: I don't remember seeing you at the last AGM. Who the fuck are you?

Ms. Julie Vagina: I'm head of mixed media for Vajazzle? We make anarchist shorts? One was on last week at the ICA's Anarchist Film Club? I'd give you my card but I'm a fucking ANARCHIST.

Higgsy: You reckon you're a fucking anarchist, do you? Anarcho-communist or anarcho-syndicalist?

Ms. Julie Vagina: Pff. Classic fucking statist shibboleth. First rule of Anarchist Club is that there's nothing wrong with rules. You can be an anarchist AND be disciplined. So, shitbonce: anarcho-fucking-syndicalist Monday to Thursday, anarcho-fucking-communist at weekends.

Jez: What do you be on Fridays then?

Ms. Julie Vagina: None of your fucking business. What, you work for social services or something?

Jez: Yeah, so what? Whoops, mind that fire extinguisher! Disorder, disorder! You on the roof! Do you fucking mind, I'm in a meeting here! Ms. Vagina, pray continue.

Ms. Julie Vagina: Fridays I'm experimenting with at the moment. Then filming it. Then destroying it. But filming the destruction. Last week I went Muslim. I've done proto-veganism, sensory deprivation, Tai Chi and *Pingu*. Now can I sit down on the fucking sofa?

Higgsy: No. You fucking can't. Because I've just set fire to it, ha ha, anarchy, death to the statist Tory scum sofa, I've got some ketamine, fancy a cider round the corner?

Mr. Vernon Spools (*News of the World*): On a Point of Order, Constable. Why are you not kicking the shit out of those rat-faced bastards by the sofa?

Det. Con. Badge Obscured (Metropolitan Police): Fuck along now, Sir, or I'll do you for obstruction. And *[produced baton]* resisting arrest. Wait a minute. Don't I know you? Aren't you a journalist?

Mr. Vernon Spools: Sort of *[produced card]*.

Det. Con. Badge Obscured: Apologies, Sir. The media are all here, your distinguished self included, so we must be seen to show restraint. Observe this small crowd of troublemakers. A pretty random mix of pissed-up students who fancy going a bit Bullingdon, and lawless squatwarts addicted to violent protest. They're not the ones we're trying to intimidate. While everyone focuses on this bollocks, we'll be kettling the tits off harmless kids and their mums, put a bit of fucking truncheon about, scare the living shit out of them, humiliate them. See how fucking keen they are for the next demo, ha ha ha. *[consulted notes]* Oh, thank you very much, Sir. Most obliged. We'll let this die down a bit and then slip along to Whitehall. There's a pacifist 'lie-in'. They're a lot easier to pick up and chuck in a fucking van, I can tell you. And in due course we'll charge them with violent disorder.

Mr. Vernon Spools: I thought you said they were pacifists.

Det. Con. Badge Obscured: There'll be violence in the van. And some disorder. I really ought to be getting along now. Anything else I can do for you, Sir?

Mr. Vernon Spools: Yeah, look. *[vouchsafed telephone number]* Any of the scallywags you nick turn out to have posh or famous parents, call me first. Usual terms apply.

Det. Con. Badge Obscured: *[saluting]* Mind how you go now, Sir.

Jez: Right, civilians! Stand well back unless you want to be singed by the righteous flames of Anarchism! We're burning effigies of Simon Cowell and fucking . . . *[observed effigies]* Carol Vorderman!

Higgsy: No, you dipshit! It's Cameron and Clegg!

Jez: It doesn't look anything fucking LIKE them.

Higgsy: They're anarchist effigies, arse swab! Stand back, I've filled them with diesel!

Moment of Conflagration.

House of Commons
Proceedings held upon the Feast of St. Cabbage,
the 21st of November 2010
PRAYERS AND SUSPIRATIONS
[Mr. Speaker upon the Booster Seat within the Chair]

Rear Gardeners' Question Time

Mr. Ed Miliband (Doncaster Awkwood): Thank you, Mr. Speaker. Could the Prime Minister please tell the House what he thinks he's blooming well doing? Because I tell him this . . .

Hon. Members: Wanker!

Mr. Speaker: Order, order.

Mr. Ed Miliband: I tell him this . . .

Hon. Members: Wanker!

Mr. Ed Miliband: Brerk.

The Prime Minister (Mr. David Cameron): Mr. Speaker, one of the lessons I learned from Margaret Thatcher and Tony Blair was this: form your mouth into a sort of beak shape – like so – to get your message across. Another lesson I learned from them was this: you've got to act early to get results.

Mr. Ed Miliband: Aha! Oho! Is the Prime Minister acting NOW then, Mr. Speaker? Is his apparent devotion to the National Interest nothing but a pathetic charade? No doubt the Prime Minister saw the recent editorial in *Political Analysis Quarterly* which brerk said, and I quote:

Mr. Cameron is by nature a moderniser. A historicist approach to Conservatism, fundamental to theorists and party activists for so long, holds no attraction for him. The Prime Minister's political credo is of minor consequence. His stature as a 'statesman', however, is a major worry. Why? Because Mr. Cameron is a spunkblob. A translucent homunculus of cock issue. A viscous plait of curdled Eton Mess. An animatronic fucking jizzflume . . .

Hon. Members: Yeah, Cameron, you wank satchel! Spermbanker's Bonus! *Strictly Come Dancing*!

Mr. Speaker: Order, order. This is most improper. The hon. Gentleman should know better than to set in train a semen-themed free-for-all. I will take no further questions on this matter. You, Sir. The slender Gentleman in, if I may say, the rather splendid suit there.

Ms. Yvette Cooper (Pontefract Ultra): Mr. Speaker, as Shadow Foreign Secretary, I would like to make the most of it, as who knows, *que será será*, but while I'm on my feet, what will this Government do about Injustices Abroad? There are fucking loads, as I have discovered, and it's really not as easy as people think. Meanwhile, the Foreign Secretary is just faffing about, pretending that everything is under control. Well, it isn't. It may interest the House to know that President Obama is one of my Twitter followers . . .

The Secretary of State for Defence (Mr. William Hague): Point of Order, Mr. Speaker. Does the hon. Lady know for certain that it is the real President Obama? Is it a Verified Account?

Ms. Yvette Cooper: I am assured it is genuine, Mr. Speaker. The avatar is a photograph of President Obama. It most certainly is not a photograph of anyone else! Does the hon. Gentleman take me for a fucking idiot? This is what President Obama sent me via Direct Message earlier today:

Hey Yvette how's it going? Sure would appreciate any thoughts on Middle East. That shit a motherfucker LOL x

Mr. William Hague: Mr. Speaker, would the hon. Lady care to tell us how 'Obama' is spelled in the context of that Direct Message? Does it in fact have two 'm's? And could she tell the House if she had a Direct Message from this 'President Obamma' yesterday telling her a joke about Hillary Clinton and a black pudding? Ha ha, idiot! It's me winding you up! You dozy bint!

[The hon. Member for Pontefract Ultra then leaving the Chamber via High Dudgeon, the Chancellor of the Exchequer entering.]

Ms. Harriet Harman (Camberwick Betspread): Ah, what felicitous timing, Mr. Speaker. As the Shadow Chancellor is on 'pub gardening leave' today, could I ask the hon. Gentleman a question? Is he familiar with the joke doing the rounds about 'Tory Cuts'? It is a play on words, you see.

The Chancellor of the Exchequer (Mr. George Osborne): Mr. Speaker, I think any day now someone's going to say something oppositional and searching. It never happens. I sometimes wish there was *[swished riding crop]* more resistance. Mr. Speaker, this country's recovery will indeed be led by a 'bunch of cuts'. These cuts will hurt, *[purred]* of course they will. But they will be progressive and fair. That's it, end of story, no returns, fuck you up the arse with a power mop. Cleggo.

The Deputy Prime Minister (Mr. Nick Clegg): Thanks, Woggy. Yeah, I just wanted to say there's more to this Government than cuts, Mr. Speaker. We have much much much more to offer, including . . . I don't know. Call it compassion. Call it vision. Call it cross-bench saucy working political lunching. Hey, don't get me started on lunch. Do you know what I had for lunch today, Mr. Speaker? Crispbread. Cock of The Christ! Crispbread! And spazzy tinted WATER. *[shook head]*. Lunch!

Mr. Ed Miliband: Mr. Speaker, I know a lot of people think Labour squandered their thirteen years in power by just being Tories with better haircuts. But that wasn't my fault, I was mostly playing on my brerk Nintendo and solving chess puzzles . . .

Hon. Members: Show us your bishop!

Mr. Speaker: Order, order!

Mr. Ed Miliband: My point, Mr. Speaker, is that the one thing, the ONE BRERK THING that Labour created to near-universal acclaim was a new network of Sure Start centres. The Chancellor promised that money for these centres would be protected. I have to tell you I now believe those assurances to be not worth the paper they were brerk shitten on. Can I ask the Chancellor this: will the £1.1-billion Sure Start funding remain in place? And if not, why so? Why so, Mr. Speaker?

The Secretary of State for Education (Mr. Michael Gove): I would like suavely to put the hon. Gentleman's mind at rest,

Mr. Speaker. Ideally with powerful hypnotic drugs, aha ha ha. Although perhaps *[adjusted hair]* a Statement to the House will suffice for now. Funding for Sure Start *[adjusted tie]* will not only remain, it will be protected by three important new safeguards. Firstly, this funding will be carefully folded into a new Early Intervention Grant. This new grant will also enfold programmes tackling teenage pregnancy, various initiatives for disabled children, and so on. For the same money. Thereby *[adjusted testicles]* making everything much better value.

Hon. Members: Great idea! Bah, what next – handouts for the pregnant disabled? You cunt, Gove, you look like a fucking peeled mushroom!

Mr. Speaker: Order, order, you blooming rowdy gits! Let's have a civilised debate, I implore you.

Mr. Michael Gove: Secondly, these Early Intervention Grant allocations will be reduced by 11 per cent next year, protecting Sure Start by making it much more competitive. And thirdly, Mr Speaker, Sure Start is covered by our new Local Authority Devolvement Protocol *[adjusted teeth]*, which will require councils to protect everything, but again with a great deal less money. So if Sure Start centres are closing, you know whom to blame, as suavely as possible. Local authorities.

Mr. Ed Miliband: Oho, brerk! I thought, Mr. Speaker, that LABOUR was to blame for everything.

Hon. Members: Yah blah garbly blah, Clarkson, Hammond and May!

Mr. Speaker: Order, the hon. Gentleman must ask a question.

Mr. Ed Miliband: I apologise, Mr. Speaker. I will rebrerk. Does the Prime Minister think he can do whatever he likes because he imagines there is an incoherent Opposition with all the brerk political purchase of the *Toy Story* cast list?

Hon. Members: To oblivion and beyond!

Mr. Speaker: Order. I implore the House not to denigrate the cast of *Toy Story*. They are much-loved characters who will long outlive the memory of this Parliament. They should be treated with reverence.

Hon. Members: I'd like to give Little Bo Peep a 'lamb shanking'! Threesome with her and the lesbian cowgirl! I've gone all Woody!

Mr. Speaker: Enough! This is outrageous. The *Toy Story* narrative holds many lessons for us. Teamwork. Life as Duty. Strength through smallness.

The Secretary of State for Culture, Olympics, Media and Sport (Mr. Jeremy Hunt): Mr. Speaker, while we're on the subject of films, may I explain why I've decided to get rid of the UK Film Council, despite its generating four times the amount of money it costs? I accept this is difficult for many people to understand. It just goes to show how awfully shockingly bloody thick many people became under the previous administration. *[to the Chancellor of the Exchequer; inaudible, possibly 'How am I doing, Woggy?]*

[The Chancellor of the Exchequer nodded his approval, put his finger unto his lips to signal discretion, then mimed 'Chinese Burn'.]

Hon. Members: You rhyming slang! Yeah, you slip of the tongue! Yeah, you total fucking shitbumper!

Mr. Speaker: Order, order now. We have all had enough of the joke about the Minister's name and its rhyming possibilities.

Ms. Amonia Makeweight (Alternatingham Satterdace): On a Point of Order, Mr. Speaker. The House deserves an explanation. What is this word that rhymes with 'Jeremy Hunt'?

Mr. Speaker: I will ignore that remark. The hon. Lady is being disingenuous and, if I may be frank, is also a cunt. I . . . *[coughed repeatedly]* Sorry, sorry – I mean, is also being mischievous. Secretary of State, pray continue.

Mr. Jeremy Hunt: Mr. Speaker, my first decision as Culture Secretary was to abolish ministerial cars, saving £250,000 a year. I wanted to send a signal that this Government is serious about getting ministerial cabs instead. Likewise with culture. Whether they be 'high-culture' offers such as quality period drama, or whether they be hugely popular soap operas. Both are cultural products – brands, if you will – and it is very much my job as Culture Secretary to enhance the offer of Britain's culture both here and abroad. I want to upgrade our culture to 'more than a world-class brand'. Or 'world-class brand platinum'. It's all at a very early stage.

Hon. Members: *[mewling, puking, infantilisation]*

Mr. Speaker: Order. Fuckretary of Cock . . . I . . . *[coughing most fitfully]* Secretary of State, continue, I prithee.

Mr. Jeremy Hunt: Culture, that's what we are interested in, Mr. Speaker. Whether it be paid for by hard-working taxpayers through the BBC, or whether it be available for a very reasonable subscription to Sky, Branded Britain offers the best offer money can buy. Which brings me to money.

[The Chancellor of the Exchequer then miming intercourse with a goose, the head thereof being trapped inside a drawer.]

Mr. Jeremy Hunt: My department is responsible for an extraordinary fifty-five quangos, the vast majority with highly paid bosses and costly bureaucracy. Well, not for much longer, Mr. Speaker. Is the House aware that the UK Film Council employs eight top executives who are paid more than £100,000? That is not culture. That is taking the piss. This kind of greed has no place in a quango, which is why *[observing the Chancellor's more urgent miming]* we must grasp this goose and fuck it.

The Secretary of State for Communities and Local Government (Mr. Eric Pickles): Mr. Speaker, I would like to add my weight to my hon. Friend's cultural Speak Your Weight machine. *[consumed muffin]* I am telling local councils exactly the same thing. If anyone's earning more than £100,000 *[burped]*, I'm saying that's unacceptable, they are just grasping *[consumed battered sausage]*, greedy bastards . . .

Ms. Caroline Flint (Femdom Valley): Chup bup whoa whoa whoa, Mr. Speaker. What about the top executives . . .

Mr. Eric Pickles: *[inaudible, consumed vanilla slice]*

Hon. Members: *[uproar with gesticulations]*

Ms. Caroline Flint: Up chup bah I will not be silenced, Mr. Speaker. Will the hon. Gentleman give way?

Mr. Speaker: Order, order. The House must settle down. This is the House of Commons, not some rubbish on at the National Flipping Theatre. Will the hon. Gentleman give way?

Mr. Eric Pickles: *[inaudible, consumed savoury flan]*

Mr. Speaker: Order! I insist – will the hon. Gentleman now give way?

Mr. Eric Pickles: *[inaudible, consumed scampi]*

Mr. Speaker: For the last time, will the hon. Gentleman . . .

[The Secretary of State's legs then buckling, causing him to collapse with great catastrophe upon the hon. Member for Dorchester Filtered. Mr. Speaker then calling for the Tarpaulin.]

Ms. Caroline Flint: My question, if I may finally be allowed to ask it, is this: why is it acceptable for executives of nationally owned banks to earn a fucking fortune in salaries and bonuses, but NOT OK for executives of public bodies? Eh? Plus, now I have everyone's attention, I would like to announce that I am going to salsa classes. *[performed a short salsa dance]* Ha-cha-cha!

Mr. George Osborne: Mr. Speaker, perhaps I can explain to the hon. Bumholes opposite how the principle of remuneration for public service works, as plainly and as cruelly as possible. *[purred]* It is perfectly reasonable for bankers to earn a great deal of money as they are FUCKING BANKERS, THAT IS THE WHOLE POINT. If a bank is de facto in public ownership, it is necessary for these bankers to receive high salaries, bonuses, etc. because banking is a competitive business and we have to attract people of the right calibre. I can vouch for these people, Mr. Speaker. I dine with them regularly. On the other hand, the chief executive of Shitbury-on-Thames? Or some quango chairman? They shouldn't need incentivising *[swished cane]* to work in the public sector. Not with all the redundancies we are seeing at the moment. Let's be truthful, Mr. Speaker, who actually cares? Some of them didn't even go to university! They'll all be out on their ear soon, eh? *[twisted the ear of the Minister of State for Policy]* Eh? Ha ha ha! I hope that is of some help, Mr. Speaker.

Mr. Ed Balls (Burly & Shitwad): Mr. Speaker, the hon. Gentleman opposite may twist the ear of his colleague. But he cannot twist the facts. And I have here *[produced document]* a list of facts I think the House may be interested in. FACT ONE: The Chancellor of the Exchequer keeps an inflatable woman in his Downing Street sex dungeon. It is modelled on Baroness Thatcher . . .

Hon. Members: Outrageous! Phwoar, Former PMILF! The Falklands Three-Hole, I've got that one!

Mr. Speaker: Order! The hon. Gentlemen at the back there must stop their obscene re-enactment of the Sinking of the *Belgrano* at once. For a start, the hon. Gentleman's penis looks nothing like an Exocet missile. No, DON'T put a condom on it, nobody's interested. Chancellor of the Exchequer.

Mr. George Osborne: Mr. Speaker, my personal affairs are of no concern to this House. If any hon. Member *[swished cane]* wishes to submit a complaint, I will see them *[indicated cellar]* downstairs. And for the record, I always do her up the inflatable bottom. It could be anyone's face.

Moment of Mental Photoshopping.

Parish Hall in the Constituency of Twickenham and Headgear

A Surgery held upon the 17th of December 2010

PRAYERS, IMPRECATIONS AND AIR-FRESHENING IN TRAIN OF THE OVER-SIXTIES AEROBICS SESSION

Dr. Vince Cable in the Orange Stackable Chair

[At the Trestle Table with the hon. Member for Twickenham and Headgear: Ms. Pippy Longsuffer, Constituency Agent, and Ms. Ingrid Kurtz, Coalition Minder.]

Ms. Pippy Longsuffer: This is Mrs. Huntingdon. She'd like your help with her local Ethnic Diversity initiative . . .

Mrs. Doreen Huntingdon: Don't I know you?

Dr. Vince Cable: I should hope SO, Madam. Ha ha. I am, after all, the Business Secretary.

Ms. Pippy Longsuffer: *[coughed]*

Dr. Vince Cable: But first and foremost the MP for Twickenham and Headgear.

Mrs. Doreen Huntingdon: Mm. I don't recognise the face. But the voice is familiar. You used to be on the *Today* programme a lot, didn't you?

Dr. Vince Cable: Yes. Yes, I did. In fact, two years ago I was voted . . .

Mrs. Doreen Huntingdon: You're not Evan Davis, though.

Ms. Pippy Longsuffer: Good Lord, no. Dr. Cable is *[fastened cardigan]* very much a ladies' man.

Dr. Vince Cable: How may I help you?

Mrs. Doreen Huntingdon: *[produced map]* This is Twickenham. As you can see, population density is marked, here, parish by parish. *[produced bar chart]* Now, an ethnic breakdown of the constituency. As you can see, the biggest section of Twickenham society I have labelled Ordinary . . .

Ms. Ingrid Kurtz: Just . . . exactly how 'big' is this 'biggest' Twickenham society would you say?

Dr. Vince Cable: What does 'Miscellaneous' mean? Who are they?

Mrs. Doreen Huntingdon: That's . . . I've just sort of lumped together all those Not Ordinaries who aren't 'Black/Blackish', 'Brown', 'Oriental and/or Australian', those I call 'The Tieless EU', etc. They're non-categorisable. *[produced map]* So here's my proposal for Rethinking Ethnic Diversity in Twickenham. Ordinary here, here and here. Brown/Oriental/Australian here . . .

Ms. Ingrid Kurtz: Fuck this. Sorry, Madam, you're going to have to leave. Either through that door under your own steam, or jammed into the fucking supermarket trolley I notice has been abandoned in the backyard, *[looked at Ms. Longsuffer]* Ms.

Longsuffer. And then pushed out into the shit-clogged, piss-stained Twickenham one-way system. You mental fucking fanny trumpet.

[Ms. Ingrid Kurtz stood up, mimed 'stuff Mrs. Huntingdon into a shopping trolley, then vigorously push the trolley'. Mrs. Huntingdon gathered her documents and left.]

Dr. Vince Cable: Wait! I wanted to tell you about Rupert Murdoch and the Ofcom Report!

Ms. Ingrid Kurtz: Just shut the fuck up about all that. You're not in the Members Bar now. You're not gossiping with some posh bird from the *Telegraph*, with a twinkle in your eye, a large Pinot Fucking Grigio in your fat fist and a hard-on.

Dr. Vince Cable: That is absolutely outrageous. I . . .

Ms. Ingrid Kurtz: Spare me. We've all seen you. The transformation's remarkable. Outside, a fucking tent with a hat on it. Inside, you head for the nearest Sloane totty in your expensive lounge suit and put on the Lumbering Charm act. You know what you look like? You look like a genial sex offender doing the Twist very, very fucking slowly.

Dr. Vince Cable: How dare . . .

Ms. Ingrid Kurtz: Stick to the script. You think the Coalition's doing a brilliant job. The Cuts are unavoidable. Tuition Fees are fucking great. David Cameron's a Political Giant.

Dr. Vince Cable: Bollocks. Cameron's an idiot. The only place he's a Political Giant is *[chuckled]* at a photo opportunity in a nursery school! *[chuckled]*

Ms. Ingrid Kurtz: We're not interested in what you fucking think. We're interested in Vince Cable the Liberal Mascot. Shit a plank, we'd have been better off with fucking Charles Kennedy in a kilt.

Ms. Pippy Longsuffer: Ah, Mr. Rutter.

[Mr. Mark Rutter approached the Trestle Table holding a large sports bag and a mobile telephone playing the theme tune from Dragons' Den.*]*

Dr. Vince Cable: Mr. Rutter. Nice to meet you. Let me first of all make it clear: I will cut that marauding bugger Rupert Murdoch down to size if it's the last thing I ever . . .

Ms. Ingrid Kurtz: What have you got for us today, Mr. Rutter?

[Mr. Rutter unzipped his sports bag, producing a Device.]

Mr. Mark Rutter: Ladies and gentlemen, my name is Mark Rutter and I would like to introduce you to the Radio Avenger, a powerful new tool in the fight against antisocial behaviour on the public highway. *[activated Device]* Let us say you are driving along, observing the speed limit, perhaps between Twickenham and Isleworth. Suddenly you are overtaken by a dangerously speeding car crammed with unruly teenagers. The windows are down. Objectionable music blares out, signalling to the world that the car's occupants have the power to listen to whatever they like and at whatever volume . . .

Ms. Pippy Longsuffer: I'll get some coffee, shall I?

[Ms. Longsuffer exited, checking her mobile telephone and locating a packet of ten Silk Cut Ultra. Mr. Rutter produced an antique Ghetto Blaster from his sports bag.]

Mr. Mark Rutter: Let's say these youths are playing a particularly vile species of Hip Hop.

[Mr. Rutter caused violent and misogynistic Hip Hop to occur on the Ghetto Blaster.]

Ms. Ingrid Kurtz: *[shouting]* Switch that fucking awful row off! Nobody wants to hear this shit!

Mr. Mark Rutter: *[shouting]* That's exactly my point!

Dr. Vince Cable: *[shouting]* I'll tell you what the TORIES don't want to hear! Me! Talking about this fucking Maoist revolution that's happening in a lot of areas like the Health Service, local government, reform, all this kind of stuff . . .

Ms. Ingrid Kurtz: *[shouting]* Shut up! Shut up, you wanker!

Mr. Mark Rutter: *[shouting]* You simply point the Radio Avenger in the direction of the offending sound system and *voilà*!

[The loud Hip Hop emanating from the Ghetto Blaster then becoming loud Easy Listening.]

Ms. Ingrid Kurtz: *[shouting]* That's it! Out! You're pissing me off now!

Mr. Mark Rutter: *[shouting]* As you can hear: Johnny Mathis! The Radio Avenger has changed stations, from *[consulted Device]* 1Xtra to . . . Smooth FM! Chummy and his mates have lost all credibility!

Dr. Vince Cable: *[shouting]* I'll tell you who HAS lost credibility! Nick Clegg!

[Ms. Ingrid Kurtz advanced on Mr. Rutter, who silenced his Ghetto Blaster.]

Ms. Ingrid Kurtz: Right, pack up your fucking Super Soaker or whatever it is, I'm escorting you from the premises. You *[indicated Dr. Cable]* stay the fuck here until I get back.

Dr. Vince Cable: You'd better show me some fucking respect. I've got the nuclear option, you know! I could take this government down if I wanted to, just by detonating myself and exploding into a million globules of bitter hatred!

Ms. Ingrid Kurtz: And don't talk to anyone.

[Ms. Ingrid Kurtz and Mr. Rutter left the room. Dr. Cable muttered to himself, rearranged the papers on the Trestle Table, stood up, walked around humming 'The Way You Make Me Feel' by Michael Jackson, attempted to moonwalk across the floor, traumatised a hamstring. Miss Polly Cadogan and Miss Holly de Quimbley, junior reporters for the Daily Telegraph, *entered the room.]*

Miss Polly Cadogan: Knock, knock.

Dr. Vince Cable: Come in, come in. You'll have to forgive me. I've just been doing my calisthenics and . . . *[saw Miss Cadogan and Miss de Quimbley]* Oh, hello.

Miss Holly de Quimbley: We wondered if we could have a word with you about child benefit or something?

Miss Polly Cadogan: Yah, we're concerned mums?

Dr. Vince Cable: Please, please, sit down. I find it difficult to believe that EITHER of you is a mother. You look so nicely turned out. Oh, I don't mean . . .

Miss Polly Cadogan: That's OK. I like your hat.

[Dr. Cable removed his Michael Jackson Fedora.]

Miss Holly de Quimbley: One two, one two.

Miss Polly Cadogan: I'm . . . Mrs. Chav . . . Mrs. Chavington, by the way. This is my fellow concerned mum Mrs . . .

Ladysovereign. Could I just get you to say something for level, Dr. Cable?

Dr. Vince Cable: Level? I'll tell you what ISN'T level. The cross-media playing field. I don't mind telling you, I am at war with Rupert Murdoch, and in me he has found his Nelson. If he, that is, were to be the Napoleon of . . .

Miss Polly Cadogan: I see you've spotted my outsize Liberal Democrat rosette, Dr. Cable. We are definitely Lib Dem mums?

Miss Holly de Quimbley: Yah, totes.

Dr. Vince Cable: *[observing rosette]* It does look very big there, nestling in your, in your . . .

Miss Holly de Quimbley: *[inaudible, possibly 'tits']*

Miss Polly Cadogan: So if you could tell us, I don't know, what you had for breakfast?

Dr. Vince Cable: . . . blouse . . . thing. Are those . . . wires coming out of your, your . . . luscious rosette?

Miss Holly de Quimbley: Breakfast?

Dr. Vince Cable: Breakfast, yes. I had some porridge in the house with Mrs. Cable, tea, no sugar. My ministerial car arrived and, with it, my second breakfast, ha ha ha – two bacon cheeseburgers and a Danish. She'd fucking kill me if she found out, the missus. Can I be very frank with you, and I am not expecting you to quote this outside: she thinks I'm at Pilates on Thursday afternoons as well!

[Dr. Cable winked at Misses Cadogan and de Quimbley.]

Miss Polly Cadogan: Oh, Dr. Cable. You're quite the rogue.

Dr. Vince Cable: *[chuckled]* I am, aren't I?

Miss Holly de Quimbley: We're quite rogueish too. But

basically we're concerned mums and Liberal Demarols . . .

Miss Polly Cadogan: Democrats.

Miss Holly de Quimbley: Mm. But if I could subliminally distract you for a moment, Dr. Cable, by inviting you to imagine my writhing, glistening, naked, cum-spangled body . . .

Dr. Vince Cable: *[indicated erectile awareness, chuckled]* That . . . oh, that actually is a very good analogy for certain relationships within Cabinet. If I may be frank . . .

[Ms. Ingrid Kurtz re-entered the room and approached the Trestle Table with a look of scepticism.]

Miss Polly Cadogan: Yes, quickly.

Dr. Vince Cable: Rupert Murdoch is a media rapist, and I am about to blow his prick and ballsack off with a shotgun. Cameron's a lazy twerp. Nick Clegg's a stuck-up ponce. The Lib Dems are trying to put a brake on the Tories' demented destruction of everything we stand for, by using reverse psychology and letting them do it. *[chuckled]* They'll realise the folly of their actions soon enough. Plus, everyone thinks I'm fucking brilliant, and . . .

Ms. Ingrid Kurtz: What did I say? What did I fucking say?

[Misses Cadogan and de Quimbley retreated. Dr. Cable called after them.]

Dr. Vince Cable: Watch this space! *[indicated trousers]* I'm going nuclear!

[Ms. Ingrid Kurtz then berating Dr. Cable most soundly with a stackable chair.]

Moment of Contusion.

House of Commons

*Proceedings held upon the Feast of the Shortest
Working Day, the 21st of December 2010*

PRAYERS AND TIDINGS OF
UNCERTAIN CONTENT

[Mr. Speaker within the Grotto]

A Christmas Cabal

*[The House decorated in most Festive fashion to mark the Rising of
Parliament, Carols uttering forth from the Band of the Royal Scots and
Gingers in the Corridor. Mr. Speaker attired as Father Christmas, entering the Chamber via the Calendar Window upon a prototype 'mag-lev'
Sleigh, this being drawn by several Reindeer in Sky HD livery. Then
alighting and entering a large translucent decorated Grotto in place of
the Speaker's Chair, then sitting upon a large Sack marked 'TOYS'.]*

Mr. Speaker: Ho ho ho, settle down now. Let's find out who's
naughty or . . .

Hon. Members: Wanker!

Mr. Speaker: . . . nice. Order! Yes, you, Sir. In the illuminated
bonnet.

Mr. Bobby Floaten (Morraleigh Drifton): Will the Prime Minister list his rethinking engagements for today? And will he accept the rethought good wishes of his backbenchers? Which I am not officially one of, but it doesn't matter, and could someone get a picture of me standing up like this, like I'm giving an important speech, only I need something to show my constituents to prove I'm actually in Westminster, not off to the West Indies later as the guest *[hit in face by Yule Log of unknown provenance]* . . . fuck, yes, point taken, mum's the word, fucking ouch.

The Prime Minister (Mr. David Cameron): Mr. Speaker, this morning I had rethinking sessions with ministerial colleagues and others. We rethought the plan to massively reduce school sports funding in the light of important new evidence . . .

Hon. Members: Rah rah, yah yah, bollocks.

Mr. Speaker: Order, ho ho ho, order. Please. I'm sure we all want to get through the business today and be with our loved ones, mince pies, etc. as soon as possible. Order, the hon. Member there will re-pant her 'mince pie' at once. Nobody is impressed with these genital revelations. I . . . dear God. Order, order. No, Madam. I don't care how many Select Committee Reports you can accommodate. Stop it.

The Prime Minister: . . . in the light of important new evidence that we were supposed to be increasing school sports for the Olympics and also for our proposed Fatbusters initiative aimed at 'huskier' young people. Later, I met economic advisers to rethink the anticipated timescale for recovery, exploring possible synergy with the Meteorological Office in the rethinking of heavy snow and its impact on our economy. Which, let's face it, is still a million times better than it would have been under the guardianship of *[indicated Opposition Front Bench]* that fucking cascade of bum plasma, Mr. Speaker.

Mr. Ed Miliband (Doncaster Awkwood): Mr. Speaker, why doesn't the Prime Minister simply admit he's complacent? Shut up, Christopher, it's NOT a fucking stupid brerk question. And get out of my head, I am Leader of the Labour Party, remember? Remember?

The Prime Minister: Well, ha ha, Mr. Speaker, it seems the hon. Nutter opposite is able to have a full and frank exchange of views IN HIS OWN MIND. No wonder people think he's fucking mad. He IS. Listen, you horror-comedy stand-up freak, you've been doing this job for the last three months. People are beginning to ask, when are you going to start?

Christopher (Mr. Miliband's Imaginary Friend): Tell him he has all the integrity of a clitoris. Tell him he LOOKS like a clitoris. Tell him he looks like a six-foot clitoris with a little fucking smirk just below the tip.

Mr. Ed Miliband: Shut up, shut up. Mr. Speaker, it is no wonder the Foreign Secretary describes the Cabinet as Thatcher's Love Buttons, because that is . . . *[consulted notes]* No further questions.

Mr. Speaker: Ho ho ho, excellent. That's the spirit. It is the season of goodwill, therefore let us cast aside our differences . . .

The Business Secretary (Dr. Vince Cable): Fuck you, arsehole. Fuck you up the Dartford Tunnel with a five-mile tailback. A five-mile tailback of fucking coaches full of incontinent pensioners.

Hon. Members: *[seasonal ill will, reflux, flatulence]*

Mr. Speaker: Order! I sincerely hope those remarks were not aimed at this Chair. I may be dressed as *[consulted label]* 'Sexy Santa', but the dignity of the House remains paramount.

Dr. Vince Cable: I apologise, Mr. Speaker. Again. I don't know why *[indicated the Prime Minister and the Deputy Prime Minister]* they don't just make me Minister Responsible for Fucking Apologies and bloody well have done with it. My remarks were in fact directed at *[indicated the hon. Member for Southampton Thrushpatch]* that cunt.

The Secretary of State for Culture, Olympics, Media and Sport (Mr. Jeremy Hunt): *[terminating game of Angry Birds]* Mr. Speaker, I can assure the House that I didn't even say anything. I was checking important emails from my contacts. Not contacts, not contacts. Civil servants, from my civil servants. I said absolutely nothing about my taking over Governmental responsibility for Mr. Murdoch expanding his interests. I regret that my learned and most hon. Colleague is no longer in a position to decide whether Mr. Murdoch may quite legitimately spend £8 billion of his own money in acquiring the rest of BSkyB, which by the way is a great brand, along with Sky HD and Sky News, not forgetting Sky Sports Extra. Once he buys it all, this will obviously be his own company. He will have bought it with again let me repeat his own money, what is the problem, of course there will be rigorous scrutiny . . .

Hon. Members: Shitclod! Fuckpump! Wanker!

Mr. Speaker: Ho ho ho, order. I believe the Business Secretary's remarks were aimed at the hon. Gentleman there. Forgive me, I don't recognise your face.

Mr. John Denham (Southampton Thrushpatch): Mr. Speaker, I am the Shadow Business Secretary! I have been an MP for literally fucking ages! You remember, I resigned over the Iraq War? I was Secretary of State for Something briefly – Innovation, I think. I have been on official aeroplanes, Mr. Speaker. I have eaten posh soufflé wearing a dinner jacket, in the company of some of the most powerful people in the world . . .

Hon. Members: Who are you? Who are you?

Mr. Speaker: Order. Ho now. I did vaguely recognise the hon. Gentleman, of course, but had him confused with our newsagent. He will oblige the House by repeating his remarks to the Minister. Let us all hear his words of, ho ho ho, principled wisdom.

Mr. John Denham: All I said was that the hon. Gentleman there, the Business Secretary, was a quivering sack of gelatinous fucking shit and that his integrity was now in tatters, that's all. I said that it is very difficult to see how David Cameron and Nick Clegg can continue to have confidence in him as Business Secretary. They should have someone like me as Business Secretary, Mr. Speaker. Someone who's prepared to stand up in this House and say, yes, we know a lot of people have reservations about News Corporation having a controlling influence over British media, but you should really watch what you say about Mr. Murdoch. If Mr. Murdoch had asked ME if he could buy the rest of BSkyB when I was Secretary of State, I would have put down my soufflé spoon, narrowed my eyes . . .

Mr. Ed Miliband: Mr. Speaker, I think what my hon. Friend is trying to say is that we agree the News Brerk decision is not to be taken lightly, that Mr. Murdoch only really liked Tony Blair, that he's not our friend any more, and that in the end it is more important to chip away at the Government than to welcome the Minister's frank defiance of Mr. Murdoch's brerk chicanery. He is a venal capitalist who has undermined the character of our nation for decades, brerk, and . . . *[consulted notes]* correction, remains a great bloke happy Christmas everyone mazel tov and salaam brerk.

Dr. Vince Cable: It is an absolute bloody liberty, Mr. Speaker. Am I to be a figure of fun even here, standing in this House, wearing this tinselly Christmas Crown and white beard? Am I? Bah humbug and bah bumshag! As for you *[indicated Secretary of State for Culture, Olympics, Media and Sport]*, you gurning fucking gonkbollock . . .

Hon. Members: Scumbag! Maggot! Cheap lousy faggot! Dee dum de-de dah de dee dum-dum your arse!

Mr. Speaker: Order now, please.

[A scuffle then breaking out before the Dispatch Box, hon. Members of the Opposition in factional disputation concerning policy on 'media monoculture' and also concerning the correct lyrics to 'Fairytale of New York'. Mr. Speaker then in demeanour most jolly summoning the Cudgellers to stifle the disorder with Quelches and Gumptions. Peace then settling upon the Chamber.]

The Secretary of State for Work and Pensions (Mr. Iain Duncan Smith): Mr. Speaker, if I may for a moment appropriate the quietness in this chamber and draw attention to my costume. Hon. Members will have inferred, I am sure, that I will be attending – shh – a fancy-dress party later as the Ghost of Christmas Past. Because, Mr. Speaker, I believe that, ultimately,

Quiet Nothingness will prevail. Listen, just listen. Shh. Silent Night. Holy Night. All is calm . . .

Hon. Members: Piss off, you whining cock stump! Yeah, you egg-fuck! Yeah, moobhead!

Mr. Speaker: Order, ding dong merrily in the name of the Infant Jesus, order! Hon. Members . . . order, order, the hon. Lady there in the Disney Cinderella gown will stop doing that with her wand immediately. Hon. Members have a clear choice here. *[indicated multiple packs of confectionery]* The Cadbury's Celebrations. Or *[indicated the Corridor]* the Royal Cudgellers. Thank you.

Mr. Iain Duncan Smith: All is calm, Mr. Speaker, as I say. I would ask a simple courtesy of those hon. Members who complain so very loudly about this Government's – shh – compassionate reform of everything. If you can't say anything nice, don't say anything at all. In the words of the great *[consulted notes]* Björk Guðmundsdóttir: 'It's oh so quiet, shh, shh.' If you're not prepared to be part of the Compassionate Society, then eff you. So be it. Prepare to be crushed and mutilated by the tanks and heavy artillery of the Compassionate Society, because none will be spared the armoured might of our righteous indignation, shh.

Dr. Vince Cable: Mr. Speaker, may I say to my *[indicated Secretary of State for Culture, Olympics, Media and Sport]* hon. Friend and Cabinet Colleague, notwithstanding the distance between us, sitting at different ends of that Cabinet table metaphorically, and from now on actually, that I sincerely – sincerely – hope that taking away the best fucking bit of my portfolio and absorbing it into his already massive box, stuffed as it is with everything from Morris Dancing to the fucking Olympics, won't signal any sort of rift within the Coalition.

Mr. Jeremy Hunt: Mr. Speaker, yes, I hope so too. I am certainly not one of those who thinks the hon. Gentleman a ridiculous sulky old codger, with his glasses balanced at the end of his nose like someone playing Professor Fucking Higgins in a local production of *My Fair Lady*. Mr. Speaker, I really hope my taking Sky off his tiny inconsequential plate doesn't mean we can't get on together.

Dr. Vince Cable: Mm. I really fucking hope that too. For my part, Mr. Speaker, I congratulate my hon. So-Called Coalition Friend and wish him well in his dealings with Mr. Murdoch.

Mr. Jeremy Hunt: Mr. Speaker, I thank my most learned and hon. Colleague. I certainly found Mr. Murdoch's son the most congenial lunch companion.

Mr. Jeremy Corbyn (Folk Islington): Mr. Speaker, is it not the case that Mr. Murdoch's attempts to control the media in Britain cloak a sinister ambition to create some sort of 'Sky Israel HD' upon the landscape of our beloved media homeland? Mark my words, in ten years' time the BBC will be reduced to a beleaguered, occupied Palestine. Furthermore, this plan by the Government to hand the World Service over to the BBC to look after is a plot more dastardly than Fidel Castro's exploding cigars. What does 'look after' mean? The BBC will be obliged to look after the World Service in the way a vet would look after an elderly and infirm dog. Plus, the insidious rise of home-grown fascism and carpetbaggers raping our public realm. Women and children and ethnic minorities oppressed. It is outrageous.

Mr. Speaker: Ho ho ho, I must ask the hon. Gentleman what he's talking about, as he's lost me and I suspect everyone else in this Chamber. What is outrageous?

Mr. Jeremy Corbyn: Everything, Mr. Speaker. Aye, everything . . .

[The hon. Member stamping his foot and singing a Chartist anthem, 'The Dirty Bastard Landlords', then refusing to stop when called upon by Mr. Speaker, then twice, then thrice, then being banished from the Chamber, then beginning a beat-boxed folk version of 'Lose Yourself' by Eminem, then being escorted from the chamber by the Bailiff and several Pursuivants in elvish Christmas costume.]

Mr. Jeremy Hunt: Mr. Speaker, the hon. and mental Gentleman could not be more wrong, even with that stupid hat he wears. Who does he think he is, Mr. Speaker – Bob Dylan? I can assure the House he is not Bob Dylan. He is Jack Hargreaves.

Hon. Members: The hon. Mentalman! The hon. Mentalman! The hon. Wanker!

Mr. Speaker: Order, ho ho ho. Come on, please. Let's have a little Christmas discipline.

Dr. Vince Cable: On a Point of Order, Mr. Speaker. Did my esteemed Colleague the Secretary for Bloody Everything Now Apparently just allude to a lunch he had with James Murdoch?

Mr. Jeremy Hunt: No. No. Absolutely no. No, no, no. OK, yes. It was quite a shortish lunch. I didn't have any pudding.

Dr. Vince Cable: Hm, in that case it doesn't sound like 'lunch' to me at all. The meeting was minuted, of course.

Mr. Speaker: Order. The, ho ho, hon. Gentlemen must address their remarks to the Chair.

Mr. Jeremy Hunt: There isn't a Chair, squitfuck, is there? Just a

Grotto, with you in it. Yes, of course the meeting was 'minuted'. There just weren't any civil servants there taking actual minutes. They were all busy doing important things. Don't worry, I've got the minutes here *[indicated head]* in my head.

Dr. Vince Cable: Oh, have you? I'm sure the House would fucking love to hear those minutes.

Mr. Speaker: Order – definitely NOT ho ho ho – order! The hon. Gentlemen will address the Grotto.

Mr. Jeremy Hunt: The minutes in my head are private. And anyway, fuck off. I have a Murdoch to go to. A meeting. A meeting to go to.

Mr. Speaker: Address the Grotto! Address the flipping Grotto!

[The Secretary of State then quitting the Chamber most hurriedly, scattering £20 notes upon the Floor of the House.]

Mr. Jeremy Hunt: Mr. Murdoch says, 'God bless you, every one.'

Moment of Snookcocking.

House of Commons

Held upon the Feast of the Blessed Duvet,
the 10th of January 2011

HANGOVERS AND SNOOZE-BUTTONING

[Mr. Speaker in the Chair]

A Presumption of Resumption

Mr. Speaker: Order, order. I'd like to welcome back hon.
Members from what I trust has been a restorative holiday. I
respectfully ask the House for its forbearance as I have been to
the doctor with my nerves and am now being treated for mild
amnesia. Questions to the Deputy Prime Minister. Yes, Sir. You,
Sir, the hon. Member for Gentleigh Dusset. Yes. *[air punch]*
Still got it.

**The Secretary of State for Energy and Climate Change (Mr.
Chris Huhne):** Mr. Speaker, as a matter of record can I point
out that, as well as representing the good people of Gentleigh
Dusset, I am also in the Cabinet. I have been an important
member of that Cabinet for months now, with my own little
chair and everything. I think I deserve a bit of fucking respect,
and would like to remind the House that I am a very tetchy

millionaire, worth much more than my hon. Friend the Deputy Prime Minister over there *[inaudible, possibly 'the back-stabbing ponce'].* If you're looking for tetchy *[indicated 'tetchy'],* you've come to the right place.

Mr. Speaker: Order. Welcome to the Annual General Meeting of the All-Party Parliamentary Group for Endangered Tribes. It has been a busy year . . . *[Intervention by the Clerk to the House.]* Yes, of course. The . . . the bank managery one there, sorry, I've forgotten . . .

Mr. Chris Huhne: Will the Deputy Prime Minister tell us what he's been up to? I'm sure we'd all be fascinated to know. And may I take this opportunity to remind the House of my bloody existence, thanks? I may have lost the contest for the Lib Dem leadership to my hon. Friend. OK. I bear no grudge. I am sure we have all read the *Sun* today and would be fascinated to learn more about 'A Large Cock Britain'.

Hon. Members: Todgers AND tits in the *Sun* now? Not on the same page, I hope. The leader's always a bit cocky, to be fair. I bet Lord Mandelson admires his column in the mirror occasionally.

Mr. Speaker: Cowabunga, dudes. Let's talk this shit through, yeah?

The Deputy Prime Minister (Mr. Nick Clegg): Mr. Speaker, may I with respect correct my hon. yet mischievous Friend? Today I launched NOT 'A Large Cock Britain' but 'Alarm Clock Britain'. There is a subtle but important difference. Mr. Speaker, we want to see people getting up early and working hard. The metaphor of an erect penis is immaterial. This is about people. People who want their kids to get ahead. You can call them people who don't want to rely on state handouts. You can call them people who need people, Mr. Speaker. You can call them the luckiest people in the world. People who don't need politicians to tell them what to think or how to live their lives. No, wait a minute . . .

Ms. Hazel Blears (Salford & Chucky): Point of Order, Mr. Speaker! *[indicated self]* The hon. Gentleman has no idea how proper folk live. I, on the other hand, used to be Minister for Folk and I can tell him with perky confidence that an alarm clock is a stupid anachronism. What next, Mr. Speaker? 'Cassette-Tape Britain'? My constituents use the alarm on their MOBILES. They are not mincing Londoners with posh retro bits and bobs in their swanky apartments, walking about nude with little pork-pie hats on, and their cats called Neville and Philip and all sorts.

Hon. Members: Fuck you, the North! Fuck you, the South! I wish they'd turn the M25 into a moat! I wish they'd turn the M1 into a fucking terraced street! Municipal Stalinists! Neo-liberalists! Come on, you salads! Howay the chips! Wankers! Wankers!

Mr. Speaker: I'd like a vowel please, Carol.

Ms. Hazel Blears: Plus, what about all these local-authority folk he's putting OUT of a job, most of them apparently in MY fucking constituency, thanks very much I'm sure? They won't need to be up so early NOW, will they? I am smiling hard, Mr. Speaker, but it is a grim smile of bitter irony. I am speaking loudly, Mr. Speaker, because I am on the Back Benches these days and I wish to remind certain smarmy barmcakes down the front that I actually did quite a lot for social mobility, including a celebrity motorcycling rally. Ee, what do you think of my new haircut? I can tell the House it's either static electricity or I'm bristling with indignation!

Hon. Members: Wanker! You look like a fucking ginger broccoli floret! What happened to the Big Cock? I nodded off.

Mr. Speaker: Whoa, whoa. This is a Book Club meeting, not a town-centre pub. Personally, I think the sexual tension is gratuitous and . . . *[Intervention by the Clerk to the House.]* I'm the what? Speaker? With all due respect, I think you'll find I was the Wimbledon Men's Singles Champion, 1992. Bring me some barley water and a fresh towel.

Ms. Hazel Blears: Mr. Speaker, the hon. Gentleman's so-called Alarm Clock Britain is not fit for purpose. It is not alarm clocks that will get this country back on its feet, it is socially mobile tap-dancing.

[The hon. Member for Salford & Chucky then descending to the Floor of the House, being joined by hon. Members of the Parliamentary tap-dancing troupe The Division Belles to perform, impromptu and freestyle, a dance to a medley of numbers from the musical drama Chicago.*]*

Mr. Speaker: *[applauding]* Bloody good. Really bloody good. Thanks so much for entertaining us. Now if I may, Madam Chairman, I'd like to say a few words about the great work done by Sea Scouts up and down the country. I . . . *[Intervention by the Clerk to the House.]* Ah, that explains a LOT. The House of Commons. Yes, yes, I remember. But it's all so different. Where's Mr. Blair? And what's Chris Morris doing at the Dispatch Box?

The Deputy Prime Minister: Mr. Speaker, this Government is formed by a coalition of two parties. We want to join the people of Alarm Clock Britain in another coalition. A coalition of the compliant. Tax cuts. Not handouts. That's right: the first ten grand completely tax-free, subject to terms and conditions. Alarm Clock Britain. You can call it progressive. You can call it fair. Whatever you want. We're easy like Sunday morning. So let's hear it for the Sleeve-rollers. The Hard Mums. The Big Dads. *[consulted phone]* Shit, got to dash. Childcare emergency, back-up nanny just bailed. Ten to one it'll be some old fucking twaddle about 'cystitis' again. Cover for me, yeah?

[The Deputy Prime Minister then quit the Chamber. Hon. Members in clamorous eagerness to address the House, seeking the attention of Mr. Speaker.]

Mr. Chris Huhne: Mr. Speaker, as by some stretch the most widely known and respected Liberal Democrat, I would like . . .
Mr. Speaker: Order, order. OK, settle down. *[mimed 'book']*
Hon. Members: Book.
Mr. Speaker: *[mimed 'film']*
Hon. Members: And film.

Moment of Charade.

House of Commons

Held upon the Concatenation of Tongues,
the 31st of January 2011

PRAYERS AND FREEMASONRY OVERTURES

[Mr. Speaker upon the Adjusted Chair]

Questionable Health Issues

Mr. Speaker: Order. I would ask that hon. Members behave in a seemly fashion during this debate. I have a physiological condition *[indicated self]*, temporary, I hope, which renders me particularly susceptible to sudden loud noises. I have been to see my GP about this, several times. He has diagnosed *[produced and read note]* 'persistent irritation'. I would crave . . .

Hon. Members: WANKER!

Mr. Speaker: Ow! Order, order. Come on. *[brandished note]* This is a professional diagnosis. From a genuinely nice GP, very helpful, if a little brusque. Oh, and who, by the way *[addressed the Secretary of State for Health]*, asked me to pass on his regards and give you this . . .

[Mr. Speaker handed a document to the Clerk of Documents,

*it thereforth being vouchsafed via the Bailiff of the House to the
Secretary of State for Health, who, being in violent conference with
the Chancellor of the Exchequer, did shift about in his seat, most
restlessly.]*

Mr. Speaker: Basically he's taken your advice, rebadged his prac-
tice as a Pathfinding Network Stakeholder, and put together
a consortium of venture capitalists and health-care providers. That *[indicated document]* is an outline bid for managing
the NHS in Camden. Controlling the budget, filtering the
patients . . .

The Chancellor of the Exchequer (Mr. George Osborne):
SHUT YOUR STUPID MOUTH, YOU BLABBERING
COCKBIN, OR I WILL HAVE YOU BLITZED INTO
HUMAN TARTARE AND FED TO MY FUCKING
PIGS!

Mr. Speaker: Ow! Ow! Order. The hon. Gentleman is right. I
recall that I was asked by our mutual acquaintance to choose
a quiet moment to pass the bidding document on. I agree, it
is much too noisy in the House at the moment. Apologies.
Although, now I come to think of it, isn't this all a bit irregular?
It did seem odd that his business associates were present during
the entire consultation. I had my vest off at one point.

Hon. Members: Wanker! Yeah, save the NHS, it looks fucking great on the posters! Hold up, I fancy a bit of this. I did a
BUPA after-dinner last month and they were all over me like
fucking RUBELLA!

*[Uproar and Tumult in the Chamber, with much waving of
Order Papers and Stethoscopes. Several Sound Bombs lobbed from*

Opposition Benches unto Government Benches, and vice versa. Mr.
Speaker in distress then summoning the Royal Cudgellers, thereby
causing quietude to settle upon the Assembled Company.]

Mr. Ed Miliband (Doncaster Awkwood): Mr. Speaker, may I
seize this moment of opportunity, which is technically a question? Brerk. I sense extreme discomfort in the Government
Benches, particularly among its minority-party Coalition partners, about this horrific plan for the NHS, brerk . . .

Christopher (Mr. Miliband's Imaginary Friend): That's it! Fuck
them up the arse with their NHS Bill. Especially the Liberals.
They deserve it, go on. Oh sure, they're in the fucking POOL,
but they're just that floating dinosaur thing nobody wants to go
on.

Hon. Members: NHS! NHS! NHS!

Mr. Ed Miliband: . . . which is why, Mr. Speaker, I'd like to ask
instead a shrill question about the resignation of Mr. Andy
Coulson, the Prime Minister's Head of Propaganda and long-
standing . . .

Christopher: Don't say 'bum chum'.

Mr. Ed Miliband: . . . brerk bum chum.

Hon. Members: Wanker! Homophobe! Wankerphobe!

Mr. Speaker: Order now, shush! The Chamber cannot hear the
hon. Member for Doncaster Awkwood's point about the NHS.

Mr. Ed Miliband: Mr. Speaker, thank you. If I may, I would like
to unleash one of my legendary stinging one-liners, revealing the
truth about this Tory Government. *[searched pockets]* Oh yes, Mr.
Speaker. Hon. Members opposite may mime 'endangered panda'
until they go pop. And, right, my question about the privatisation of the NHS is . . . bugger, where's my question?

Christopher: My God. You really are a useless punnet of cock mince, aren't you? Remember I told you to go to the toilet before we left? I bet you left the question in the bathroom. Oh, man. What a blithering, nurdling, smeary, fumbling papfuck you are. I hate you. 'Brerk.'

Mr. Ed Miliband: While I locate the question, Mr. Speaker, let me brerk this. If the Prime Minister really DOES still have confidence in Mr. Coulson, who has technically just resigned because he is linked in the public imagination to a police investigation into phone-tapping at the *News of the Brerk* . . . well. If he does, then I tell the Prime Minister this: he looks silly. He's clearly a very poor judge of character. *[searched Order Papers]* So, as I say, we should have no further confidence in HIM. Mr. Speaker, the Prime Minister should now do the right thing and resign at once, taking his brerk horrible Government with him, and let us forget about Mr. Coulson. And remember to get on with saving the NHS. Bloody hell, where's my bloody question? It was on a sheet of A4.

Hon. Members, Christopher: You knobhead! You arsepump! You lop-sided, incompetent plume of shit!

Mr. Speaker: Ow, order! Please keep the noise down, it's making me feel . . . weird.

[The hon. Member for Doncaster Awkwood then searching the Floor of the House for his Question, then aware of his brother, the hon. Member for South Shields Ocado, waving a sheet of paper with a Question upon it.]

Mr. Alan Johnson (Long Division & Baffle): Mr. Speaker, it is with great regret that I have to inform my hon. Friend that I am resigning as Shadow Chancellor. To be honest, I have had quite enough bullying from *[glanced at the Chancellor of the Exchequer]* certain bastards opposite. And frankly I can tell them that however clever they think their sums are, they often don't add up. Even with a calculator and a civil servant. I now plan to spend more time with my tropical fish, but would like to assure my hon. Friend . . .

The Prime Minister (Mr. David Cameron): Oho, Mr. Speaker! Aha, Mr. Speaker! *[mimed fistive violation]* The hon. Gentleman criticises me for giving a key role to Mr. Coulson, the widely respected former editor of the *News of the World*. Yet Mr. Coulson resigned from that newspaper AGES ago over phone-tapping, about which he knew nothing. Is the hon. Gentleman suggesting that Mr. Coulson's apology to Mr. Murdoch wasn't enough, and that he must now apologise again? What signal does this send out to the global media-baron community? That we don't trust them? I would remind the House that global media barons are the lifeblood of our fucking economy!

The Secretary of State for Health (Mr. Andrew Lansley): Mr. Speaker, if there are no further questions on the NHS I'd quite like to slip off, if that's OK. The wife and I have to be in Cirencester first thing.

The Prime Minister: And yet now, Mr. Speaker, we hear that the Shadow Chancellor has jumped ship! Fuck my old boots, as I believe the saying goes, the hon. Member for Doncaster Awkwood has only been Leader of the Opposition for five minutes. What about HIS judgement of character?

Mr. Ed Balls (Shitwad & Burly): Mr. Speaker, it is not for me to put myself forward – for the second time, incidentally – as a heavyweight Shadow Chancellor. My hon. Friend and Party Leader will want to consider the matter very carefully, I am sure. Perhaps he will surprise the House by choosing, I don't know, Delia Fucking Smith to be Shadow Chancellor, or a seahorse in a jar . . .

Mr. Chuka Umunna (Strem Ends): Point of ORDER, Mr. Speaker. Wha' if man were to appoint a DJ to the post? That would be most terribly amusing, na fink? He would be like a 'DJ Shadow Chancellor'. Oh yeah, I see you, baby. Shaking that ass. Shaking that ass.

Ms. Louise Bagshawe (Poshoe & Yumbly): *[emphatic flailing]* Mr. Speaker, if the booty being adduced in support of the hon. Gentleman's faux-street proposition is notionally mine, I can assure him my bottom has remained inert throughout this entire debate. I'm more of an indie girl. Chick lit. White wine. Hinterland. Perhaps the hon. Gentleman would care to tell the House if HE ever shared a bong with Blur, or gave any of them an 'executive massage'.

Mr. Ed Balls: . . . HOWEVER!

Mr. Speaker: Ow! The hon. Gentleman will please moderate his voice. I'm getting quite short of breath here.

Mr. Ed Balls: However, if my hon. Friend would like me to take over as Shadow Chancellor for the time being, fine. Whatever. Happy to oblige. Would have been nice to be fucking asked the first time, but no matter. Pointless dwelling on that now.

Mr. Ed Miliband: Good, yes, Mr. Speaker. That is exactly what I was about to suggest . . .

[The outgoing Shadow Chancellor and the incoming Shadow Chancellor did then hurriedly exchange places upon the Opposition

Benches, with collateral disgruntlements and resentments. The
Secretary of State for Health signalling his intention to quit the
Chamber, with much deference to the Government Benches and the
Chair.]

Mr. David Miliband (South Shields Ocado): Mr. Speaker,
before the Secretary of State for Health leaves us, may I ask him
a *[produced sheet of paper]* question?

Mr. Speaker: Yes. But I would be obliged if you would ask it very
quietly. I fear I may be having an attack of the vapours.

[The hon. Member for Doncaster Awkwood then, having crawled
along the Floor of the House and ascended the Opposition Benches to a
position behind the hon. Member for South Shields Ocado, did snatch
the Question and return to his place. Hon. Members then howling
with derision and acclamation and blowing vuvuzelas, Mr. Speaker
clasping his hands over his ears.]

Mr. Ed Miliband: *[presenting middle finger to the hon. Member for*
South Shields Ocado] Mr. Speaker, the question to the Secretary
of State is this: what happened to the Reading of the Health
and Social Care Bill? I believe it was to have taken place in
Parliament today.

Hon. Members: *[screaming, shouting, air horns]*

Mr. Speaker: *[inserting earplugs]* That's it. While I still have the
strength, I am excusing myself from the rest of this debate. Mr.
Clerk, please advise me when it is safe to take these out, I can't
hear a thing. Lovely. Carry on.

Mr. Andrew Lansley: What? *[indicated innocence and irrita-*
tion] There WAS a Reading of the Bill. Earlier on. In bloody
Parliament. Copies were made available in the Members'

Dining Room. Now why don't you all just piss off and leave me alone? I have to travel to Cirencester in the morning.

Mr. John Healey (Chuckle & Brotherly): Oh, is that why the Dining Room was closed for lunch? 'Private Function' it said. And may I ask why the bollocking hell I was not present for this lunchtime Reading of the Bill? I am only the Shadow Secretary of State for Health! I had to send out for fucking sandwiches! Oh, *[patting jacket]* and I seem to have lost me wallet now . . .

Mr. Andrew Lansley: Mr. Speaker . . . *[Mr. Speaker asleep.]* Mr. Clerk, I absolutely bloody resent the implication that I have been charged with somehow 'sneaking through these NHS reforms on the sly and not cocking it up if I want to stay Secretary of State for Health'. That is an outrageous slur. The truth is this: you really can't get that many people in the Dining Room.

Mr. John Healey: Bah, this isn't working. Hold on, I'll try turning it round and you catch the other end. Who read the Bill then?

Mr. Andrew Lansley: It was read in its entirety by Mr. Martin Jarvis. He's very good. Does a lot of stuff for Radio 4 . . .

Mr. John Healey: Oh bother, I'm getting in a right pickle here. Who HEARD the reading?

Mr. Andrew Lansley: Key people. Important commissioning people in the healthcare industry. There was a former Labour Health Secretary there nodding along in agreement, so you can take that bloody sarky look off your face, matey boy. Some people from the media were present . . .

Hon. Members: Fucking Murdoch again! He's like the Wizard of Oz, behind the curtain! Yeah, or paywall! Shut up, he's probably having this taped, and I for one do not wish to be barred from the Members' Dining Room – they do bloody nice roly-poly!

Mr. Andrew Lansley: The media representatives were all off the record, relax. Honestly, I really don't know what all the fuss is about. We are simply acting on the evidence, some of it utterly compelling, from private contractors who say the NHS is not fit for purpose.

Mr. John Healey: Never mind your stupid evidence. If you want actual evidence, read these reports *[produced takeaway menus]* . . . well, obviously not these. But if I WERE to be holding the right bits of paper, they would include research from economists at Imperial College demonstrating quite clearly that allowing private companies to cherry-pick the NHS must lead to a fall in clinical quality. Oh, now how did I get me arm trapped down me trouser leg like that? Botheration.

The Deputy Prime Minister (Mr. Nick Clegg): I agree with the hon. Gentleman, despite the fact that he clearly can't stand still for fifteen seconds without suffering a physical-comedy catastrophe. Not only is this Bill a rushed, ill-considered bag of . . . I don't know, call it FUCK MUCUS. But also, obviously, enforced competition will make it harder for NHS staff to work collaboratively in multidisciplinary teams and across organisa-tional boundaries. As Leader of the ACTUAL Opposition, I condemn in unequivocal terms this *[received Chancellor of the Exchequer's shoe in face]* . . . Yes, now I recall that even before the Liberal Democrats helped form the most successful Coalition since the Beatles, we were always going to get rid of Primary Care Trusts. *['double teapot']* Look, OK? Some people out there are saying these reforms strike at the very heart of the NHS:

the GP's allegiance to his or her patient. Now you can call these critics dinosaurs. Call them tortoises. Call them bummers. They are all these things. They are highly critical, dinosaur-bumming tortoises. What I am saying is this, and I'm quoting myself here:

You can't look after the clinical wellbeing of a patient if at the same time your decisions don't lead to financial consequences. It's a very simple idea.

So there you have it. Of course we'll listen. Of course we'll reflect. Listen and reflect: now that DOES sound like something you'd hear late at night on Radio 4, ha ha, when doubt and anxiety drive away sleep . . .

Mr. John Healey: I agree with Nick. Not all of it. The first bit, certainly. I never listen to Radio 4 unless I'm on it. Could someone give me a hand with these trousers?

[The Shadow Chancellor then straining to pull the arm of the hon. Member for Chuckle & Brotherly from his trousers, and punching him.]

Mr. John Healey: Ouch. Fuck. 'To Me, To You': THAT sounds like Radio 4. Oh, I've dropped me hammer on me toe now.

Mr. George Osborne: May I welcome the hon. Gentleman to his new role as Shadow Chancellor? He is indeed a heavyweight opponent. If I could offer some advice, I would suggest punching the hon. Gentleman just here, beneath the ribs.

Mr. Ed Balls: I thank the hon. Gentleman for his kind words. *[punching the hon. Member for Chuckle & Brotherly]* He reminds me of some aristocratic arsehole in a film about the French Revolution, savouring a public execution. Mr. Speaker . . .

Mr. Speaker: *[asleep]*

Mr. Ed Balls: Shit a brick, it's like the Mad Hatter's Tea Party in here. With *[indicated Mr. Speaker]* Little Jimmy Osmond over there as the fucking Dormouse. *[indicated the Chancellor]* You! The papers are full of stories about tax havens and tax dodgers and tax amnesties for big corporations and your fucking mates in the City. Instead of squeezing the poor like so many cheap washing-up sponges that have totally lost their cleaning power, now there's a recession on – which incidentally dates back to 1996, when the Tories were in power – why don't you squeeze the rich? You should be going after the non-doms, the banker wankers, the fat cats!

Mr. George Osborne: Oh, ha ha ha. The hon. Gentleman wishes to see a fat cat? I suggest the next time he's at a school fête he queues up to have his face painted to resemble a baby tiger by a bored supply teacher who smells of patchouli. Then he should look at himself in a fucking mirror. *[quitting his place, taking with him a box]* Now if you'll excuse me, I have to . . . present some points at a 'reception'.

Hon. Members: Box! Box! Cherchez Dynamitey!

[A great commotion then swelling within the Chamber, the Clerk of the House waking Mr. Speaker in great agitation.]

Mr. Speaker: Ugh. What? Oh, yes, Cherchez Dynamitey is hereby invoked. I challenge the Chancellor to declare if he be a Vile Papist or no. And to ask, with all the House:

Hon. Members All Together: What's in the Box – is it Dynamite?

Mr. George Osborne: Yes.

Hon. Members: *[aghast]*

Mr. George Osborne: I thought it would be a bit of a hoot to bring in an actual case of dynamite. It's quite exciting. I got it from the MoD, although naturally I had to sign a waiver. Apparently it's extremely volatile. I'll show you . . .

[Hon. Members silent, Mr. Speaker observing with trepidation. The Chancellor then with extreme care and slowness removing the lid from the box, then registering great fearfulness.]

Mr. George Osborne: BANG! Ha ha ha!

[The House shrieking in alarm, then laughing most uproariously at the revealed contents of the box, to wit, diverse sex toys. Mr. Speaker collapsing within the Chair.]

Moment of Paramedical Summoning.

House of Commons

Held upon the Contiguation of the Blessed Contingents,
the 17th of February 2011

POLLED OPINIONS AND BANTERINGS

[A Guest Speaker in the Chair]

Prime Minister's Listening Time

The Bailiff of the House: Oyez, oyez! I bring news concerning Mr. Speaker, who is indisposed due to *[consulted note]* 'a sprained wrist and melancholia'. Be it herefore known that a Guest Speaker has accordingly been invited to oversee the Proceedings of this Chamber by the Secretary of State for Communities and Local Government, Mr. Eric Pickles. This invitation being an exemplar of the Big Society, which has been recently and most solemnly commended and ordained by Her Majesty's Government . . .

Hon. Members: *[grumblings, mumblings, fumblings, otherworldliness]*

The Bailiff of the House: Oyez, oyez! I have a note here from Mr. Pickles, who incidentally is also indisposed:

Hello. You all right? Sorry I am not in the House today. I can't be everywhere at once. Though to be fair, even if I fly business class I occupy two seats. Ha ha, joke.

Now I believe that what will keep the Big Society idea going is sustainability. People are happy to volunteer their time, but they have to earn a living too. If you don't believe me, ask Lord Wei of Shoreditch. He's the bloody Big Society Tsar, and even HE'S gone down from three days a week to two. It's all about independence, and paying those pesky bills. I exclude pensioners from all this, obviously. We have a few little surprises for THEM round the corner, as some of you know.

During the coming week I will be hard-earning a living as an Alarm Clock Briton, touring constituencies up and down and all over the bloody country, talking to people about how they see the Big Society and Alarm Clock Britain, what they think it might all mean, going off early in the morning, ha ha, joke.

Ladies and gentlemen, the Big Society depends on ordinary-shaped people like you stepping up and saying, 'I could do that, and don't even bother paying me!' As the usual Mr. Speaker is off with some bloody thing or other, I have arranged a Volunteer Speaker. You all know her as the colourful lady who sells souvenirs outside the Houses of Parliament and who, OK, can get aggressive at times with the religious shouting. But she has offered to do it for nothing, so please welcome as Volunteer Speaker Mrs. Pearly Queenie Bunting.

[Then entered the Volunteer Speaker, garbed in raiments of most unwholesome aspect, redeemed by mother-of-pearl attachments and a Beefeater Hat, carrying a bag of London Souvenirs for sale and making her way to the Speaker's Chair.]

Mrs. Volunteer Speaker: Hooverneer! Hundun Hooverneer! Getcha Big Ben, getcha Big Ben! Clock on a stick, clock on a stick, and there will be a Calamitous Spanking of the World, and Godly Rage, amen! Repent! Repent!

Hon. Members: Well, this is a refreshing change. Yes, someone who speaks her mind. Well, you know what they say – you don't have to be mad to work here, as long as you maintain a few lucrative outside interests.

The Secretary of State for Environment, Food and Rural Affairs (Mrs. Caroline Spelman): Mrs. Speaker, last month I stood before the House and announced that the Government was pressing ahead with consultations on how Britain's forests might be more efficiently managed, or possibly sold off in the future. There was some pretty hostile coverage, I have to say. Headlines such as 'Forest Chump' and 'Fuck Off, Woodentop'. Some very rude questions were asked in this House too . . .

Ms. Mary Creagh (Wakefield Irritated): Mrs. Speaker, as Shadow Secretary for *[consulted lapel badge]* Environment, Food and Rurality, let me repeat what I said to the hon. Lady at the time. If this Government thinks it can divert the entire country from the *[glanced at the Chancellor of the Exchequer]* cruel buggering of our educational system, health service and social-security infrastructure with some bonkers plan to sell the forests, and a subsequent U-turn to show it is sensitive and responsive, then it is barking up the wrong arse. I mean, tree.

Mrs. Volunteer Speaker: Be quiet! You! Were you there? Were you there when they crucified my Lord? Teddies! Dressed as Bobbies! Getcha Teddy-Bobbies! You!

Mrs. Caroline Spelman: Thank you, Mrs. Speaker. And may I ask the hon. Lady who the sodding bumhole she thinks she is? Nobody even knows how to pronounce her name!

Ms. Mary Creagh: Point of Order, Mrs. Speaker. It is pronounced 'career', but shortened. Plus, I think she'll find very few people know how to spell HER stupid name, wanker, no returns.

Mrs. Volunteer Speaker: No! No! Flip the kipper, we're doing the Lambeth Walk – OY! If you don't behave yourself, it's the cells, Queenie! Oh yes. Gherkin in a Snowglobe! His Spears of Fire and his Chariot of Flame! Next!

Mrs. Caroline Spelman: Mrs. Speaker, hon. Members may also recall that I stood here a week ago and told you that people were getting worried about nothing and to just shut up. Today, I have three announcements to make. *[consulted note from the Prime Minister's Office]* 'Firstly, tell them the consultation about selling off forests is in the fucking skip. Apologise to any hon. Members who'd been planning to buy shares in England's woodland, we'll sort something out in due course. Then, confirm that all clauses relating to the Forestry Commission will be taken out of the Public Bodies Bill or whatever official-sounding bollocks Sandra's fried up with her wonks at the Strategy Unit. Then tell them a panel will be set up to advise on the future of forests. Don't make any jokes about wood panels. And try for once not to sound like Mary Fucking Poppins having an enema . . .' Ah, wait, Mrs. Speaker. I see what's happened here. This is more of a note to me, actually. Sorry.

Hon. Members: Wanker! What a humiliation! I'd better get the deposit back, my consortium's already worked up plans for a fucking eco-town on ten square miles of Marston Vale!

Mrs. Volunteer Speaker: Hooverneer, Hundun Hooverneer!

Hello, Sir, how are you today? Can I interest you in a Cockerney Sparrer? Look, he's got a little Arsenal cap and scarf, very chirpy, £14.99. I have seen things. There are no lies in Deuteronomy. THERE ARE NO LIES IN DEUTERONOMY!

Mr. Owen Favours (Ladderscale): Would the Prime Minister list his engagements for today? And will he acknowledge that this is the *[consulted note]* 'Most Listening Government Since the 1940s'?

The Prime Minister (Mr. David Cameron): *[asleep]*

Mrs. Volunteer Speaker: Eye, Wobbly Bridge, Tate, St Paul's! Hundun Hooverneers! Don't fall asleep, love, that's how they got poor old Brian Haw! Horses in the sky! Horses and monsters!

The Prime Minister: *[awakening]* Mm. Apologies. It's this bloody Arab Spring. I've been listening on behalf of Her Majesty's Government to all sorts, round the sodding Alarm Clock Britain clock! 'Hello, Mr. Cameron? Sorry it's so late, but my colleagues and I in Egypt wanted to pick your brains about democracy and free speech . . .' I mean, you do your best, explain how democracy works. How large public forums such as Tahrir Square, indeed Parliament Square, are a magnet for mischief-makers shouting dangerous nonsense about people with blood on their hands and all that. I tell them: get security to lock it down, but NB, keep it open for the tourists, they're key. You'd be astonished how many times they apologise and say they've got the wrong number. AND I'm having endless meetings with my Middle East Peace Task Force. While you lot are on half-term, I'll be flying out to show solidarity with various regimes – and various oppositions to various regimes – with a diplomatic team of defence-logistics exporters . . .

Hon. Members: You're drumming up business for the weapons trade? Boom boom! Are you utterly without shame, you simpering amoral clusterbombfuck?

Mrs. Volunteer Speaker: Shut up! They arrested poor Brian as soon as this shitty Government got in! 'BLAIR IS A WAR CRIMINAL.' That's what he used to say. He bought one of my Teddy-Bobbies, put a little T-shirt on it saying 'TEDDY-BOBBIES AGAINST BOMBS'. Behold the Whore of Babylon, who bringeth misery and constipation in her wake!

The Prime Minister: With the greatest respect, whoever the fuck you are . . . *[consultation with the Clerk of the House]* I see. *[inaudible, possibly 'Tell that toerag Bercow that if he doesn't turn up for the next Session, he can consider himself hoisted up the greasy chimney with his own fucking petard']* I am speechless, Mrs. Speaker, at this synthetic outrage over my mission to reinforce peace and freedom. Democracies have a right to defend themselves. And with British industry's Arab Spring Sale now on, our arms customers would surely be demented if they DIDN'T snap up our two-for-one offers on a range of democracy-preserving devices.

Mr. Andy Burnham (Mersey & Emotional Side): Point of Order, Mrs. Speaker dough. Who'll be in charge while the Prime Minister is abroad? That *[indicated the Deputy Prime Minister]* numpty shitclogger?

The Prime Minister: Who's in CHARGE? We live in the Age of the Blackberry, the Internet, the Wii Fit. And a much more accommodating Civil Service recently. Please. Piss off. I remain in charge, obviously. I am the fucking Prime Minister.

Mrs. Volunteer Speaker: Libya will be next, Brian used to say! War follows oil! The clock on the stick is ticking, up the apples and pears, buy a postcard at least, Sir, are you from Continental Europe? Punk talking to policeman! Diana, bit orangey but that's how she was! Punk talking to guardsman! Punk talking to Diana! This was all written down! In blood!

Mr. Ed Miliband (Doncaster Awkwood): Mrs. Speaker, let me seize this moment to talk about the economy and the Government's broken promises.

Hon. Members: Wanker! Crypto-Goth! Replicant!

Mr. Ed Miliband: I tell you this. No, sorry. I ASK you this. The snow, the snow the Government blamed for a stalled recovery has now melted away. I wonder, Mrs. Speaker, what the brerk Prime Minister and his pathetic entourage of . . .

Christopher (Mr. Miliband's Imaginary Friend): Don't say anything weird. Say 'fuckers' or 'bastards' or 'shitheads' or something. Say something ordinary.

Mr. Ed Miliband: . . . yes, what will the Prime Minister and his pathetic entourage of brerk SINISTER DANCING CLODS OF SEXGRISTLE blame Britain's faltering economy on NOW? The wrong kind of Retail Index, Mr. Speaker? The wrong kind of shopper? The wrong kind of electrons in the atmosphere? Let me remind the Prime Minister . . .

Christopher: Christ in a Vauxhall Viva, don't mention the polls. You'll look like a complete fuckwit when they change. We've discussed this.

Mr. Ed Miliband: Just look at the polls, Mrs. Speaker. *[brandished Farrow & Ball catalogue]* Tories now ten points behind!

This is Mrs. Thatcher all over again, Mrs. Speaker! She was doing really badly when she began her savage campaign of cuts and privatisations. Well, I tell you this, brerk. This is not the 1980s. Mrs. Thatcher only did so well shortly afterwards because she took us to war, bypassed the unions and had the full backing of Rupert Murdoch. And in THOSE days, let me remind the House, Labour in Opposition was absolutely blooming useless!

Christopher: Fuck it, that's me. I'm retreating to your stupid hippocampus. Don't bump into anything, you total gimpoid, I hate you.

The Prime Minister: Mrs. Speaker, we inherited an economy based on 'state multiculturalism', yet who even knows what I am talking about?

The Deputy Prime Minister (Mr. Nick Clegg): True that. Mrs. Speaker, we have to reduce the deficit. Call it 'debt'. Call it 'intergenerational theft'. Call it 'sclerosis of the Treasury Ballsack'. It's all the same to me. Plurality. Freedom. Choice. That's why I'll be voting YES to AV in May. Then we'll see how far personal reputation can influence politics.

The Secretary of State for Education (Mr. Michael Gove): Mrs. Speaker, may I suavely purchase one of those delightful little plush riot policemen? And may I bring an *[adjusted cummerbund]* urgent matter to the attention of the House? Hon. Members are well aware of my finely tailored, relentless quest to end central-government control of our schools, which is why I am seeking a total of fifty new powers to *[adjusted cloak]* ease these freedoms into a properly guided reality. Could we have a *[adjusted eyebrows]* show of hands?

Mrs. Volunteer Speaker: And the number of heads upon the Beast of Parliament shall be 666! Who's for the Gentleman in the top hat? He's got a lovely face!

[A Show of Hands then was counted at thirty-five favouring the Secretary of State.]

Mrs. Volunteer Speaker: Armageddon, the Final Battle! Dragons! Dragons and snakes with the heads of sharks! Who else wants to buy a souvenir?

[A Show of Hands then was counted at nought.]

Mr. Michael Gove: Thank you, Mrs. Speaker. Credit card OK? Ha ha ha!

The Prime Minister: Right, I've had enough of *[indicated Mrs. Volunteer Speaker]* hairy Mary from the dairy, thank you. Mr. Bailiff, arrest that woman and have her charged with causing a Public Nuisance. While the Opposition flails around trying to work out what we've just done with the vote thing, let me introduce the newest resident at Number 10. *[produced box]* Oh, don't worry, it's not dynamite! It's Larry.

[A Cat then being presented to the House by the Prime Minister. Hon. Members crowding about to catch a glimpse, with much sympathetic murmurings and endearments. Interruptions from the hon. Member for Sheffield Masturbeighton's dog, Twatter.]

The Prime Minister: Yes, we got him from animal rescue. His job is vital, of course. To *[indicated hon. Liberal Democrat Members]* deter the rats.

[Twatter then in sudden and most fierce pursuit of Larry, attacking

the legs of hon. Members. Pandemonium with much screaming, the
Royal Cudgellers then being summoned with urgency.]

Hon. Members: That's not a Labrador, that's a fucking
Staffordshire terrier! Someone run it through with a sword!
Blunkett, you great heaving tit, where did you buy this cunt,
the fucking PUB?

Mr. David Blunkett (Sheffield Masturbeighton): The bloke said
it was kosher! I said it felt a bit small for a Labby, and he said
it was the new miniature kind! You can't ever get him past the
kebab shop!

Mrs. Volunteer Speaker: Let them alone for they be blind leaders
of the blind! And if the blind lead the blind, then all shall tumble into the Ditch of Hell! Pitchforks! Fiery Furnaces! Repent!

[Then entered with great force and decisiveness the Royal Cudgellers,
euthanising Twatter most expeditiously, then calming the Assembled
Company with measured and appropriate physical repression in
the service of Free Speech, arresting Mrs. Pearly Queenie Bunting,
confiscating her trading licence and delivering her unto Psychiatric
Attendants.]

Moment of Democratic Governance.

Number 10 Downing Street

Held upon Dress-Down Friday, the 25th of February 2011

MEMES AND FEEDBACK

[The Prime Minister's Senior Adviser on the Spacehopper]

Inaugural Meeting of 'Cabinet Casual'

[Hon. Members of Cabinet and Senior Advisers, having surrendered all shoes, ties, jackets, telephones and other gadgets at the door, did enter the Cabinet Room to find the table and chairs removed and the space furnished with artificial grass and a number of orange Spacehoppers. The Prime Minister's Senior Adviser welcoming the Assembled Company upon a blue Spacehopper, in demeanour most chillaxed.]

The Secretary of State for Education (Mr. Michael Gove): What ghastly humiliation *[adjusted kaftan]* have you prepared for us this time, 'Steve'?

The Prime Minister's Senior Adviser (Mr. Steve Hilton): That's it, come in. *Wilkommen, bienvenue,* welcome. Make yourselves comfortable.

The Secretary of State for Communities and Local Government (Mr. Eric Pickles): Are you taking the piss, lad? *[brushed crumbs from Hawaiian shirt]* Because if I sit on one of them things either IT'S going to fucking burst, or I am, or both. *[remained standing, consumed pie]*

Mr. Steve Hilton: This is the first of what I hope will be a very productive series of 'Cabinet Casuals'. No shoes, no agenda, no minutes. Just a few guys and *[indicated Home Secretary]* Theresa, hanging out, *[mimed Frisbee-throwing]* gently tossing ideas to one another. Exploring parts of the policy landscape we've maybe only previously seen from the 'HD Policycopter'. *[exchanged fistbumps with Prime Minister]*

The Secretary of State for Environment, Food and Rural Affairs (Mrs. Caroline Spelman): *[entering, in Care Bear pyjamas]* Sorry I'm late. It's been manic. You know Kevin Costner's been on CNN, dressed as Robin Hood? Complaining to the world that we're selling off Sherwood Forest to the Sheriff of Nottingham? Bloody nightmare.

The Chancellor of the Exchequer (Mr. George Osborne): Here's *[mimed malicious Frisbee throw]* an idea. Shut up and do your fucking job. Or we'll find someone else to be Piñata of the Month.

The Prime Minister (Mr. David Cameron): Ho whoa whoa. I'm sensing some scepticism in this room about 'Cabinet Casual'. This is unacceptable. We discussed the initiative quite thoroughly the other day. The need for a top-down, bottom-up, vertically integrated 'John Lewis' approach to, to . . .

Mr. Steve Hilton: To everything, exactly. This is a chance for us to come together, build a narrative. Share that narrative.

Own that narrative. George, chill the fuck out, man. Pull up a Spacehopper.

[The Chancellor of the Exchequer seizing a Spacehopper with much impatience, then producing a flick knife, then most furiously stabbing the Spacehopper into emphatic deflation.]

Mr. George Osborne: Here's! My! Narrative! Steve! Fuck! You! And! Your! Stupid! Fucking! Californian! Reach-around! Bullshit! *[cast aside husk of Spacehopper]* I'm off. Not that it's YOUR problem, of course, but I've got the Fucking Economy parked outside on a double yellow. Enjoy your gently bobbing little circle jerk. I have a delegation of librarians to torment.

[The Chancellor of the Exchequer then quitting the Cabinet Room, puncturing the Spacehopper beneath the Secretary of State for Defence, pushing the Secretary of State for International Development from his, and cackling most heartily. The Prime Minister's Senior Adviser then signalling to the Assembled Company to ignore these Disruptions and gather round. Hon. Members of Cabinet then slowly converging in pneumatic increments.]

The Prime Minister: Don't take any notice of Woggy. Been in a strop for two days. Ireland's getting on his wick. He feels very badly let down by their economic failure, actually.

The Foreign Secretary (Mr. William Hague): Sod 'em and begorrah!

The Secretary of State for Health (Mr. Andrew Lansley): I'll tell you what makes me bloody cross, if we're talking casually about narratives, Steve. People say I'm 'masterminding' the destruction of the NHS. Yet they also accuse me of being stupid. I can't be both, can I? Mastermind and stupid. Can I?

The Home Secretary (Ms. Theresa May): I must say *[oscillating]*, I like this Spacehopper more than I'd expected.

Mr. Steve Hilton: *[clapping]* Great, great. I wonder if we could now transition from 'relaxed' to 'relaxed and focused'? We've got a lot of shit ahead of us this year. We need to be prepared. We need to COMMUNICATE our principles, OK? We need to DEFEND these principles. Show people we BELIEVE in ourselves. Then we need to FORCE our principles onto the fucking Statute Book. This process is called GOVERNMENT.

Assembled Company: *[nodding, bobbing, wobbling]*

Mr. Steve Hilton: I was being ironic.

Assembled Company: *[retrofitted ironic laughter]*

Mr. Steve Hilton: Two words: 'short' and 'listen'.

The Deputy Prime Minister (Mr. Nick Clegg): *[to the Prime Minister]* Two words: 'cock' and 'gobbler'.

The Prime Minister: Shut up.

The Deputy Prime Minister: Two words: 'bollock-faced' and . . .

The Prime Minister: Just be quiet, Nick. Very irritating. This is important. Steve got me elected. Not you, Nick. Not fucking you. Me. Now grow up.

[The Deputy Prime Minister then bouncing firmly and uncertainly away from the Prime Minister, most furious of countenance.]

Mr. Steve Hilton: So, communicating effectively. Top line: keep it short. 'Communication' has five syllables. *[swivelled on Spacehopper]* 'Hypnotise' has three. You want to reduce workers' rights? Don't communicate. Hypnotise. Just dangle Bob Fucking Crow in front of them and start counting backwards from 1978. Keep it SHORT. No more than twenty-one words in a sentence. If you can't read it through without drawing breath, fuck it, it's shit.

Mr. Eric Pickles: *[inaudible, consumed baked bean and cheese melt]* . . . more than *[inaudible, consumed pickled egg]* fucking lucky, son!

Mr. Steve Hilton: My very point, Eric, you incorrigible, irrepressible fucking blue whale. Short is better than fat. Motto: If it doesn't fit on Twitter, cram it up your shitter. Our mission, ladies and gents: nudge the narrative of this country's future into line with our . . .

The Secretary of State for Culture, Olympics, Media and Sport (Mr. Jeremy Hunt): Steve, sorry to interrupt, but we did all this 'nudge' stuff last year. Shouldn't we be moving on? I'm not sure how much more 'behavioural prompting' I can take, frankly.

Mr. Steve Hilton: Excellent. Frankness is a powerful, powerful spanner in the human toolbox. I admire your independence, Jeremy, I do. Ladies and gents, did you know that Jeremy's the only Cabinet Member NOT coming to the Thinking Spa next week?

Mr. Jeremy Hunt: What Thinking Spa? I knew nothing about this. Of COURSE I'm coming. I'm DOWN. Ink me in. I must have got my diaries . . .

Mr. Steve Hilton: There IS no Thinking Spa, you fucking cheese straw. So. Nudge, yes. Keep it short. But, people, if we're going to *[mimed 'tug of war']* pull the country with us, we need to LISTEN.

The Jazz Chancellor (Mr. Kenneth Clarke): *[awakening]* Wap

bap fiddly biddly widdly tsh-tsh ka-dap bap bapsolutely, daddio. It's only blap bap by wabbeda wabbeda listening to cats
that you dig what those cats wabbeda wabbeda want.

Mr. Steve Hilton: Ken, who gives a shit what your manky old cats
want? I'm saying we need to be active listeners. Not passive listeners. We need to fucking 'listen' the public into submission.

Mr. Kenneth Clarke: Tsh-tsh. What the fuggeda fuggeda huggery
buggery are you jiving on about? It hup bup bap drap ka-blap
doesn't make any psst thrap bop de-bip bop huggeda muggeda
wubbeda habbeda SENSE.

Mr. Steve Hilton: OK. Let's pause. Andy, you're worried you'll
be seen as some *[inviting sceptical laughter]* dim, terrified stooge
charged with selling the most unpopular Government proposal
since the Poll Tax.

Assembled Company: *[sympathetic murmurings]*

Mr. Steve Hilton: So let's, yes, let's 'interrogate that notion'. Let's
splay that notion wide open and give it a 'policyoscopy'. Andy,
why don't you and I jam this one through?

Mr. Kenneth Clarke: *[asleep]* Psh tsh wabbeda hurdle glap,
daddio.

Mr. Andrew Lansley: Oh God, not again. Not again, Steve.

Mr. Steve Hilton: I'll be The Public. You can be the Secretary
of State for Health. For now. This *[handed a cricket bat to the
Secretary of State for Health]* is your point, OK? The point you're
trying to get across. Right. Explain the NHS masterplan to me.
I'll be the listening public.

*[The Secretary of State for Health then gingerly taking the cricket bat,
then adopting a stance most uncertain.]*

Mr. Andrew Lansley: Ladies and gentlemen, I yield to no man, or woman, in my admiration for the National Health Service . . .

Mr. Steve Hilton: When are you going to do my fucking cataracts? I'm eighty-three next month!

Mr. Andrew Lansley: Ah, yes. But. The sooner we move the NHS into the twenty-first century, the sooner we can do your cataracts. Look, I love the NHS too. But it was founded a very, very long time ago. Hard to believe that there were still ration books then, and smog, and only one channel on the BBC even if you had a television set . . .

Mr. Steve Hilton: I can't fucking 'look', can I? I can't fucking SEE! I've got CATARACTS!

Mr. Andrew Lansley: The . . . ah ha. So, ladies and gentlemen, we stand at a crossroads. Behind us *[indicated 'behind']*, the old NHS with Hattie Jacques as Matron and no problems with car parking. To the *[indicated]* left and right . . .

Mr. Steve Hilton: You think we don't know what you're up to? Marketisation, you gulping charlatan. Take that gormless fucking look off your face. I'm not the old bloke with cataracts now, I'm a young, savvy nurse.

Mr. Andrew Lansley: Ah, I yield to no one in my ha ha twinkly admiration for nurses . . .

Mr. Steve Hilton: I'm a male nurse. And I can tell you that if the private sector get their hands on my beloved NHS, the poor, who are actually really, really ill, will be in mixed wards with plaster falling from the ceiling and mouse shit everywhere. Meanwhile, the rich, who just have a slight headache or want a mole removed, get armed guards, a Jamie Oliver tasting menu and *[indicating the Secretary of State's kimono]* monogrammed fucking kimonos . . .

Mr. Andrew Lansley: *[akimbo in kimono]* Now wait a minute. You're not listening to me. I am telling you that none of this is going to happen . . .

Mr. Steve Hilton: And let's pause it there. Everyone, how did Andy do?

Ms. Theresa May: Well, if I'm being honest I thought he seemed unconvincing, even when his kimono came undone.

The Deputy Prime Minister: Wanker. You're all wankers. Especially *[indicated Prime Minister]* him.

The Prime Minister: Oh, I know! Steve, Steve! I know. He didn't do anything with his point. The cricket bat. He just sort of twiddled it.

Mr. Steve Hilton: Dave's bang on the money, as usual. Andy made no attempt to get his point across. Here, Andy. Pass me the cricket bat.

Mr. Andrew Lansley: No. Because I know what's going to happen.

Mr. Steve Hilton: But we DON'T know what's going to happen, do we? That's the nature of political *[indicated 'everything']* shit. One minute you're Secretary of State for Health . . . *[accepted cricket bat]* Now. Andy. You be The Public and I'll be the Secretary of State. OK?

Mr. Andrew Lansley: You're going to hit me with that cricket bat. Don't think I don't know. I'm not an idiot.

Mr. Steve Hilton: And let's begin. Ladies and gentlemen, as Health Secretary I have to tell you a hard truth. If we are to preserve the NHS as a public service, free at the point of delivery, we must fix it. Urgently. We must repair it. And repurpose it.

Mr. Andrew Lansley: Bah, bollocks! You just want to break it up and sell it off! I'm a fifty-eight-year-old heart surgeon, by the way. Called, er, Bond. James Bond. Why don't you tell us the truth, Secretary of State?

Mr. Steve Hilton: I hear you, Mr. Bond. I understand your scepticism. You were lied to by Labour for years. This Government is more honest, more responsive. We listen. We are listening to you now. So what we're going to do, actually, is park our NHS reforms for now.

Mr. Andrew Lansley: Wow, are we? I mean, are you?

Mr. Steve Hilton: Oh yes. We need to get this right. So we'll park these reforms for a month or two, listening all the time, then come back to you. The opinion polls might be better then, and we can have another go. If they're not, we'll keep listening until they are. So from this moment on, Mr. Bond, I promise you, we're listening. Listening hard. From now until, say, June at least.

Mr. Andrew Lansley: Brilliant, so does that . . .

Mr. Steve Hilton: Ah ah. You can't ask me any questions until then because I am listening. I can't listen and answer your stupid fucking questions at the same time, can I?

Mr. Andrew Lansley: But that . . .

Moment of Reverse Sweep.

House of Commons

Held upon the Eve of Swapsie Fainites,
the 15th of March 2011

PRAYERS AND MORPHIC RESONANCE

[The Speaker's Chair Left Blank]

Prime Minister's Speaking Time

[Hon. Members having taken their seats, wriggling one against another in anticipation, Mr. Speaker entered the House, nodding most gravely to the Officers of the House, conferring upon hon. Members a look of profound disdain, then taking his seat upon the Booster Seat within the Chair, whereupon he discovered Sellotaped to the Dispatch Box a large Photoshopped image of Mrs. Sally Bercow in pornographic attitude.]

Hon. Lady Members: Men are wankers! Down with Post-Feminism! This is shameful shit! I would!

Hon. Gentlemen Members: Wanker! Pornography exploits men too, you know, now I'm wondering if she has a shaved pussy! I would!

Mr. Speaker: What is the meaning of this . . . this outrage? Who

248

is responsible? I demand to know. I am the flipping Speaker and I compel hon. Members to respect and obey me!

Hon. Members: *[diverse insolences with physical suggestiveness]*

Mr. Speaker: You, Sir. The hon. Member for Clungepool & The Wrekins. I notice you, Sir, cannot make eye contact. Perhaps if you spent more time in this Chamber and less time 'bunking off' with your mates, you would have a better grasp *[indicated pornographic image]* of the buttocks. I mean, Affairs of State.

Mr. Mark Pritchard (Clungepool & The Wrekins): Mr. Speaker, I object in the strongest possible terms. YOU, not I, have been absent from the Chamber. I have been here for at least half an hour looking at pornographic pictures of your wife. There has been a lively debate on the subject. Granted, I may have left the Chamber to visit the Gentlemen's WC for five minutes, but where have YOU been, Mr. Speaker? Discussing political philosophy with Daniel Fucking Barenboim, perhaps.

Hon. Members: Fight! Nude Wrestling Match! Blind Man's Buff! Nude Blind Wrestling Match! Spot the Blind Dog! Pin the Tail on the Nude Blind Man! Nude Jousting on Big Blind Dogs! Sausagey Sausage!

Mr. Speaker: Order, I say. I will not put up with this most hideous and vulgar affront to my dignity.

Mr. Mark Pritchard: *[held aloft a copy of the* Evening Standard*]* Mr. Speaker, hon. Members now have a pretty accurate account of the current state, and extent, of your dignity. We have all read this profile of Mrs. Sally Bercow, in which she says:

> **I could never have imagined how sexually exciting it is to lie naked in our bed, in our beautiful apartment above the Houses of Parliament, waiting for Big Ben – that's my nickname for John's**

todger – to strike. Since he became Speaker we've both been propositioned endlessly. I'm more bangable, he's more bangable, we've both been going at it hammer and tongs. Sometimes he comes into the bedroom wearing just his Speaker's robes and a pair of socks, barking 'Order, order!' in a gruff, sexy way . . .

Hon. Members: *[laughter, distracted visualisation, self-awareness]*
Mr. Speaker: Order, order!
Hon. Members: Ooh, fuck me! Fuck me, Mr. Speaker! Ha ha ha!
Mr. Speaker: *[standing on Booster Seat]* This is an absolute bloody disgrace! I command the entire House to give way on this matter! Give way, I say!
Mr. Mark Pritchard: We will not give way. You are all over the papers with your robes and your socks and your penis. It is preposterous. You're not fucking sexy, Mr. Speaker!
Hon. Members: You're not fucking sexy, Mr. Speaker!

[The hon. Member for Bolsover Oneside then producing his penis and, with it, indicating Mr. Speaker.]

Hon. Members: Cock visible!
Mr. Speaker: Order. Order. Er, hello? Excuse me? Yes, I'm talking to YOU. How dare you! The hon. Gentleman will withdraw that cock at once. It's . . . and pointing at me, Sir? Oh, this is intolerable. Bailiff, the Bloody Mary!
Mr. Dennis Skinner (Bolsover Oneside): I ent doon owt. It just sort of slipped art. *[inaudible, possibly 'Fook you, an your bloody prefect's aircoot. You look like a fooking acorn, you silly coont']*

[The Bailiff of the House called outwith for the Sergeant-at-Arms to fetch the Chest of Jacobean Persuasions. The Chest having been

brought inwith was duly opened. The Bailiff then presenting the Bloody Mary to the House, Mr. Speaker descending to the Floor and with great solemnity inspecting it. Hon. Members of the Cabinet then entering the Chamber and taking their seats upon the Government Benches, the Prime Minister peremptorily removing the Booster Seat from the Chair, then taking his place upon it.]

The Prime Minister (Mr. David Cameron): Right. Enough of this nonsense. Skinner, put your old man away. Nobody's given it a second glance since 1986. Bailiff, have the Chest removed. Give Skinner one in the bollocks with the Mace if he does it again. Bercow, take your seat by the Dispatch Box.

Mr. Speaker: What in the name of blithering balls is going on here, Prime Minister?

The Prime Minister: *[most hurriedly]* Upon the Eve of Swapsie Fainites I do hereby claim the Speaker's Chair and call Swapsies.

Mr. Speaker: Fainites! Fainites!

The Clerk of the House: Oyez, oyez. The hon. Gentleman was tardy with his Fainites. Under the provisions of Swapsie Fainites, the appellant may cause Swapsies to occur without hindrance, unless Fainites be called before Swapsies. This not being the case, the Swapsie must stand.

[Mr. Speaker then trudging most angrily to the Prime Minister's seat and sitting down to much jeering, the Chancellor of the Exchequer flicking him with a ruler.]

Mr. Swapsied Speaker (Mr. David Cameron): *[addressing mobile telephone]* Steve, yeah, I'm in. Catch you later. Defo. Sweet. *[terminated call, addressed Government Benches]* We've got a lot of shit to get through today. We need to be prepared. We need to COMMUNICATE our principles, OK? We need to DEFEND these principles. Show people we BELIEVE in ourselves. Then we need to FORCE our principles onto the fucking Statute Book. This process is called GOVERNMENT.

Hon. Members: Scandalous! This is exactly how Nazi Germany started! This is exactly how *X-Factor* started!

Mr. Swapsied Speaker: Silence in the Chamber! Clerk, please take up the Mace and present it with great force to any hon. Member who interrupts me. I am feeling imperious and a little bit sexy today. *[indicated pornographic image]* And please remove that stupid bloody picture of an octopus swallowing a French loaf or whatever . . . oh, I see. Ha ha ha.

The Swapsied Prime Minister (Mr. John Bercow): That is no octopus, that is an image of bizarre sexual congress Photoshopped to accommodate the face of my lady wife! Harumph!

Mr. Swapsied Speaker: Order, I would remind the Swapsied Prime Minister that I am the Swapsied Speaker for this Sitting of the House, and ask him most respectfully to shut his fucking cakehole. Oh, I'm sure that *[indicated Opposition Benches]* you bags of themeless arsecack have been VERY happy to have the Oompah *[indicated the Swapsied Prime Minister]* Loompah here as Speaker for this initial period of actually genuinely fantastic Coalition Government. Taking Urgent Questions from backbenchers? Encouraging scrutiny? Well, let me tell certain hon. Members that they are NOT 'all in this together'. The House of Commons is NOT a coalition. It is a Conservative-controlled national authority.

The Deputy Prime Minister (Mr. Nick Clegg): That's right,

David. With, I would remind all hon. Liberal Democrat Members, a VITAL centre-left counterweight at its heart. Now, you can call it . . .

Mr. Swapsied Speaker: Oh shit off, Nick, you tragic clown. Ouch. Sorry, I didn't mean to say that out loud. I apologise. My hon. Friend is of course welcome to brief the *Guardian* or indeed anyone else about how his principled objections to a privatised NHS have 'paused' the Health Bill, if that's what keeps his Party Members happy. But I can assure him that the only vital centre-left counterweight at the heart of THIS Government is *[indicated trousers]* in my tented boxer shorts, dudes!

The Chancellor of the Exchequer (Mr. George Osborne): On a Point of Order though, Mr. Speaker: are Lib Dems ever really happy? Every single one I've met looks like they've just been given some very bad news by their fucking oncologist. *[cackled]*

Mr. Ed Miliband (Doncaster Awkwood): Mr. Swapsied Speaker, after the most vicious Budget since King William's Window Tax of 1696, does the . . .

Mr. Swapsied Speaker: Yeah, I'm going to have to stop you there, Lanky Kong. My job as Swapsied Speaker is to ensure this House 'sticks up' for the ancient right of Free Speech, literally. In accordance therefore with a recently rediscovered Parliamentary By-Law, any hon. Member wishing to address the Chamber must be in possession of this, *[produced antique staff, handed it to the Chancellor of the Exchequer]* the Venerated Stick of Stoke.

Mr. George Osborne: Mr. Swapsied Speaker, I accept this Stick of Stoke and the power it confers *[hit Swapsied Prime Minister with*

Stick]. And now I'd like to take this opportunity to answer those who have criticised my Budget.

[The Chancellor of the Exchequer then crossing the Chamber, laying about Opposition Members with the Stick of Stoke. Who, protesting most vociferously, were cautioned by the Clerk of the House to remain silent or face further Sanction via the Mace.]

Mr. George Osborne: Mr. Swapsied Speaker, certain mincing bedshitters have accused my – correction, this – Government of callousness. Callousness! *[punched Chief Secretary to the Treasury]* Our emphasis on 'squeezed middles' and off-the-record remarks about 'Chav Britain'. As though we have nothing but contempt for the poor. Fuck! *[smote Dispatch Box with Stick]* Why then are we striving so earnestly to help POOR motorists, POOR taxpayers, POOR housebuyers? I for one commend today's editorial in Mr. Murdoch's *Sun* newspaper, which says:

By George, we think he's got it! After months of campaigning by the *Sun* for a cut in fuel duty, Mr. Osborne has delivered. It is a victory for common sense. A victory for motoring. That's why 18-year-old Tanya is sprawled across this truck bonnet, her young body contorted in sexual palsy. It's time to say:

NO to the enemies of enterprise and harmless nudity.
NO to the forces of stagnation, especially the BBC.
NO to AV, which makes THREE things to say NO to.

[Hon. Members in favour of the Alternative Vote system then protesting silently, in trepidation of the Stick of Stoke and the Mace, with complex mimes upon the theme of Electoral Reform.]

Mr. Swapsied Speaker: Order. Questions to the Swapsied Prime Minister!

The Foreign Secretary (Mr. William Hague): Mr. Swapsied Speaker, does the Swapsied Prime Minister agree that the Government's policy on Libya is just fucking brilliant? Measured, and increasing, military intervention will have the tyrant Gaddafi out very quickly, I am sure. So, let's have less scepticism. More 'smart' bombing. Less politically motivated concern for civilian casualties. More unqualified support for those irregular rebel forces we see in the newspapers relaxing during cigarette breaks in the oilfields.

Hon. Members: *[mimed 'wanker']*

The Swapsied Prime Minister: Right, well, OK, as we're playing some silly game and a question has been asked of me, allow me to explain why I think a ceasefire is the priority here. Surely . . .

Mr. Swapsied Speaker: Order. With respect, shut your wobbling fucking gob. The Stick is with the Foreign Secretary.

Mr. William Hague: Yes, and while I'm up can I confirm that, whatever's being whispered in the private bars of Westminster and the sex clubs of Soho, I have definitely NOT 'lost my mojo'. Watch this.

[The Foreign Secretary then throwing the Stick to the Secretary of State for Defence, then removing his trousers and underpants, then taking to the Floor of the House, performing in his head the 'Theme from Shaft' by Mr. Isaac Hayes, murmuring only those lyrics subject to immediate mental recall, with much pelvic melisma.]

The Hon. Member for Sheffield Masturbeighton's Guide Dog Naomi: Sausages!

Mr. David Blunkett (Sheffield Masturbeighton): Quiet, girl, or they'll do you. It sounds like Hague's got his pants off again. We could be here all fucking night.

Mr. William Hague: Shaft!

The Secretary of State for Defence (Mr. Liam Fox): *[indicating Stick]* Oh, at fucking last I get to say something, do I?

Mr. Swapsied Speaker: Order, shut up!

The Swapsied Prime Minister: With respect, the hon. Gentleman has the Stick of Stoke. It is perfectly . . .

[Intervention with Mace. The House in Adjournment for ten minutes to accommodate the removal by Tarpaulin of the Swapsied Prime Minister, the continuation of the Foreign Secretary's interpretative dance, and the seizing of the Stick by Mr. Swapsied Speaker.]

Mr. Swapsied Speaker: Order. As I seem to be in possession of both the Chair and the Stick, I'd like to make a direct appeal to everyone who's thinking about starting their own business. Now is the time to do it. This month sees the launch of StartUp Britain.

Mr. William Hague: Shaft!

Naomi: Sausages!

Mr. Swapsied Speaker: Yes, if you've wanted to start your own business for absolutely yonks, or if you're working for a big firm but know you could do a better job on your own, or even if you're about to be made redundant because of the very necessary deficit reductions and can't bear the idea of sponging off the State like some fucking human leech, StartUp Britain is for you.

Mr. Dennis Skinner: Pointer Order or someowt. This Foreign so-called Secretary is a bloody laffenstock. Daft bugger's got a face like a mahoganised cat's ARSE!

The Secretary of State for Education (Mr. Michael Gove): *[coughed; inaudible, possibly 'Just to confirm we're replacing EMA at £500 million a year with something more discretionary and suave for £180 million which will help more poor pupils as there will be more OF them'; coughed; adjusted spectacles]*

Mr. William Hague: Shaft! You damn right!

Naomi: Sausages! Sausages! Woof! Woof!

Mr. Swapsied Speaker: StartUp Britain. I think you'll agree it sounds slightly more substantial than 'Wake-Up Britain' or whatever it was that *[regarded the Deputy Prime Minister]* died on its arse last month.

The Deputy Prime Minister: Alarm Clock Britain. *[inaudible, possibly 'You total shit, you'll be smirking on the other side of your fucking frankfurter face after the AV referendum']*

Mr. John Hemming (Birmingham Hardly): Mr. Swapsied Speaker, I would like to back up Nick's statement about Lib Dems being at the heart of Government, with particular reference to myself. I am a Lib Dem MP, as several of you may know, very much NOT at the heart of Government, ha ha! However, I wondered if I might get a couple of lines in the papers by being brave enough to use Parliamentary Privilege to name famous people cited in superinjunctions? Certain publications are keen for someone like me to stand here with a straight, fat, pompous, oily face and announce that Sir Fred Goodwin, Ryan Giggs, Rolf Harris, Richard Hammond, Simon Cowell, oh, and I see my mistake here – not in possession of the Stick, fuck.

[The Bailiff then smiting the hon. Member for Birmingham Hardly most calamitously in the guts, the Stick of Stoke rebounding with much force, then calling for the Tarpaulin.]

Mr. Swapsied Speaker: Yes, so. StartUp Britain. Our business is your business, particularly if your start-up is in either the health or education sectors. We're even bringing enterprise zones back, so if you suddenly discover you live in one, let's go!

Mr. William Hague: John Shaft!

Naomi: Sausages!

[The Chancellor of the Exchequer then having approached the Chair from behind did snatch the Stick from Mr. Swapsied Speaker, brandishing it before the Dispatch Box.]

Mr. George Osborne: Right, you motherfuckers! Bailiff, stand down. I'll keep order now. The world, the nation, the House of Commons, the *[regarded Mr. Swapsied Speaker]* party are in the mood for strong, cruel leadership. I demand silence!

Naomi: Sausages! Sausages! Sausages!

Mr. William Hague: He's a complicated man that no one understands . . .

Moment of Dilemma.

Olympic Delivery Authority

A Meeting held in the Ozymandias Suite,
New Stratford, upon the 24th of March 2011
PRAYERS AND THE SACRIFICIAL
SLAYING OF A BULL
[Lord Coe in the Uncomfortable Chair]

An Address by the Mayor of London

Mr. Boris Johnson: *Feminae et viri. In Roma dicebatur 'obliti privatorum, publica curate'. Nulla recognitio inter vos. Optime. Re vera obliviscite si infixi meum* 'todger up the nanny'. *Ego Boris, Praefectus Londonii sum, observantiam exigo. Ecce Bojo! Ho ho ho!*

Authority Representatives: Jesus in the One and Nines, why is that bumbling tosser talking in fucking LATIN? What a wanker. It's so he can take the piss, say what he thinks, present himself as a much cleverer version of David Cameron. The only Latin I remember is Edmundo Ros, and to be honest even then it might have been Santana.

Mr. Boris Johnson: *Roges, cur iste ineptus caudex loquetur in lingua* *scelesta Latino, quod masturbator! Respondo — ut melius celarem meam ambitionem esse Princeps Britanniae, quod nemo me intelleget. Caudices!* Twatwits! Bumclangers! *Adeo sperno vulgum et eorum obesitatem, maculas, horrendos vestes cum signis et aliis scriptis. Exempli gratia,* 'Messi' *aut* 'Fatface'. *Me obstupet. Certe, sperno vulgum. Vulgum autem amare debeo. Stultis persuadere debeo ut mihi faveant anno proximo. Optio horribilis est.* Ken Bastard Livingstone *inaugurans Ludos Olympicos? Recordans* Norman Fucking Wisdom, *vestitus paululum parvo pretio? Hercle, procul absit!*

Authority Representatives: What a hefty, shuddering ball valve. What's he saying about Livingstone? Not sure, but I don't think it's very complimentary. He can bloody well talk, he's got a face like a massive fucking unbaked loaf. Still, he definitely has the Nutty Catholic vote sewn up. But why . . . why is he inside a Cadbury's Creme Egg costume?

Mr. Boris Johnson: *Roges autem, cur Praefectus Londonii vestitus in ingento Cadbury's Creme Egg habito? Ho ho, ea interrogatio iusta est. Illum ovum foris gerere debeo usque ad finem Ludorum Olympicum, propter pactum Sponsoris Officialis Chocolatis. Saluto ludos in eo ovo. Ludi vivant! Ovum vivat! Londinium vivat!*

Authority Representatives: Oh God, suppose he's gone completely fucking mad? Maybe he thinks he's becoming some sort of cult figure. Well, he's very nearly right.

Mr. Boris Johnson: *Sed feminae virique, abhinc MMVIII, Londonium factum melius est. Paulum maior est, carius in habitationem sed etiam commodissimum cum, et in, se. Omnibusibus dearticulatibus. Duis rotis* 'Be a Barclays Banker Like Boris' *curri. Magis veniet. Volo aedificare insulam artificiosam in Tamese. Non* *solum ad festivos togatos cum amicis, sed etiam ad edificationem Londoniorum. Posse aedificemus fanum animalem, aut museum. Studeo togatis festivis. Pareo insignis in toga!*

Authority Representatives: Bloody hell, '*omnibusibus de-articulatibus*'? I know what's going on here, he's listing his achievements as Mayor. Got rid of bendy buses, introduced Boris Bikes and . . . well, that's it really. What next, toga parties for his fucking mates on an artificial island in the Thames? Is that what he's saying? Fuck knows, fancy a pint? *Nunc est bibendum*, ha ha ha! Yeah, *bendibusibus*, ha ha ha!

Mr. Boris Johnson: *Ludi Olympici sunt opportunitas aurea Londonii ad quatendum mammas suas in fenestra tabernae mundis. Nobis est fructendas mammis aureis. Magnopere honoro illum, Prime Minister, certe – etiam debeo monere illum suam condicionem ad* 'cap housing benefits' *posse causare* 'Kosovo-style social cleansing'. *Mr. Cameron educatus esset in Etona, ego quoque, sed eheu habet tantum potestatem ingeniosum quantum cancer pancreaticus. Iste* sillybollocks *est. Est quoque* massive spam dildo . . .

Authority Representatives: I wonder what 'spam dildo' is Latin for? I got the first bit, about London jiggling its golden tits in the window of the world, I went to Charterhouse. Are we getting in Kosovan cleaners now? Brilliant, their builders were really bloody cheap during Phase One construction. Yeah, three cheers for de-unionised labourers, Chinese dissidents and unpaid interns!

Mr. Boris Johnson: . . . *sed possum pendere ex sui favente ad meam Candidaturam Praefacturam. Scit si non teneam victoriam, liberaturus sum ad sequendas alias opportunitates. Sto pro portis Troia*

261

HQ, exigens eum facere proelium pro officio Conservative Party Leader. *Superam Hector/*Fucking Cameron the dim clacking little twerp *deinde trahere corpum suum circum Parliament Square a tergo mea Boris Bike. Ha ha ha!*

Authority Representatives: He really doesn't like Cameron much, does he? I heard that 'something happened' at Eton. Well, I'm sure it was perfectly proper, they have a very level playing field there.

Mr. Boris Johnson: *Feminae virique, valde* fucking *calidus est in hoc ovo. Debeo nunc ire. Bene facto in Olympicos. Certus sum futuros esse pars legaciae in officio Praefacti Londonii. Nisi significabunt initium viae longae ad 'Numero X Downing Street'! Fortuna tibi sit, vale!* Cheers!

Moment of Exit.

House of Commons
Held upon the Eve of the Ideological Bifurcation,
the 20th of April 2011
PRAYERS AND FLOURISHES
[Mr. Speaker upon the Booster Seat within the Chair]

In the Merry Old Land of Nod

Mr. Speaker: Order, order. I would like to make a short announcement.

Hon. Members: Wanker! Is the announcement that you're a short wanker? Have you got the R2-D2 gig in that new *Star Wars* musical?

Mr. Speaker: Oh God, what's the point? I was GOING to say that this month is a very special one for the nation. We have a Royal Wedding to look forward to, come on. Let's put aside our differences and rejoice. I'm sure we all wish the happy couple a comfortable and adequately funded life together.

Hon. Members: God save the Prince! Rule Britannia! I couldn't care LESS about the fucking Royal Wedding, so I bought an I Couldn't Care Less About the Royal Wedding commemorative mug! Hypocrite, you're just pissed off you didn't get an invite!

Brideshead! Roundhead! Fat turd! Smug prick! Republicant!

Mr. Speaker: Also, I am constitutionally obliged to announce – with heavy heart, it has to be said – that hon. Members are now allowed to use their mobile phones for *[consulted note]* 'bread, skimmed milk, butternut squash (not too big this time), baby oil, gin'. Oh, wait. Apologies, *[consulted correct note]* 'micro-blogging and social networking'.

Mr. Aeneas Upmother-Brown (Weston-super-Cilious): Mr. Speaker. Firstly, will the Prime Minister list his engagements for today? Secondly, will he confirm the Government's exciting new plans to measure the Happiness of the Nation? And thirdly, may I offer my services as a very upbeat kind of straight white guy, late fifties/early sixties, wife's family owns most of Buckinghamshire, totally committed to making Consensus Democracy work?

Hon. Members: Wanker! Bum fountain! Fucktrope!

Mr. Aeneas Upmother-Brown: *[consulted Twitter account]* I say. Well, I never. Bingo. I've actually BEEN Minister for 'Tourism, Architecture and the Small Business Helpline' since June of last year. That would explain all the paperwork and so on. Marvellous. Well, in that case I can absolutely assure the Prime Minister of my undivided . . .

The Prime Minister (Mr. David Cameron): Mr. Speaker, I thank my hon. Friend for his good wishes and his diligence, whoever the fuck he is. This morning I had meetings with ministerial colleagues and others. Blah blah, loads of bloody calls about Arab shit, I've got Sam niggling in my ear about getting tickets from Stiffy for the Bahrain Formula 1, standing around at Number 10 greeting sodding pensioners smelling of mints and

264

piss, nurses, arms manufacturers – honestly, it never stops. Have you any bloody idea what it's like, having to listen to people for hours on end, frowning and nodding? It's exhausting.

Hon. Members: Wanker! Vodaphone! Top Shop!

Mr. Speaker: Order, order. There is absolutely no point in hon. Members simply shouting out trade names . . .

The Clerk of the House: Yo ho, Mr. Speaker. I believe it is a reference to a campaign by UK Uncut to highlight aspects of tax management in the context of the deficit reduction, yo ho.

Mr. Speaker: Order. Let me tell the House that I will not tolerate anti-Semitism in any form, either actual or non-actual. Prime Minister, pray continue.

The Prime Minister: Mr. Speaker, may I correct the impression that there is to be some sort of Happiness Index set up by this Government to measure well-being? I cannot stress firmly enough that this Government doesn't give a flying toss if you're smiling or not. The index will measure people's ability to *[executed flourish]* 'flourish', Mr. Speaker. We need to find those people who are depressed, perhaps, disabled, whatever. Encourage them to flourish, if necessary by means-testing their benefits. Flourishment is nourishment. For the unhappy. For the economy. For Britain.

Hon. Members: *[unhappiness, depression, discreet flourishment]*

The Prime Minister: And talking of 'unhappy', Mr. Speaker, I notice my hon. Friend the Deputy Prime Minister is looking very glum. Perhaps he has seen the latest predictions for the AV Referendum. It must be *[pelvic thrust]* HARD knowing you sacrificed so much for some footling, semi-skimmed electoral reform that nobody's interested in because your political reputation is resting on it and they'd rather see you *[rotated pelvis]* squirm than vote AV, which is why they're sticking with winners like me and *[pelvic thrust]* FIRST *[pelvic thrust]* PAST *[pelvic thrust]* THE *[pelvic thrust]* POST!

Hon. Members: *[attempted pelvic-thrusting and rotation, some dizziness and falling over]*

The Deputy Prime Minister (Mr. Nick Clegg): Mr. Speaker, it is up to the People of Britain on May 5 to decide what kind of voting system they want. For, really, what is the Alternative Vote an alternative TO? Call it the status quo. Call it stifling sectarianism. Call it *[indicated the Prime Minister]* a squirting cock of treachery and betrayal. Well, Mr. Speaker, maybe there IS an alternative. No coalition lasts for ever.

Hon. Members: *[handbags, bumbags, love handles, secret puddings]*

The Prime Minister: Mr. Speaker, the hon. Gentleman may sulk as ostentatiously as he likes. His face looks like a toddler's sketch of sadness. I say to him, Mr. Speaker: diddums. Boo hoo, twat off, nobody needs you now, you're fucking box-office poison.

Hon. Members: Turn that frown upside down! Yeah, turn that pout inside out! Yeah, shove that moue up your fucking FLUE.

Mr. Oliver Letwin (Midsomer Boxset): Mr. Speaker, might I respectfully offer to my hon. Friends the suggestion that these slight, these very slight differences of approach might better be aired at my next Policy Pop-In? I have . . .

[The Chancellor of the Exchequer then performing a clawhold upon the hon. Member for Midsomer Boxset.]

The Chancellor of the Exchequer (Mr. George Osborne): Mr. Speaker, might I respectfully offer to my hon. Dickhead the suggestion that everyone just shuts their clacking cockshafts until after the Elections and the Referendum? The Prime Minister, Deputy Prime Minister and my hon. Friend here *[performed inverted facelock upon the Chief Secretary to the Treasury]* are due to meet tomorrow anyway, are we not? Ha ha ha!

Mr. Ed Miliband (Doncaster Awkwood): Oho, aha, Mr. Speaker! Is this the famous 'Quad' the papers are all talking about? Brerk? The Coalition's so-called 'inner circle'?

[The hon. Member for Doncaster Awkwood's Imaginary Friend Christopher then returning to cognisance with much haste from the hon. Member's hippocampus.]

Mr. Ed Miliband: Because, Mr. Speaker, brerk, first of all, a quad cannot be circular. That is basic geometry. And if we cannot trust the Government on basic geometry, what can we trust them on? It is a scandal, Mr. Speaker, and one which . . . I'm not going to tell them, Christopher, be quiet, I'm trying to make a point here.

Christopher (Mr. Miliband's Imaginary Friend): Shut up! Just shut your stupid mouth! Oh, that's right, you have to breathe through it because of your stupid fucking deviated septum. Don't make a joke about the Quad. Don't mention your operation. Be quiet. Because your personal rating goes down a percentage point for every ten seconds you remain visible, you total wankblanket.

Mr. George Osborne: Mr. Speaker, may I offer my best wishes to the hon. Gentleman for his forthcoming operation? Restricted breathing can *[purred]* cause acute discomfort and/or sexual excitement.

Mr. Ed Miliband: I can assure the hon. Gentleman there will be none of that, thank you very much. I am having it done on the NHS.

Mr. George Osborne: I'm sorry, Mr. Speaker, I didn't understand a word the hon. Gentleman said. He sounds like an anteater, with sinusitis. In a sack, down a fucking well.

Hon. Members: Wanker! Aardvark! Nasal drip!

Mr. Speaker: Order, no, no, no. I will not tolerate this vulgar abuse and . . . wait. What Elections? The hon. Gentleman mentioned Elections earlier.

The Clerk of the House: Yo ho, Mr. Speaker. I believe the hon. Gentleman was referring to next month's Elections. They are to be held on the same day as the No to AV Referendum, yo ho.

Christopher: Hammer them on the NHS. They're on the back foot. Come on. Fuck your nose job.

Mr. Ed Miliband: Mr. Speaker, people are asking: why am I having this operation on my deviated septum? It's certainly not because political commentators say I sound like a ha ha wasp in a shoebox. Far . . .

Mr. George Osborne: *[cautioned the Clerk of the House to be silent, mimed 'throat-cutting']* Mr. Speaker, I of course assumed that you were advised of the imminent Elections. On the same day as the No to AV Referendum there will be Elections for council seats throughout the country . . .

Mr. Speaker: Yes, yes, of course. I think you'll find I have my finger very firmly . . .

Mr. George Osborne: . . . and for the position of Speaker of the Commons. I'm sure, Mr. Speaker, I echo the sentiments of all hon. Members in this Place when I wish you the very best of luck in what promises to be a *[punched the Jazz Chancellor]* tough contest.

The Jazz Chancellor (Mr. Kenneth Clarke): *[awakening]* Mm wabbeda wabbeda fuck? Yes, Mr. Speaker. So the glap bap *Daily Mail* and the moggeda fuggeda tss-tss ga-flap bap *Sun* call me the huddler muddler bop-bop drr-bobbler glap bobbeda Yobs' Friend, doo bop dee-doo they? Pff. Pff. It's tss-tss splap bap muggery buggery MEANINGLESS! I'll tell you wabbeda who IS the gobbeda flobbeda wobbeda Yobs' Friend, Mr. Gap-Bap Spackeda Spackeda Speaker: the squee bubbela drr-fuck-fuck ba-bap babbeda *SUN*.

Mr. Speaker: Order, order. This is most extraordinary. Is the hon. Gentleman telling me I am to audition for my own flipping job? This is the blooming House of Commons, not *Britain's Got Talent*. Mr. Clerk! Why the blithering arse was I not informed of this Election of the Speaker?

[The Chancellor of the Exchequer then signalling to the Clerk of the House to remain silent or forfeit his testicles.]

Mr. George Osborne: If I may, Mr. Speaker. A list of candidates has been available for some time in the Members' Vestibule. You'll be delighted to hear that your name is at the top of that list.

Ms. Nadine Dorries (Double Bedfordshire): Point of Order, Chancellor of the Exchequer. Is my name on it? Because at the end of the day I represent the common-sense heart of the Big Society . . .

Mr. George Osborne: Yes. Sure. Ha ha, the hon. Lady's name IS on the list of candidates. Of course. *[inaudible, possibly 'You* *poor, dim, grim-faced trollop']* Along with the . . . that hon. Member at the back there asleep and . . . someone who's not here at the moment.

Mr. Speaker: But this is flipping ridiculous! At no point . . .

Ms. Nadine Dorries: Do you mind? I was doing the talking, thank you very much, Mr. Speaker For The Time Being. Of course, I am deeply honoured to be considered for this important Office of State. If, *[irritated hair]* and I obviously stress it is a BIG IF, if I was to land this one, it would mean the world to me . . .

[The hon. Member for Double Bedfordshire then inviting the Approval of the House made her way to the Chair, where she did execute a firm Double Teapot before Mr. Speaker. Who, enraged at her impertinence, did stand and perform a Return of Teapot.]

Mr. George Osborne: I have to leave the Chamber now, Mr. Speaker. But I must speak plainly. I won't be nodding at the Chair on my way out.

Hon. Members: *[aghast, agog]*

Mr. Speaker: Whoa whoa whoa there! No! All hon. Members MUST nod at the Chair upon exit. The Compendium of Constitutional Niceties is very clear on this point.

[The Chancellor of the Exchequer then quitting the Chamber, pausing before the Chair as if to nod, then not nodding most flagrantly, then giving the 'V-sign' to Mr. Speaker, then mouthing 'Fuck you' by way of explanation, then cackling most heartily, then quitting the Chamber.]

Mr. Speaker: Order. Right, don't think I don't know what's blooming well occurring here. I know exactly what's going to happen. I'll chase after the Chancellor of the Exchequer to insist that he return to the Chamber to nod at the Chair. Which, may I remind the House, he DID NOT DO. Meanwhile, *[indicated the hon. Member for Double Bedfordshire]* Elsie Bloody Tanner there is going to pinch my Chair and then everyone's going to take the . . . sod it, what do I care any more, yes, take the FUCKING MICHAEL!

Hon. Members: It's uncanny! It's like he can see into the future! Wanker!

Mr. Speaker: Order, order. I would therefore *[cleared throat]* like to deliver a short speech I have prepared for a contingency *[cleared throat]* such as this. *[produced Reading Glasses, consulted sheaf of paper]* Artisan bakery. Boutique B&B. NO. TV? Host panel show. *Bercow's Britain. Bercow's British Bakery. John and Sally's Breakfast Drop-In. Breakfast with the Bercows. Breakfast in Bed with the Bercows. Bercow & Co. Bercow's Westminster Chimes* . . . oh, wait. *[consulted alternative sheaf]* Yes, sorry. This is the right one. Ladies and gentlemen, the permanence of our great institutions depends on continuity. Continuity and firm direction . . .

Hon. Members: Make-up! Wardrobe! Wanker!

Mr. Speaker: Bah, then, and humbugger. I will leave the Chamber now. I may not return. Who knows what the future holds? Next year, some of us will still be here. Others will be *[blew nose]* absent. I want you all to know what a tremendous privilege it has been to preside over these solemn and momentous gatherings of the nation's elected representatives. You are tribunes for the greatest nation on Earth . . .

Hon. Members: Hear, hear! He's right, we are fucking brilliant,

I've actually got a lump in my throat! Go private, I would, really.

Mr. Speaker: . . . a true reflection of our increasingly diverse society. Where once this Chamber would have been filled with aristocratic landowners as far removed from today's Man – or Woman! – in the Street as it is possible to imagine, well . . . look at it now. Filled to the FUCKING BRIM with high-earning, tax-dodging, shareholding, middle-class wankers with backgrounds in Journalism or the Law. I am off to meet a publisher, and in due course will blow the lid off this seething wormery of lies and malice. Bollocks to the lot of you.

[Hon. Members observing with great insouciance, Mr. Speaker then most stropfully indicating his quitting of the Chamber via High Dudgeon. The hon. Member for Double Bedfordshire making herself comfortable upon the Chair.]

Mrs. Self-Appointed Speaker: Wait! How bloody dare you! Come back here and nod to the Chair!

[Mr. Speaker then halting in static agitation, tormented by Constitutional Dilemma, hon. Members chi-iking and jeering most mercilessly, then returning to face the Chair, nodding most curtly and then quitting the Chamber, hon. Clerks to the House and the Bailiff in his train.]

Mrs. Self-Appointed Speaker: Ha ha ha! Right, then. I'm in charge now. I want all questions, remarks and what-have-you addressed to the Chair, plus I am spitting feathers here, can someone get me a latte, and some of those nice . . .

Hon. Members: *[chatting, tweeting, exiting the Chamber]*

The Prime Minister: Oh, listen. Before you all go. All this bloody nonsense on the Internet, stirring the shit about our very necessary NHS reforms. Hon. Members may be interested to know that one of the most eminent doctors in the land, Dr . . . *[consulted note]*

Hon. Members: Up yours, William Hartnell was the best one! Piss off, Cameron, you drizzled fucking cake, nobody believes you! Lansley, your head looks like a giant poisoned fucking toe!

Mrs. Self-Appointed Speaker: Order, order. I am not having this sort of behaviour. Hey, you! Nod to the bloody Chair if you're going. Your head, I mean, obviously. Nod your head. Oh, that's disgusting. Typical Labour. No wonder the world's economy went right out the trousers.

The Prime Minister: . . . Dr Inverhouse, a widely respected, crusty old medic with a tweed suit and a big beard. Him. Well, he has issued a statement saying this:

. . . although I most certainly do not endorse the Government's reckless, brainless solution to that problem.

No, sorry. It's the bit before that:

Of course the NHS needs to be more efficient. The system is currently failing too many people in hospital and residential care.

Ms. Angela Eagle (Electric Ladyland): This Government cannot be allowed to get away with this big bag of utter giblets! Privatisation is not the answer! How many private companies are bidding to run Accident & Emergency departments? Eh? Eh? You . . .

The Prime Minister: Calm down, dear.

Hon. Members: *[shrieking, chanting, ululation]*

Mrs. Self-Appointed Speaker: *[inaudible]*

The Prime Minister: *[smirked, exchanged fistbumps with Front Bench]* Yes, dear. You, dear. Calm down. Calm down. Let the 'Winners' on this side of the House speak. *[exchanged High Five with Foreign Secretary]*

Christopher: Here's your chance. He's quoting Michael Winner. Car-insurance ad. 'Calm down, dear, it's only an accident.' Ask that twatbubble if he's really saying the Government's plan to fuck over the NHS has been arrived at by 'accident'. Oh, oh, I know! Ask him if he's saying the Government's NHS reform is a CAR CRASH! Take the piss. Go on. GO ON!

Mr. Ed Miliband: Oho! Is the Prime Minister saying, when he says, 'Calm down, dear,' that he thinks he is as well known as Michael Winnet?

Christopher: Winner. WINNER. You arse sponge.

[The Chamber now emptying, the Prime Minister engarbed as 'The Stig' leading out hon. Government Members amid cries of 'Calm down, dear!' The hon. Member for Camberwick Betspread leading out hon. Opposition Members amid loud mutterings of disapproval.]

Mrs. Self-Appointed Speaker: Order, bloody cheek, do you mind? Nod to the Chair! Nod to the effing Chair!

Mr. Ed Miliband: Because I tell the Prime Minister this: he is no Michael Winner. He is David 'Loser'.

Christopher: Fuck this. Jesus, I hate you, you're stupid. If you need me I'll be hanging out in your stupid deviated septum, banging my head against the stupid walls.

[The hon. Member for Doncaster Awkwood then quitting the

Chamber, clutching his nose. Mrs. Self-Appointed Speaker then surveying the Chamber, counting three unconscious hon. Members remaining, to wit the hon. Member for Sheffield Masturbeighton, the hon. Member for Bolsover Oneside and the Jazz Chancellor. Mrs. Self-Appointed Speaker then returning to her former place on the Government Benches.]

Ms. Nadine Dorries: Thank you, Mrs. Speaker. Yes, I would very MUCH like to propose my Sex Education Ten-Minute Rule Bill. Mrs. Speaker, we as a society have a constant struggle with sex. Not all of us, obviously. Some of us have absolutely no problem regarding sex, especially within the sanctity of marriage. But I want to talk about young girls, who are getting considerably more pregnant than their counterparts in Europe because of unacceptable sexual activity, which in my book is often punctuated with both question and exclamation marks.

[Hon. Members asleep. The hon. Member for Sheffield Masturbeighton's guide dog Yorkshire Lass in drowsy vigilance.]

Ms. Nadine Dorries: Our society is saturated in sex. It sometimes feels like one of those old children's programmes on the television, before they were over-sexualised, where society is the hapless contestant and sex, i.e. the green gunge from the Gunge Tank, is sploshed over the contestant/society's hapless head. It is about time we started talking about abstinence, and that is exactly what my Ten-Minute Rule Bill is all about. Saying Yes to abstinence and No to gunge.

The Jazz Chancellor: Hzz bzz wabbeza wabbeza zz-zz bzz.

Ms. Nadine Dorries: At the moment, girls aged thirteen to sixteen are taught about safe sex with condoms and bananas, although, OK, that seems a bit cautious even to me. Well, from now on these girls need to be told to tidy their rooms, put away their skimpy tops in favour of something sensible and to be taught that saying No to sex with boys and their bananas is a cool thing to do. You may say, 'Well, why don't we educate boys and tell them that sexual harassment is wrong and to stop leaning on girls like that?' And I say: face facts, boys will be boys. If after all this advice I'm giving them girls get pregnant, they only have themselves to blame.

Mr. Dennis Skinner (Bolsover Oneside): *[passed wind in a heavy northern accent]*

Ms. Nadine Dorries: My main advice is the Ten-Minute Rule. We need to say to them, look, if a boy gets his banana out, say OK, we can have sex, but only if you go and stand still in the garden for ten minutes with your trousers and pants off. If after ten minutes his erection is intact, fair enough. But it won't be. Trust me, I have used this technique on a number of occasions. All those in favour!

The Hon. Member for Sheffield Masturbeighton's Guide Dog Yorkshire Lass: Woof!

Ms. Nadine Dorries: All those against! Brilliant! Carried. Right. I am off to tell the sexualised media about this . . .

[The hon. Member for Double Bedfordshire then quitting the Chamber, nodding most gravely to herself. The remaining hon. Members unconscious in consensus.]

Moment of Nothingness.

Number 10 Downing Street

Upon the Feast of the Bartered Bride, the 5th of May 2011
DISTANT THUNDER
[Messrs. Cameron and Clegg in the Garden]

Prime Minister's Kettling Time

[The Prime Minister and the Deputy Prime Minister approaching the double lectern at a saunter, exchanging pleasantries.]

The Prime Minister (Mr. David Cameron): Remember what Steve said. Hit the positives, block the negatives. Accomplished much in one year, real challenges lie ahead. Steady as she goes. All good. Shit. *[indicated the Deputy Prime Minister's Downstairs Area]* Look. Your flies are undone, you utter bloody chav.

The Deputy Prime Minister (Mr. Nick Clegg): I'm not looking. Pathetic, Dave.

The Prime Minister: Don't pause like that. Steve reminded us literally five fucking minutes ago. Say 'halloumi' or 'prosecco' in the gaps, it helps keep the face socially mobile.

The Deputy Prime Minister: Halloumi, halloumi, fuck you up the hairy socket with a boom microphone, *[waved to hon.*

Members of the Press] prosecco halloumi, you cunt. I don't even understand how Sensei Steve on his sodding Spacehopper gets to boss ME around. He's your bloody guru, not ours.

The Prime Minister: Oh, come on. You're the one all over the *Daily Mail* with your transcendental meditation and your crying, you big halloumi ponce. Anyway, stop moaning. We just prosecco gave you the Social Mobility Strategy to launch. I thought you liked all that bumfluff. What was it called again?

The Deputy Prime Minister: 'Opening Doors, Breaking Barriers.'

The Prime Minister: Brilliant, yeah. Sounds like a demo that's turned violent. Perhaps you can claw back a few students with THAT. Hey, maybe wear an ironic T-shirt in the Commons from now on, ha ha ha, prosecco prosecco!

The Deputy Prime Minister: Mm. Maybe it'll say, 'My Party Went into Coalition and All I Got Was This Piece of Shit Social Mobility Strategy.' Halloumi bollocks to you.

The Prime Minister: Still, this is what you asked for, yeah? A Referendum. After today, we owe you lot prosecco bugger all.

The Deputy Prime Minister: I certainly didn't ask for it to be called the fucking Say No to AV Referendum. Anyway, the polls don't close for hours yet. There might be a late surge. Prosecco.

The Prime Minister: Oh please. Halloumi, halloumi, do me a favour. Who's going to vote for AV? You. And your fucking Twitter followers. The only late surge you'll see is when you're having one off the wrist in the conservatory at two in the morning, listening to Puccini and crying like a harpooned seal. Prosecco halloumi. *[returned the salutations of journalists, gave 'thumbs up' sign, indicated the Deputy Prime Minister, mimed 'wanker']*

The Deputy Prime Minister: Look at them. The 'press pack'. Bunch of prickgobblers. What do you and the Murdoch lot talk about at your stupid dinner parties anyway? Prosecco. Halloumi.

The Prime Minister: Depends who's there. Cars, a bloody LOT actually. Bit of politics. Regulatory prosecco procedures for the halloumi media. All sorts. None of your fucking business, no offence. Prosecco.

The Deputy Prime Minister: Yeah, well, you should watch your step.

[The Prime Minister and the Deputy Prime Minister then stopping upon the Lawn, then looking at one another, in countenance most daggers and handbags.]

The Prime Minister: What halloumi the fuck prosecco are you talking about?

The Deputy Prime Minister: These dinner parties of yours. Prosecco. Halloumi. You need to be very careful about your boundaries, Dave. Very fucking careful indeed.

The Prime Minister: Boundaries? Prosecco, you tit. Have you forgotten what's happening in September? The deal we made a year ago? You get your little referendum, you agree to have the whole halloumi electoral map redrawn. They say your lot could lose a quarter of your seats. I mean, it SOUNDS dramatic, but I'm not sure anyone would really notice. Prosecco, prosecco.

The Deputy Prime Minister: Halloumi wanker. I think YOU'LL find that the entire political fucking LANDSCAPE is being redrawn while you eat jugged hare and joke about 'pikeys' with that shit Clarkson. The world's changing, Dave. You can call it 'Blue Labour'. You can call it 'Red Tory'. You can . . .

The Prime Minister: Nick, you can call it Mopsy and take it to the fucking Royal Academy Summer Exhibition. It won't make a halloumi bit of difference, mate. After today nobody's going to be interested in *[dug the Deputy Prime Minister playfully in the ribs]* political *[shoulder punch]* pluralism. Ladies and gentlemen, thanks for coming. When Nick and I stood here a year ago and promised to work together in the national interest, we knew it would be one heck of a journey.

The Deputy Prime Minister: That's right, Dave.

Moment of Confection.

Acknowledgements

Thanks to my wife Eileen for all the research and support. Thanks to Hannah Griffiths and everyone at Faber for wanting to do this. Thanks to Asa Bennett for his invaluable and inventive Latin translation.

But mostly thanks to my lovely brother Paul. A decade ago, we started a satirical website, Martian FM. I did the writing, he did everything else. One of our regular features was a sweary Parliamentary spoof called 'Hansard Late'. Without Paul, nobody would have seen it. So cheers, man.